I HAVE STRUCK

MRS. COCHRAN

WITH A STAKE

TRUE CRIME HISTORY

Twilight of Innocence: The Disappearance of Beverly Potts · James Jessen Badal

Tracks to Murder · Jonathan Goodman

Terrorism for Self-Glorification: The Herostratos Syndrome · Albert Borowitz

Ripperology: A Study of the World's First Serial Killer and a Literary Phenomenon · Robin Odell

The Good-bye Door: The Incredible True Story of America's First Female Serial Killer to Die in the Chair · Diana Britt Franklin

Murder on Several Occasions · Jonathan Goodman

The Murder of Mary Bean and Other Stories · Elizabeth A. De Wolfe

Lethal Witness: Sir Bernard Spilsbury, Honorary Pathologist · Andrew Rose

Murder of a Journalist: The True Story of the Death of Donald Ring Mellett · Thomas Crowl

Musical Mysteries: From Mozart to John Lennon · Albert Borowitz

The Adventuress: Murder, Blackmail, and Confidence Games in the Gilded Age · Virginia A. McConnell

Queen Victoria's Stalker: The Strange Case of the Boy Jones · Jan Bondeson

Born to Lose: Stanley B. Hoss and the Crime Spree That Gripped a Nation · James G. Hollock

Murder and Martial Justice: Spying and Retribution in World War II America · Meredith Lentz Adams

The Christmas Murders: Classic Stories of True Crime · Jonathan Goodman

The Supernatural Murders: Classic Stories of True Crime · Jonathan Goodman

Guilty by Popular Demand: A True Story of Small-Town Injustice · Bill Osinski

Nameless Indignities: Unraveling the Mystery of One of Illinois's Most Infamous Crimes · Susan Elmore

Hauptmann's Ladder: A Step-by-Step Analysis of the Lindbergh Kidnapping · Richard T. Cahill Jr.

The Lincoln Assassination Riddle: Revisiting the Crime of the Nineteenth Century · Edited by Frank J. Williams and Michael Burkhimer

Death of an Assassin: The True Story of the German Murderer Who Died Defending Robert E. Lee · Ann Marie Ackermann

The Insanity Defense and the Mad Murderess of Shaker Heights: Examining the Trial of Mariann Colby · William L. Tabac

The Belle of Bedford Avenue: The Sensational Brooks-Burns Murder in Turn-of-the-Century New York · Virginia A. McConnell

Six Capsules: The Gilded Age Murder of Helen Potts · George R. Dekle Sr.

A Woman Condemned: The Tragic Case of Anna Antonio · James M. Greiner

Bigamy and Bloodshed: The Scandal of Emma Molloy and the Murder of Sarah Graham · Larry E. Wood

The Beauty Defense: Femmes Fatales on Trial · Laura James

The Potato Masher Murder: Death at the Hands of a Jealous Husband · Gary Sosniecki

I Have Struck Mrs. Cochran with a Stake: Sleepwalking, Insanity, and the Trial of Abraham Prescott · Leslie Lambert Rounds

I HAVE STRUCK MRS. COCHRAN WITH A STAKE

SLEEPWALKING, INSANITY, AND THE TRIAL OF ABRAHAM PRESCOTT

Leslie Lambert Rounds

The Kent State University Press KENT, OHIO

© 2020 by The Kent State University Press, Kent, Ohio 44242
ALL RIGHTS RESERVED
Library of Congress Catalog Number 2020027548
ISBN 978-1-60635-409-4
Manufactured in the United States of America

LIBRARY OF CONGRESS CATALOGING-IN-PUBLICATION DATA
Names: Rounds, Leslie L., author.
Title: I have struck Mrs. Cochran with a stake : sleepwalking, insanity, and the trial of Abraham Prescott / Leslie Lambert Rounds.
Description: Kent, Ohio : the Kent State University Press, [2020] | Includes bibliographical references and index.
Identifiers: LCCN 2020027548 | ISBN 9781606354094 (paperback) | ISBN 9781631014291 (epub) | ISBN 9781631014307 (pdf)
Subjects: LCSH: Prescott, Abraham, 1815?-1836--Trials, litigation, etc. | Trials (Murder)--New Hampshire. | Sleepwalking. | Insanity (Law) | Cochran, Sally, -1833.
Classification: LCC KF223.P74 R68 2020 | DDC 345.742/02523--dc23
LC record available at https://lccn.loc.gov/2020027548

24 23 22 21 20   5 4 3 2 1

CONTENTS

Acknowledgments   vii
Introduction   ix

PART I: THE MURDER

1 The Killing   3
2 The Cochran Family   10
3 Sally and Chauncey Cochran   15
4 Nighttime Attack   24
5 The Prescott Family   33
6 Indictment and Incarceration   41

PART II: ABRAHAM PRESCOTT'S TRIALS

7 The Prosecution Presents Its Case   55
8 The Defense's Opening Argument   73
9 The Defense Discusses Sleepwalking   86
10 The Avery Connection   96
11 Mental Illness in the Prescott Family   104
12 The Physicians Begin Their Testimony   113
13 More Physicians for the Defense   122
14 The Prosecution Rebuts   128
15 The Defense Begins Its Closing Argument   138
16 Closing Arguments Conclude   149
17 Verdict and Retrial   158
18 Reprieve, Riots, and Execution   168

PART III: SOMNAMBULISM, INSANITY, AND
PRESCOTT'S LEGACY

19 New Hampshire's Need for an Asylum   183
20 The Sleepwalking Defense Evolves   189
21 The Insanity Plea   198
22 The Question of Responsibility   206

Epilogue   212
Notes   218
Selected Bibliography   250
Index   259

ACKNOWLEDGMENTS

My deepest gratitude goes out to my parents, Robert and Barbara Lambert, who, from our earliest days inspired me and my two sisters to love history and to seek the deeper personal stories behind the well-documented public pageant. My husband, Emory, and our five grown children deserve immense credit for patiently listening to iterations of Sally's tragic story—over and over—yet always urging me to persevere. "Ma," Harriet Boulris Rooney, and Beverly DeMontigny, too, believed in me and never failed to remind me of their faith. I'm very grateful to Donna-Belle and James Garvin for jump-starting this project and to Richard Shaw and Mary Duran Cronkhite for filling in important details at the finish. My knowledgeable coworkers, Tara Raiselis and Carolyn Roy, provided so many important details along the way. Will Underwood, now retired, and Dr. Elizabeth De Wolfe had just the right advice, and Valerie Ahwee made excellent use of her eagle eyes, all serving to help me craft a better, more readable story. Finally, I thank all the girls and young women who came before, who deliberately stitched their history into their delicate and now iconic embroideries at a time when women's lives were often only recorded as nameless, impersonal tally marks on census pages.

INTRODUCTION

There were many points of agreement between the witnesses at the trial. Eighteen-year-old Abraham Prescott came from a family whose members were poor and unsophisticated, and sometimes even violent with each other and with their neighbors. It was a family of a decidedly lower class than those who lived in the neighborhood of the Cochran farm. Prescott was often surly, and more than one person had seen him unmercifully beat the cattle in his care. He wouldn't make eye contact with anyone. Because he rarely spoke in front of people, there was plenty of disagreement on whether or not he was as smart as other boys his age, but many people thought that Prescott was something of a dullard. No one considered him friendly, but other farmers in the area thought he was a hard worker and that counted for a lot.

Sally Cochran was known to be a good neighbor and, like her husband, Chauncey, she was both respectable and respected. The Cochrans were among the first settlers of tiny Pembroke, New Hampshire, and the family had always behaved properly. Cochran men had frequently held leadership roles in the town. They were known for their modern, profitable farms and successful businesses. Cochran women were modest, hardworking, made fine helpmeets for their spouses, and diligently raised industrious children—all that was expected of women of the era. There was no hint of scandal.

The true nature of the dreadful incident that preceded Sally Cochran's murder was less clear even than Prescott's motivation for killing her five months later. He claimed he'd been sleepwalking on the January night when he took up an ax and beat the sleeping Cochrans nearly to death. That the Cochrans believed that claim was a cause for talk in the neighborhood. Not everyone thought it wise to let a boy like that live in the family's home.

Still, the tale of the January incident was a strange enough story that newspapers across the region ran it, including comments from the family physician who treated the injured couple. He believed it must have been "a remarkable case of somnambulism." Tales like that were common enough in newspapers, used as filler between dense, lengthy descriptions of international affairs, with editors gravitating toward the unusual or remarkable local stories that arose occasionally. But the coverage for Prescott's January attack was brief. The murder and subsequent trials would generate much more attention in the press.

What happened on a sunny, warm Sunday morning in June would create such a lasting impact in the peaceful rural community that a granite marker would be erected years later on the site of Sally Cochran's killing. The lust for revenge would inspire riots, and cause a second young woman's death. Prescott's attorneys, in their effort to find some kind of viable defense strategy, would describe at trial numerous other strange tales that offer remarkable insight into the thoughts and beliefs of early nineteenth-century Americans. Their stories especially illuminate a slowly emerging understanding of mental illness, but also a continued confusion as to compassionate ways to handle those afflicted. The concern that a mentally deranged youth was unfairly executed would inspire a movement, driven by one of Prescott's defense attorneys, to build New Hampshire's first asylum for the insane. Later, the same issue would influence New Hampshire's unusual legal definition of insanity. Prescott's failed claim that he had been sleepwalking would inform the defense, less than a decade later, of another man and result in his acquittal in spite of an abundance of evidence of his guilt.

Then all of the tragedy and all of the controversy would quietly be forgotten. Even within Cochran's own family, her story would gradually disappear until none of her descendants remembered her life or the remarkable events that resulted in her death. All that would remain to mark her brief existence would be two gravestones with her name carved into them, separated in distance by a few hundred miles, and an elaborately embroidered sampler that she completed as a schoolgirl, donated a century and a half later to the Saco Museum. But the story,

rediscovered, includes an unusual amount of detail for events that occurred at a time before newspapers provided much coverage of local
news. While those details make it possible to recreate the events with
surprising accuracy, it is the many interwoven social issues of Sally Cochran and Abraham Prescott's tragic tale that make it important to re-
tell the story of the crime that ended her life.

However, those issues and their lasting impact also create a surprising complexity. Prescott's legacy is worthy of attention, but the ripples
have spread wide in the nearly two hundred years since he struck down
his employer. To keep the story moving forward, it is divided into three
parts: the murder, the trials, and, finally, the impact Prescott's legal odyssey had on both the treatment of the insane in New Hampshire, and
on the evolving (and sometimes astonishing) use of insanity and somnambulism as legal defenses.

Crimes from the early nineteenth century can be hard to research.
Newspaper coverage was spotty and suffered from inaccuracies. Di-
arists may have recorded their impressions of the crime and its af-
termath, but few diaries remain and Prescott's crime didn't generate
enough popular interest to attract attention outside the region. A
transcription of the first of Prescott's two trials exists, revised a couple of years afterward and reissued later in the century. None of the
people who were close to the events left any record of their feelings or
experiences. Much can be surmised from a knowledge of the quality of
people's lives in the area at the time. Sadly, much more will never be
known.

PART I

THE MURDER

Thus was her life's blood spilt.

—ABR'M PRESCOTT'S CONFESSION,

of the murder of Mrs. Sally Cochran, of Pembroke, N.H.

—June 23, 1833. By a private individual at the Bar.

Period broadside

THE KILLING

I have struck Mrs. Cochran with a stake!
—Abraham Prescott, shortly after the killing

Sunday, June 23, 1833, dawned pleasant and delightfully dry, a welcome change after what many had considered to have been a cold, "backward" spring. The sky was a brilliant blue—a "bluebird sky" it was called—without a cloud in sight. The weather in Pembroke, New Hampshire, a small village located not far from the state capital in Concord, had been discouragingly rainy for almost a full week before, finally clearing on Saturday, but even that day was darkened by the threat of a storm after lunch. Sunday seemed glorious.[1]

At about 9 A.M., thirty-two-year-old Chauncey Cochran settled himself in the quieter of his front downstairs rooms (they proudly called it the "clock room," drawing a little attention to the fact that they were one of the relatively few local families who owned a clock) to read the latest on the Avery trial. Rev. Ephraim Avery's murder trial had ended just three weeks before in Fall River, Massachusetts. Everyone had been talking about it for months.

Eighteen-year-old hired farmhand Abraham Prescott said nothing as he walked through the room into the back part of the house, where he found Sally, Chauncey's young wife.[2] Cochran, engrossed in his reading, barely noticed him passing by. Prescott was a boy of few words. After a several minutes, the teen came to the door, failing, as always, to make any eye contact, to ask whether or not Mr. Cochran would like to go with his wife to pick strawberries in a pasture owned by Cochran's younger brother, James. Cochran refused. Not troubling to ask more about his wife's plans, he returned to the dense prose of the newspaper. If he heard his wife and Prescott leave, he didn't mention it later. The trial of Reverend Avery was very distracting. The minister had been accused of murdering a young female mill worker. There was plenty of evidence that he'd had a secret sexual liaison with her—she was several months into a pregnancy when she was killed, and many had seen them meeting illicitly.[3] The titillating scandal had riveted the attention of New Englanders for months: Avery wasn't just a married man with children but also a minister, and thus surely a paragon of virtue. The local connection, that Avery had been arrested late in the winter in nearby Rindge after a very long, slow chase across New England, made people in Pembroke especially interested in the minister's sordid story. Cochran had just borrowed the long newspaper account from a neighbor so he was happy to let his wife go with Prescott, leaving him to pay full attention to the tale.

Prescott offered to accompany Sally Cochran's strawberry picking. Picking strawberries may even have been his suggestion in the first place. They'd go into James Cochran's pasture, a meadow that lay about three hundred feet away from the quiet dirt lane that fronted the Cochran farm and in view of three or four houses and from a couple of the Cochran's wide-open, back-facing windows. She left her two young children, Sarah and Giles Newton, aged almost four and two and a half, in the care of the young hired girl who was about eleven, and her mother-in-law, Lettice, who had shared the family home since being widowed a decade earlier.

It took Sally Cochran a few minutes to get ready while Prescott waited impatiently. Not wanting to spoil her Sunday best dress, she switched into an older cotton gown. The deep meadow grass might still be wet from the rain and she wasn't going to ruin her expensive silk dress while picking strawberries. The sleeves of both her stylish gown and her second best were gathered into very large, batting-stuffed caps that expanded like balloons over her upper arms, but tightly enclosed her forearms.[4] They were fashionable but not very practical for strawberry picking or rambling through the tall grass—they seriously limited the motion of her arms—but it was the style that everyone was wearing.

After pulling on her small cape, she fastened it closed with its hook and eye. She repositioned the large tortoiseshell comb she was using to hold up her long brown hair before tying on her calash, a lightweight, collapsible bonnet on a reed frame, hoping to shield her face from the warm sun. Her summer calash would have been made of either silk or an attractive cotton. Long strips of thin, fragile reeds ran through pockets sewn onto the underside of the fabric, shaping the bonnet into an inverted U. The calash would expand nicely over her piled hair, but when she took it off, it folded perfectly flat for storage. Then she gathered her basket and followed Prescott out the back door, through the barn and down the rutted farm lane, carefully stepping around the piles of cow manure, which would have ruined her hand-sewn slippers.

If she was concerned about heading out into the meadow with a young man just ten years her junior, she didn't mention it. Prescott had, after all, lived with them since he was fifteen. If he was sometimes a little surly or harsh to the cattle, or if the terrible incident of last January worried her a bit, she believed she knew him very well, almost like a son, or given the closeness of their ages, perhaps more like a younger brother. On a sunny June morning it was impossible to detect even a hint of danger in strolling through familiar nearby meadows, searching for the tiny, sweet berries—so welcome after the long winter—that were hidden beneath the tall grass.

The meadow was alive with passing songbirds, the buzzing of crickets, and the whirring flights of small insects that leapt before the couple as they started down the steep hill behind the house, but not after all into James's pasture as they'd first intended. In the distance, Great Brook, full from the week of incessant rain, rushed over smooth granite stones and provided the cheerful background noise of running water. The scene couldn't have been more placid and idyllic.

The pair wandered downhill away from the farm, into a more distant meadow, where they thought the strawberries might be most profuse. Side by side, they bent and pushed apart the sharp green blades of grass to reveal the berries growing on vines against the ground. Nearly an hour had passed by the time they reached the rail-and-brush fence that Prescott and Chauncey Cochran had recently worked on. Prescott suggested that the berries on the other side of the fence were larger and easier to find and Sally Cochran's basket was still only partially filled.

Cochran was encumbered by her dress and petticoats, so she elected to make the longer walk, all the way around the fence and into the field. She moved ahead of Prescott, bending and searching for the berries, her fingers stained red with their juice. He paused at the opening in the fence, distracted by something he found there. She kept intently picking the berries, conscious that it was getting late now and that, even though it was Sunday, many chores awaited. She'd need a full basket of berries to feed the entire family. A sudden noise just behind her drew her attention and she glanced up curiously. Prescott was now very close to her, grinning. He was *not* interested in the berries. Fear rising, she pushed him away. He was no longer smiling. The peril was instantly, horrifically obvious to her.

She dropped the basket, too frightened even to scream. He grabbed at her, her flowing skirt in easy reach. She struggled to free herself, her heart pounding in dread. As he dragged her inexorably to him, her calash came loose and tumbled to the ground, landing beside the bright red splash of her spilled basket of berries. She dodged away, hampered by her gown and petticoats, but desperate to escape. Terror flooded through her and now her movements seemed to slow down as Prescott's sped up. She twisted free again, but the deep grass made it difficult to even start to run and he quickly gained a firmer hold on her, this time grabbing a fistful of her hair. She didn't notice the pain of the comb being torn from her hair as his swinging fist connected with the side of her head. The force of the blow momentarily stunned her, giving him the opportunity to fling her facedown onto the grass. She drew in breath to scream as she tried to scramble to her hands and knees.

His face livid with fury, Prescott snatched up a three-foot-long, rough-cut wooden pole and swung it. The first blow of the post crashed down on the back of her head. The explosion of pain was instantaneous but mercifully dimmed as the sounds of the summer morning receded and the darkness engulfed her.

Chauncey Cochran was deeply engrossed in Reverend Avery's troubles when his mother came to the door to tell him that she was hearing a very strange noise coming from the barnyard—maybe there was an animal in distress? He reluctantly left to investigate. As he stepped out onto the rough-cut granite doorstep behind the house and looked across the dirt yard, past the well sweep, toward the open barn door, he felt a little tickle of fear at the bizarre sounds that reached him—not animal but distinctly, disturbingly human. He anxiously followed the whimpering and occasional loud moaning through the barn doors, across the cool, hay-scented, dimly lit length of the large building to the shed at the far end that opened onto the lane leading downhill to the pasture. Prescott lay sprawled in the doorway, suddenly silent now that Cochran, bewildered, loomed over him. Not seeing his wife around, Cochran's confusion swiftly turned to alarm. "What are you about, Abraham?" he asked, panic rising in him as he suddenly noticed the spray of bloodstains across the teen's white shirt.

"I have struck Mrs. Cochran with a stake," Prescott wailed. "I have killed her!" Stunned, Cochran demanded that the boy lead him to her. Prescott cried that he had left her in the brook field where they had gone, but he wouldn't get up to lead Cochran to his stricken young wife. When Cochran ordered him to run and show him where she lay, Prescott still refused, but then with great reluctance rose and started down the lane for the field. Along the way he offered a further, halting explanation over his shoulder. While picking strawberries he'd been seized with a toothache, he said. Unable to help her find berries because of the pain, he had instead sat down on a tree stump and then somehow fallen asleep. When he awoke, he realized that he had killed her—while asleep.

"Will you have me hanged?" he wailed.

"I believe the devil has got full possession of you!" Cochran screamed. Alternately shoving the teen forward and sometimes having to drag him, they made unsteady and frustratingly slow downhill progress to the still-peaceful meadow, then over a fence and into the steep smaller field nearly all the way to the brook. And then Cochran came upon his wife's calash, the broken comb from her hair, and the spilled basket of crimson strawberries, lying abandoned on the matted grass. If he'd entertained some belief that this was all a strange lie, his hopes were crushed. Prescott stopped abruptly, then pointed to some brush about thirty feet away down under the brow of the hill; the thick foliage barely concealed Sally Cochran's body but the path to it, through blood-smeared grass, was obvious. The uncut hay lay flattened, as if it had already been mown. The spot, in spite of being within shouting distance of several homes, was secluded, far down the hillside from where people usually picked berries.

Wide-eyed and groaning with terror, Cochran raced forward. His wife lay facedown in the deep grass. Her hair, usually contained by the large comb, was now tumbled down and matted with a profusion of bright red blood that spilled horribly out onto the grass and soaked into the back of her dress. Two lethally deep, gory indentations crossed her exposed skull, clearly showing the strength of the blows that had struck her down. He felt for her pulse. Finding a faint beat, he gently rolled her onto her back. She took a shallow gasping breath that momentarily sparked his hope. She was still alive, though deathly pale and completely unresponsive.

"Alarm the neighbors!" he screamed. Prescott cowered and refused. Frantically, Cochran yelled at him again and again, then sprang furiously at the boy when he didn't respond. Prescott finally took off running, but not in the direction of the neighbors. Cochran now raised his voice between sobs, screaming desperately for help. As he called, his wife continued her irregular, shuddering breaths that seemed too shallow and labored to sustain her life.

Several minutes had passed by the time his nearest neighbor, Timothy Robinson, arrived and then, horrified, ran to fetch Dr. Samuel Sargent. By the time another neighbor, Henry Robinson, reached Cochran a few minutes later, his wife's brief life had ebbed away; aged only twenty-eight, Sally was dead.

Nearly all of the other nearby neighbors now began to arrive on the scene: Jonathan Robinson; his three adult daughters, Lucy, Belinda, and Clarrissa, and his grown sons, Timothy and William; Sally's stunned younger sister, Mary Jane—the wife of Chauncey's brother (and across-the-road neighbor) James; and then William Abbott Jr. One after another, in shocked horror they disbelievingly examined the site of the murder: the trampled grass, the broken hair comb, the spilled basket of strawberries and the abandoned calash, and viewed her blood-soaked body. Each of the visitors to the scene of Sally's murder considered what might have happened and drew conclusions based on what they saw. The question of whether or not there had been a struggle between Prescott and Sally occupied everyone's minds

Mary Jane joined her brother-in-law in fanning the gathering blackflies away from Sally's face and gaping wounds. She gently smoothed her sister's skirt and folded her lifeless hands across her chest. Later she would occupy herself by picking through the matted grass to find one of her dead sister's missing knob earrings. Abbott, too disturbed by the scene to remain, went to find Prescott, his still-flattened path through the deep grass easy to follow. He discovered the young man in a nearby pasture, lying facedown with his bloody shirt and vest pulled off and wadded under his head for a pillow. Though the teen was sobbing violently, Abbott noticed that there were no tears on his face. "What is the matter?" Abbott demanded, the irony seemingly escaping him, or perhaps he was feigning confusion in an attempt to force a confession out of him.

"I have killed Sally," the boy sobbed.

Shaken, Abbott asked him how he could have done such a thing. Prescott related the same story he had told Chauncey, about falling asleep with a toothache and then awakening to discover the dying young woman in the brush.

"Why have you taken off your shirt?" Abbott asked.

Prescott said that he had thought to use it to hang himself since he supposed that they would hang him anyway. After William Fowler arrived on the scene, the two men escorted Prescott back to the Abbott home, where unrestrained, Prescott passed the rest of the day, seemingly unperturbed by the stream of locals on their way to visit the death scene who stopped in to view the now even more notorious youth. Abbott noted that the young man seemed to sleep well that night.

Sally Cochran would be buried in the small, shady, stone-walled cemetery just down the lane from her home, joining her much younger sister, Betsy, who died as a toddler, on March 22, 1823, and whose birth and death Sally had recorded on the embroidered sampler she began as a schoolgirl in 1818. The cemetery was also only a few house lots away from her parents' home. Her mother, Jane, would be buried there just four years after Abraham Prescott cut short Sally Cochran's life.

The sudden, brutal death of this young farmwife stunned the community and set into motion an unusually long legal odyssey for Abraham Prescott, at a time when even capital cases were typically prosecuted within a few weeks of the occurrence of a crime. Its repercussions would echo on for decades.

⚵ 2 ⚶

THE COCHRAN FAMILY

We are likely to be very happy in one another
—Cotton Mather

Sally and Chauncey Cochran had been closely related even before their marriage. They were both descended from the same Protestant forebears. The first member of their family who came to New Hampshire was probably Deacon John Cochran. He was part of a group of Scotch-Irish settlers, five shiploads of them, who arrived in Boston in the late summer of 1718.[1] After inquiring of Massachusetts officials and New Hampshire Governor Samuel Shute about the availability of land, large groups of several parishes decided to pack up and leave for the New World together.

Cotton Mather, a well-known Boston minister who, fortunately for future historians, kept a diary, first commented on the new colonists in a letter to a friend: "We are comforted with great numbers of our oppressed brethren coming over from the North of Ireland unto us. They sit down with us, and we embrace them as our own most united brethren, and we are likely to be very happy in one another."[2] Unfortunately, the reality quickly became much grimmer. Even if they had had access to land, the emigrants had arrived way too late to plant and grow their own food. Many had spent most of their money to secure passage. Americans found themselves having to provide support to the newcomers in a variety of ways they could ill afford. The new arrivals were unaccustomed to and surprised by how bitterly cold a New England winter could be.

With the coming of spring, and still trying to find a place to finally settle, members of the group learned of an area to the northwest, many square miles of rolling land that was said to abound with nut trees. They relocated there. It offered more hope for the future than staying on with people who were eager to see the last of them. At first they called the settlement Nutfield, in what is now Londonderry, New Hampshire, on the far southern edge of the state. In making this move to what was then the frontier of the New World, they began to fulfill a role both Governor Shute and Cotton Mather had imagined for them when their exodus to America was first contemplated: the unwitting new settlers could now serve as the imperiled buffer between their settled areas and the often-threatening Native Americans to the northwest.

The early settlers cleared the land and planted apple trees. Londonderry claims to have been the first place in America where potatoes were planted.[3] The new settlers, rebuffed by the more established colonists and probably becoming all too aware of their hazardous location, kept largely to themselves, at least through the early years of the settlement. They tended to marry within their group since new settlers to the area who didn't already have some link to the original emigrants were unusual. The initial area of Nutfield was vast: it included present-day Manchester, Derry, Hudson, Windham, and Salem, New Hampshire.[4] It was there that Deacon John Cochran settled.[5]

Both Sally and her husband, Chauncey Cochran, were descendants of Deacon John.[6] Now that the family had established a foothold in America, each successive generation of Sally and Chauncey's direct forebears would acquire land either through ambition and drive or the lucky happenstance of being an eldest male and inheriting family property, the pattern of primogeniture that remained extremely common in the New World.[7] The ownership of land and the potential wealth that went with it was a key difference between the later fortunes of the Cochran and Prescott families.

Sally Cochran's father, Moses, born in 1767, was a great-grandson of Deacon John. His forebears had remained at the site of the first settlement for four generations. Moses married "Jenny" Jane Cochran in 1797. Her mother was a great-granddaughter of Deacon John, but her ancestors had relocated, in the mid-eighteenth century, to the area of Pembroke, which was just being developed at the time. Among things dauntingly required to be performed by the settlers of that new town were "the enclosure of 1,000 acres with a suitable fence to protect herbage within two months; to build a bridge across the Great Suncook River at the isle, within one year; and each one to build a house upon his share or lot, and have a family settled there, within two years, from the date hereof."[8] This appears to have been an immense amount of work to expect from the small group of settlers. The only good news in the ambitious assignment is that the "great" Suncook River is more of a wide stream than a major river, so the building of a bridge could be accomplished fairly readily. The enormous length of fencing that was required was probably first satisfied by stacking split rails, held in place by vertical posts or "stakes," or even with roughly piled brush or tree stumps.[9] The stone walls that would come to define the landscape of rocky New England were much more a work in progress, crafted over the active farming life of the land as rocks pushed up by frost with each successive winter were dragged to the edges of fields and piled up, although properly built walls were more of an art than just a stone pile.[10]

After their marriage, second cousins Jenny and Moses Cochran probably initially lived with one set or the other of their parents. Setting up a new household immediately after marriage in the post–Revolutionary era was relatively unusual. The typical household of the period was often a noisy, complicated, blended mix of parents, children, stepchildren, grandparents, unmarried siblings, nieces and nephews, boarders, hired help, slaves, apprentices, and sometimes orphans.[11] Having a lot of adults in a household could make a significant difference in the management of the vast amount of work that had to be done every day, even though the presence of all those extra people also meant more mouths to feed and more laundry to manage.

By 1810, Moses and Jenny Cochran and their three surviving children were established in their own home in Londonderry.[12] At that point, Sally Cochran was just five years old, and Jenny was pregnant with Mary Jane, who would be born on Sally's sixth birthday. Sally and Mary Jane would share a particular bond beyond having the same birthday. Mary Jane would later marry Sally's husband's younger brother and move in right across the lane, making the young women both sisters and sisters-in-law to each other.

Like most women of her day, Jenny Cochran spent much of her childbearing years either pregnant or nursing.[13] She was nearly eighteen at the time of her marriage, and her first child, James, was born on the day before her nineteenth birthday. When her last child was born in 1824, she had just recently celebrated her forty-fourth birthday.[14] Large families were the rule rather than the exception, although by around 1800 family sizes began to slowly diminish from their previous impressive eighteenth-century levels.[15] At the beginning of the nineteenth century, the average family consisted of seven children (a number that had dropped to 3.5 children by 1900).[16] Little was known about birth control in Federal America, except that breast-feeding was generally recognized as being helpful at prolonging the time before another pregnancy. Rhythm as a method of birth control was a failure because, rather surprisingly, the female reproductive cycle wasn't very well understood. No one seemed quite certain about when in their cycles women were most likely to conceive or, more importantly, not conceive. Men of the time were far more aware of when their farm animals should be bred than when they ought to avoid intercourse with their wives if they wanted to limit family size, a concept that was almost certainly of more significance to women than men. Giving birth to so many children with limited medical care proved lethal to many women.[17] Widowers who were coupled with second, third, or even fourth wives weren't at all unusual.

Large families could provide a handy source of workers, albeit young and inexperienced, but the continued subdivision of family farms and usable land was already putting pressure on the New England landscape by this period. While the all-too-common specter of young death made it unlikely that all of a family's children would survive to adulthood during the era when Moses and Jenny Cochran were having their children, childhood mortality rates had actually fallen below those of both a previous generation and, surprisingly, of several generations to follow. (The rising childhood mortality of the nineteenth century paralleled the move from farms to cities, which turned out to be much less healthy places for children to live.)[18] For Sally and Chauncey, large Cochran families had little impact on their well-being. That would not be so in the Prescott family.

Chauncey Cochran's background overlapped significantly with his wife's. His father, James, was her uncle, her mother's elder brother. James was born in 1768 and in 1788, married Lettice "Letty" Duncan, who'd been born in 1764.[19] Lettice gave birth to seven children. Her youngest two were Chauncey, born in 1801, and James, born three years later, who would marry Sally's younger sister, Mary Jane. All three of Chauncey's older brothers were dead by 1819. That left Chauncey as the eldest surviving son when his father died that year, perhaps suddenly, since he didn't leave a will. Chauncey inherited a large portion of the family farm. However, the fact that his younger brother lived just across the lane probably means that the farmland was subdivided when the elder James died.

The Cochran family, like many of its era, had seen marriages between relatives.[20] However, the close intermingling among Cochran cousins was more than was typical and no doubt at least partially reflected the way their forebears had remained somewhat separate from non-Scotch-Irish settlers. With the final marriages between first cousins Sally and Chauncey and Mary Jane and James, that close relationship became even tighter. Sally and Mary Jane Cochran likely envisioned a future where their offspring, so near in age, would grow up side by side, double first cousins and next-door neighbors both. The events of June 23, 1833, put an end to that dream.

⊰ 3 ⊱

SALLY AND CHAUNCEY COCHRAN

The fairest bloom of sublunary bliss.
—"On Life, Death, and Immortality," stitched
on Sally Cochran's sampler

The world into which Sally Cochran was born on February 24, 1805, would have been instantly recognizable to her grandparents or even her great-grandparents. The Industrial Revolution, which would soon bring enormous, life-altering change to the New England countryside and its residents, was still in its infancy.[1] While some progress had already come to southern New Hampshire, farm and village life was only just starting to be noticeably affected by the time of her death in 1833.

Coming in about the middle of her mother's ten children, but the eldest surviving girl, Sally Cochran would have taken on the unending burden of female work as a very young child. Once she reached school age, she was probably assisting with laundry (an arduous, multiday process that was completed each week), care of the garden, cooking, child care, and some of the sewing, the complexity of the jobs evolving as Sally grew up and her mother's time was increasingly taken up with the other children, who kept arriving at such regular intervals. The 1810 census reveals that the Cochran household didn't include any live-in hired help, or even the useful presence of an adult female relative, so it was just Sally and her mother available to complete the enormous amount of work involved in running a household.

But the Cochrans were financially secure, owned land, and valued education for their children. Around the time that Sally turned thirteen, after having attended the public schools since she was about five, she was sent to the Pinkerton Academy to receive the more refined education that a private school could offer. The Pinkerton Academy advertised in 1817 in the *Farmer's Cabinet,* the local newspaper, that "The female apartment in this academy will be opened on Monday the 26th of May, instant; wherein will be taught all the useful and ornamental branches of female instruction usually attended in similar institutions. At the same time an additional instructor will be placed in the male apartment. The tuition is two dollars a quarter. Board may be had in respectable families, within a convenient distance of the Academy, on reasonable terms." While there were other private schools in the region that educated girls, the Pinkerton Academy was the school that was located closest to the Cochran family while they lived in Londonderry.

When she was a child, the education offered to young girls differed hugely from place to place and family to family.[2] In many New England towns, public schools operated and offered at least a rudimentary education to both boys and girls. These schools often also provided girls with some needlework instruction, and many girls stitched at least a simple sampler while attending, demonstrating their mastery—still critical for nearly all future homemakers, as girls were destined to be— of basic sewing skills. Students attended two terms a year, summer and winter, until they reached the age of about ten to twelve. After that, if they weren't intending to pursue a higher level of education (and few did), they might continue to attend school for a few more years for just the winter term, when little farm work competed for their time.[3]

Early public schools were dark, cold to frigid in winter, and overly hot in summer. They featured desks, or sometimes just rows of benches, and little else. The schoolmaster or mistress was frequently only slightly older than the many scholars, creating a dynamic that could vary from merely chaotic to violent. The students were grouped by ability, with "classes" cutting across a wide range of ages. Each class would be given assignments, usually rote memorization followed by recitation, often as a group, which ensured that the less skilled or motivated could advance without having actually learned much.[4] These were the type of schools that the Prescott children also attended, at least intermittently. Both Sally and Chauncey Cochran began their education in public schools, but with their higher socioeconomic status, they moved on to private academies.

The education provided by town schools often didn't extend beyond training comparable, at best, to about an eighth-grade level. Most male students who participated in higher education, beyond the public grammar schools, were eventually bound for college and the professions. For the less affluent, whatever schooling they had received when crops weren't being harvested and weather permitted travel to school was followed by an apprenticeship to learn a trade, boarding out as a farm worker, as Abraham Prescott did, and later resettling on a family farm if they were fortunate enough to inherit one, or after about 1820 in New England, perhaps a job in a mill.

Private schools offered an alternative for those who could afford to pay the tuition. Male scholars would learn more advanced mathematics and science, grammar, Greek and Latin, handwriting, possibly French, history, geography, and often some type of study of classical literature. When they had reached an appropriate level of preparation, usually in their mid-teens, college would follow for many of the young men. Although Chauncey Cochran didn't attend college, maybe because of his father's early death, his schooling helped prepare him for the complex tasks of modern farm management.

Girls coming from higher socioeconomic groups were welcomed at some of these private academies. A few of the more forward-thinking schools offered girls an education that was nearly as academically focused as what they were providing to young boys. But most academies, and especially the smaller schools that were female-run and home-based, also instructed young women in the "female arts," which usually included painting, drawing, general sewing, decorative sewing, and music and dance instruction.[5] College after an academy education was not an option for young women in the early nineteenth century—none accepted females until Oberlin College in Ohio admitted four young women in 1837, followed almost immediately by Mount Holyoke College.[6] The goal of private schooling really depended on the attitude of a young woman's parents, but providing the refinements that might ensure a good marriage was often a major motivation.

While she attended Pinkerton Academy, Cochran worked an intricate and artistic "family register" (genealogical) sampler that remained in her family for another century and a half, a poignant reminder of her short life. Cochran's sampler differed sharply from earlier schoolgirl embroideries. The first known examplars, as they were originally

known, appear to date from around the time of the reign of Queen Elizabeth I, and were stitched on long, narrow pieces of linen. The stitchery
may have been intended primarily to preserve complex patterns that
might be used to embellish the edges of clothing, and the examplars
remained unframed, rolled up for future reference.[7] Or, since records
are nearly nonexistent, samplers may always have been teaching exer-
cises, whereby young girls practiced embroidery under the guidance of
skilled female instructors.[8] By the eighteenth century, samplers were
assuming a more rectangular shape and often incorporated a wide
variety of different types of stitches, not just patterns, demonstrating
the maker's mastery of the complex, intricate language of embroidery.[9]
Late in the eighteenth century, some samplers had become exceptionally artistic, featuring complex, artful designs that were pleasing to the
eye, but often included just a half-dozen or less different needlework
techniques. These were most often stitched on loom-woven linen that
was even in weave, a critical factor as most of the stitchery involved
counting the threads of the ground to identify the proper placement
of each stitch in order to ensure tidy, perfectly even work.[10] Expensive
imported, naturally dyed silk threads would be used to render patterns
that were typically created by teachers who blended elements copied
from other instructors, borders that were specific to their regions, and
design elements that were all their own.[11]

As the girls stitched, one of their group would often read to the others from some suitably instructive and uplifting text, or the girls would
use the time to chat. When Cochran began her sampler, she sat side
by side with twelve-year-old Margaret Anderson of Londonderry, a
distant cousin, who worked a virtually identical piece that year, both,
no doubt, designed by their teacher.[12] Their samplers are among eight
from the school that have been identified, a relatively large group of
survivors for a school of its size. Leafy vines surrounded the sections
that contained their names, and satin-stitched, checkerboard cornucopia in the bottom corners sprouted attractive, complex floral borders
that reached up the sides and met at the top.

Copying a style that had originated in Lynn, Massachusetts, a couple of decades before (and likely brought to Londonderry by a former
student-turned-teacher), Sally Cochran stitched in the names of her
family members and their birth dates.[13] Although her sampler incor-

porates the design elements that were typical for her school, Cochran also would have participated in planning her needlework, likely choosing some of the elements (such as the whimsical basket at the center bottom) and selecting the colors of silk thread that she wanted to use, creating a design that was unique to her. Hers is one of the most colorful of the group. Several other girls kept their samplers nearly monochromatic.[14]

Schoolgirl needlework was often presented to a girl's parents when completed and then proudly exhibited on a wall in the family home. When young men came to court, the needlework subtly advertised that their daughter had all the tools to make a good wife. Displaying the pieces inevitably led to damage from smoke and sunlight over the years. Most samplers that have survived are faded and stained. However, Cochran's sampler remains brightly colored, so it probably didn't spend very many years on display. After her early death, her parents or husband may have tucked it away, not wanting to look every day on this powerful reminder of her innocent childhood. The birth—and death—dates of her youngest sister, Betsy Cochran, are recorded on it, even though those events, especially the toddler's death in 1822, occurred after the sampler was considered finished. (Someone also updated Margaret Anderson's sampler, even adding the date of her own death in 1844.)[15] Cochran stitched a highly unusual and especially somber—and prescient—motto on her sampler:

Each moment has its sickle and cuts down
The fairest bloom of sublunary bliss.

Her verse was a shortened version of a long poem by British poet Edward Young that had first appeared in print in the mid-eighteenth century. Although death-related sampler verses are quite common (one begins "When I am dead and worms eat me—"), Cochran's verse is not known to have appeared on any other schoolgirl embroidery and is the only somber one of those associated with the Pinkerton Academy and the Adams Female Academy, which replaced the school in 1821, when the trustees of Pinkerton voted to stop accepting females.[16]

Sally Cochran's sampler is the only remaining object that can be definitively associated with her life. Its artistry demonstrates a very high

level of accomplishment with the needle that would make it an especially sought-after textile among collectors. Completion of her sampler
probably marked the end of her education.

Perhaps as early as 1818, Moses and Jenny Cochran and their children packed up and moved to Pembroke, New Hampshire. Their move
may have been partially motivated by the severely cold weather and
drought that had afflicted New England and most of the eastern United
States over the past few years, especially in 1816, known as "the year
without a summer."[17] Many farmers were pushed into bankruptcy and
near starvation by crop failures during those years.[18] It's also possible
that a Cochran family farm became available in Pembroke at that point.
The 1820 census of Pembroke shows Moses as the eldest male adult in a
household that also included an older woman, probably a widowed relative. Since Jenny was from Pembroke, she had many family members
there who could now provide her with assistance as her family grew in
size. This may have helped relieve the burden on Sally, too.

If Sally and Chauncey Cochran hadn't already known each other well,
they were now thrown into much closer contact, since their homes were
less than a half mile apart, alongside the same country lane. When his
father died on July 31, 1819, Chauncey became, at seventeen, the head
of the Cochran household, taking over management of the family farm,
under the supervision of a male legal guardian until he reached twenty-
one, where his mother, Lettice, continued to live. At that time, it was
very common for a man to spell out in his will that his wife would have
entitlement to certain rooms in the house, use of the well, even milk
from a cow, as long as she didn't remarry.[19] Lettice Cochran continued
on, much as she had, although Sally became the mistress of the house
when she married Chauncey. But since James hadn't left a will, neighbors were appointed to inventory his possessions, providing evidence
of a substantial collection of mixed livestock, numerous farm tools and
household goods, including three feather beds and two much less com-
fortable chaff (straw) beds, many chairs, some silver spoons, two spinning wheels, and a loom. The clock the Cochrans were so proud of must
have been one they bought later as it was not included on the list.

On November 26, 1828, Sally and Chauncey Cochran were married,
most likely in the parlor of her parents' home.[20] She was twenty-three
and he had just celebrated his twenty-seventh birthday. Their close

family members gathered to celebrate the occasion, but it was a low-key affair. No honeymoon journey followed their exchange of vows. Sometime soon after, Sally Cochran packed her few possessions and they were carted down the road to her new husband's home.[21]

The Cochran family farm that she moved to after her wedding stood on a quiet dirt-and-grass country road, some distance from the center of town on what is now known as North Pembroke Road. It was situated at the top of a hill that sloped away from the road, gently at first, and then dropping off much more steeply as the land approached the fast-moving Great Brook, now called Ames Brook. Although the Cochran home hasn't survived, a map created in the 1890s shows it was located on the front edge of their property.[22] It sat close by the side of the road, with a big and then a smaller extension at the rear of it. Just a short distance behind that stood their large barn with an attached shed at the back of it.

Constructed by Chauncey's father in 1789, the house was built in the post-and-beam manner, like all homes of its era, with enormous framing timbers pegged together and assembled atop a dry laid-stone foundation over a hand-dug cellar hole.[23] Given the distance to Great Brook, it had a dug well, probably the same one that remained on the former Cochran land until it was finally bulldozed in 2012, capped with an enormous stone to keep animals (and small children and desperate housewives) from falling in. There were windows on all four sides of the house. The house, with its huge center chimney, may have been either a Cape Cod–style, one-and-a-half-story structure or more likely, given the Cochrans' prosperity, a full two-story house with several rooms on the first floor and four bedchambers on the second.

The home was surrounded by a garden, "mowing fields," and behind those, a large pasture. Usually farmers reserved their better fields for hay and ones that were rockier or steeper for pasture, and Cochran's back pasture was both rocky and steeply sloped. Hay was the primary crop of New England farms in the early nineteenth century, at first just natural meadow grass, but increasingly in Cochran's era, fields were planted with far superior English hay. The Cochrans kept cattle, cows, and pigs. They probably also kept chickens and turkeys, animals that were frequently raised on mixed-agriculture New England farms.[24]

The rural farm of the 1820s and 1830s remained a largely self-suffi-cient operation. Sally acted as a partner to Chauncey in the farming business, although there was a fairly sharp division between male and female tasks. He managed the larger farm stock, the hand mowing of the hayfields, plowing and planting, the marketing of farm products that he had produced, the construction of fencing, the maintenance of the buildings, and the vast, nearly all-year-long task of acquiring sufficient firewood to heat the drafty house in winter and fuel the always-burning kitchen fire year-round. Larger homes, as the Cochrans' probably was, could require an enormous mountain of from fifteen to twenty cords of firewood a year.[25] Nearly every other task was in Sally's domain.

Like most farmwives, her work truly was never done. It would have included, among other things, watching the children, laundry (a job that even included the nasty job of making soap), cooking for family and farm workers, preparing milk and butter for sale, baking bread, caring for the smaller livestock, especially poultry, overseeing the kitchen garden, spinning and then weaving wool and linen, housecleaning, and sewing all children's clothing, some of Chauncey's attire, and most of her own.[26]

Cooking alone consumed an enormous amount of time. Cochran was responsible for providing three meals a day, with the largest one served at midday. She prepared these meals over an open fire, bending over pots suspended from a metal crane attached to one side of a big kitchen fireplace. Once or twice a week, she also baked, using an oven built into the side of her fireplace. She'd first kindle a fire in the oven, let it burn long enough to fully heat the bricks that lined the space, then carefully shovel it out. Foods to be baked would be put in successively with those that needed the highest heat going in first. On a big baking day, the oven might need to be heated twice. In summer, all this cooking and baking would have left the kitchen unbearably hot. Cochran was also responsible for all the tasks associated with dairying. This included thoroughly scrubbing and scalding the pails used to collect the milk, milking the cows twice a day (which could easily take an hour or so each time), straining the milk, churning butter, and possibly making cheese. The enormous amount of work that had to be completed by the average early nineteenth-century farmwife like Cochran was daunting.

Given all of these activities, Cochran was clearly a very busy young woman. Of course, she had help from her mother-in-law and, in addition, her hired girl. From at least 1830 until her death, Cochran was aided by a young girl, who was recorded on the 1830 US federal census as being between five and ten years of age. Chauncey mentioned the girl, although not by name, in his testimony, saying she was about eleven years old in 1833. Given her very young age—most hired girls were more like twelve to eighteen years old—Sally probably had to train the child herself.[27] She may often have seemed more hindrance than help since she had to first be painstakingly taught how to complete each chore, and then watched closely to make sure it was being done right. Often hired girls came from poorer families, and being hired out might provide them with a steady if small wage (although many worked for just room and board) and living conditions that were generally better than what they were able to get at home.[28] Since Cochran's household help was even younger than the usual, Sally was probably also serving as much as a mother figure to the child as an employer.

After the Cochran children began to be born, the dynamic changed. While pregnant or nursing, Sally was no longer readily available to help her husband with his farm chores. Following in the footsteps of her maternal forebears, Sally Cochran must have been nearly overwhelmed by the large volume of work that she faced. The farm was well-established and her husband could now afford some additional help. About three years before her murder, Sally became something of a surrogate mother to another hired hand who joined the family and resided in their home with them. Abraham Prescott came to work for the Cochrans.

NIGHTTIME ATTACK

The January transaction
—Abigail Calef

On the cold night of Sunday, January 6, 1833, Abraham Prescott went to bed in his chamber before the Cochrans retired because he knew that he would be needed earlier than usual the next morning. As in homes all over New England, Monday would be washing day—always highly challenging in the coldest days of winter—and he might have to help haul the water.[1] But around 11 P.M., long after other members of the family had also gone to bed, he got up, went into the clock room to light a candle, then back to the kitchen, where he rekindled the fire in the fireplace. Since all of Prescott's activities on this cold night were documented only from what he would report, it's impossible to know if he was awake or asleep during his wanderings, although his actions seem highly purposeful for a sleepwalker to accomplish.

It was very cold in the Cochran house on that January night. Although the past few days had been warmer than usual, with the snow melting, making sleighing (the typical form of winter transportation) difficult, the nights were well below freezing.[2] Most households buried their large daytime fires in ashes before retiring, "banking the fire," in order to preserve some hot coals for morning. Even if the fire in the Cochrans' expansive kitchen fireplace was burning fiercely, the heat from it wouldn't have warmed even that room significantly—nearly all of the heat went up the massive chimney rather than back into the room. On cold days, fires would be kept burning in all the fireplaces, but even the best-appointed houses rarely had more than four or five, and by eleven at night, the fires would have faded to mere glowing embers anyway. The temperature inside the house would approach or drop below freezing on cold nights like this one. (Many diaries of the eighteenth and nineteenth centuries comment on water solidly frozen in jugs when people arose in the mornings, and Prescott's nighttime adventure took place in an era when winters were far more severe than typical twenty-first-century ones.)

Prescott almost certainly didn't have a chamber with a fireplace; those heated rooms would have been reserved for Sally and Chauncey's bedroom and for the chamber where Lettice slept. He may even have slept on one of the chaff mattresses in front of the kitchen fire instead. It's not surprising that Prescott's first thought, when he got up in the middle of the night (either awake or sleepwalking), was to kindle a fire and try to get a little warmer. With each breath, frost clouded the air around his face.

Even once he had the fire burning well, the room remained unpleasantly cold. Since he was chilly, dressed for bed as he was, only in the long shirt he'd also worn all day, Prescott took up the candle, crept quietly into Chauncey and Sally's bedroom and picked up a buffalo skin robe. He may have taken it off their bed since it's hard to imagine they wouldn't have wanted to enjoy its warmth as they slept. Buffalo robes had just recently become commonly available and were much appreciated.[3] The couple slept through his stealthy nocturnal visit. Then he lay down, with it wrapped around him, by the blazing fire.

He may have dozed. A little later, he rose up again and went out to the woodshed, located behind the back of the house, where he found the ax that was used for splitting kindling. Whether he had to go outside for this, or if the woodshed was part of the extension behind the house, isn't clear. He then returned to the main house and silently reentered the Cochrans' bedchamber, holding the candle out before him to light his way. The smooth wooden handle of the ax was icy cold in his grip.

He set the candle down. The light splashed across the forms of the Cochrans, resting quietly under a mound of bedclothes. Both were soundly sleeping, Sally on her back and Chauncey on his left side, when Prescott began to rain a series of blows down upon their unprotected heads with the ax, quickly beating both of them unconscious. Blood droplets sprayed across the blankets and onto his shirt, the walls, and the plaster ceiling as he swung the ax up and down. Panting from the heavy work, he fled the room, heading for the outside door, off the kitchen, where he dropped the crimson-stained weapon into the snow. Hearing groans now coming from the bedroom, he crept back there. The bloody bedclothes looked black in the dim candlelight. Sally Cochran was unconscious, but Chauncey, severely injured and bewildered, was trying hard to rise up onto his hands and knees, though still encumbered by the coverlets that trapped him. Failing in his brief struggle to free himself, Chauncey collapsed.

Whether or not he had been asleep when he attacked the Cochrans, now Prescott was fully awake and alarmed by what he saw. Either he was astonished at their severe injuries and wondering how and by whom they had been attacked, or he was equally surprised that he hadn't quite managed to kill them as he'd perhaps planned. Whatever his thoughts at this moment, Prescott went to awaken Lettice, who slept in an adjoining room and was the only remaining adult in the house. He told her that—while sleepwalking—he "didn't know but he had killed Chauncey and his wife."[4] Presumably, if he had attacked them while asleep, he shouldn't now have known how or by whom they'd been injured, so his comment seems revealing.

Lettice Cochran faced a horrific situation. She was in the house, in the dead of the night, with a strong young man who had just badly beaten her son and his wife—the splatter on his hands and shirt providing ample evidence of what he claimed. She must have wondered what he would do next. Her first thought may have been to get him out of the house until some help could come. She sent Prescott to fetch the neighbors. The closest were Jonathan Robinson, who lived with his three unmarried daughters, Lucy, Belinda, and Clarrissa, and William Abbott Jr., both of whom had homes just across the road. Even though her youngest son lived across the street as well, the three houses all in a row, she didn't send Prescott there, almost certainly not wanting to risk him attacking another of her children. When the Robinsons arrived, they immediately sent Prescott to fetch Dr. Samuel Sargent, the same physician who would be called to tend Sally only five months later. They, too, probably wanted him out of the house.

Sargent came quickly, bringing Prescott back with him. The boy settled onto a chair near the fire, uninvolved in the chaotic scene as the doctor and the neighbors bustled about, trying to minister to the injured couple, mopping up the blood and bandaging their wounds. Except for load moans he emitted every now and then, Prescott was all but invisible, not helping, but not trying to escape either.

Sargent later testified, "I was at Chauncey Cochran's on the 6th of January, 1833, at five minutes before twelve at night; staid about three hours; found Mr. Cochran and his wife both badly wounded and insensible; they remained so when I left. In six or seven hours I saw them again, when they had partially regained their senses. Mr. Cochran was wounded severely on the right temple; his eyes swollen so that he could not see; Mrs. Cochran was bruised from the nose across the cheek. Prescott was about there, his appearance much as to-day, and he sometimes expressed anxiety and moaned. I prepared, at the request of the family and neighbors, an account of the case for the 'New Hampshire Patriot,' and my name was signed to the article. I thought it probable he had got up in his sleep; knew of no difficulty in the family."[5] Dr. Sargent recognized that this was a remarkable story and that publicizing it (and thus himself) wouldn't do any harm to his medical practice. It's not especially clear, however, why Chauncey Cochran would have wanted the story of Prescott's attack to appear in the newspaper, unless it was to confirm for all who wondered that this was, indeed, a case of sleepwalking, as he and Sally accepted. Chauncey, of course, was recovering from his injuries and may not even have been consulted by Sargent before he contacted the newspaper.

If Prescott had struck the Cochrans with the sharp blade of the ax, it's hard to imagine why neither of them was killed. It seems more likely that he used the blunt side of the ax head as his weapon. He may even have beaten them with the flat side of the ax. That both of the Cochrans took many hours to regain consciousness is ample evidence that the blows were applied with real force and caused significant head injuries. But neither of the couple had any defensive wounds on their hands, as they would have had if the first blows Prescott inflicted were truly tentative and they had had time to untangle themselves from their bedcoverings. However, the force Prescott applied wasn't lethal as it easily could have been. Since they had no defensive wounds, it's likely Prescott hit them hard enough to knock them unconscious with the first strikes. What happened next seems almost inexplicable, even given the seemingly warm relationship the Cochrans had with their unpredictable farmhand. They decided that they would keep the teen on with them.

They apparently believed that they knew Prescott well and could trust him, and that the violent assault wasn't—couldn't be—his fault. The story of Prescott's attack was picked up by other newspapers in the region. Those that covered the tale reported it as "an extraordinary example of somnambulism," seeming to fully accept, as the Cochrans must also have, Prescott's claim that he had been sleepwalking.[6] Even if the Cochrans fully and completely believed that Prescott wasn't responsible since he had brutally and nearly lethally attacked them while sleepwalking, they must have been deeply concerned that he could do this again, since it was therefore presumably something he might be subject to and couldn't control. When he had recovered from his injuries, Cochran paid a visit to Prescott's parents to confirm that their son wasn't in the habit of sleepwalking. At the time, they told him that it had never been a problem. That, at least, helped diminish the Cochrans' worries about the teen. It also confirms that they had embraced the sleepwalking explanation.

By the 1830s, with the Industrial Revolution swiftly changing the face of New England, and new understanding developing in the fields of medicine and the just-blossoming study of psychiatry, science was coming to have an increasingly important role in the thinking of sophisticated and well-educated people.[7] To accept that Prescott's bizarre attack had a scientific basis—it happened during somnambulism— rather than a criminal explanation was to think in a modern way, and the Cochrans were modern people.

Later Chauncey would describe Prescott's attitude toward the January attack: "He appeared to be very sorry; I believed it; told him he ought to be very thankful that he did not kill us; he made no answer; would look down, and was not inclined to talk about it; there had been no misunderstanding between prisoner and myself or wife; he had resided three years in the family; his deportment was very good; he was obedient and kind; have known him to get water instead of my wife, after she had started for it; prisoner was eighteen years old the same month of the accident; always thought he was bad tempered; sometimes abused the cattle; never quarreled with any of the family; always treated the children affectionately, and never refused to perform labor; we never put anything hard upon him after he had done his day's work; I always stated he was good and capable; never complained until recently of his bad temper; don't know that I requested others to refrain from speaking to him of the winter transaction; never censured him for it; gave him no money to appease him."

That Cochran contradicted himself, describing Prescott as "good" and as "bad tempered" and "obedient and kind" but also someone who persistently abused animals confirms his continued confusion about the Jekyll-and-Hyde character of the boy. Cochran appears to have regarded him as unpredictable and perhaps not wholly likable, but a good worker who could be relied upon to complete his farm chores. Yet it seems improbable that the Cochrans would keep him there, living with their young, vulnerable children, given the potential threat he represented after that January, only because he was a good worker.

If, when he committed the attack, Prescott was awake, then that would be an even better reason to end their connection with him. Prescott was clearly not a completely mild and harmless young man, and his behavior had seemingly been getting worse after that strange and violent January night. Cochran would later report that Prescott "sometimes had beat my cattle unmercifully; had reproved him often for that, and on such occasion he never made much reply, generally looked down and cross; had latterly grown rather more severe in his treatment of the cattle."[8] But even that, almost inexplicably, doesn't seem to have raised any special concern in Cochran.

However improbable, it might be argued that the Cochrans kept Prescott in their employ because he was—somehow—blackmailing them (as implied by Chauncey's comment, "Gave him no money to appease him"), but there's no hint in the later trial records or newspaper coverage of anything negative about the Cochran family. If Prescott had been blackmailing them, there would need to be some type of offense that Prescott could have observed, and then might have been willing and able to use against the Cochrans. It needed to be something so ruinous that the Cochrans could accept and ignore the obvious danger of the "winter transaction" for fear of their own misbehavior being made public.

Two possibilities for this exist: one, that Chauncey was engaged in some type of criminal activity that, if revealed, would result in a scandal if not a prison term. But Chauncey, at this time, was a self-employed farmer, didn't have access to large sums of other people's money, and appears to have had little opportunity to commit a crime. Very soon after Sally's death, Chauncey moved with his children to a town just north of Bangor, Maine, a considerable distance. He would spend the rest of his life there and was always regarded as an upstanding pillar of the community, so presumably was reputable, at least after his wife's death.

The second possibility is of a sexual liaison between Sally and Prescott, or even more scandalously, between Chauncey and the teen. If Chauncey and Prescott were engaged in a sexual affair, then both their names and reputations would be severely tarnished by the release of that information, but surely Chauncey would have far more to lose than Prescott.

It is unlikely that many would have believed Prescott if he had made such an accusation. Reputation of both accuser and accused was a key consideration, as recently proven by the acquittal of Reverend Avery in the face of damning evidence of his guilt, most of it based upon the message left by his victim, who was, of course, a mere female mill worker and thus perceived as socially and probably also morally inferior to Avery. Prescott came from a family that was regarded as untrustworthy as some witnesses would testify at his trials, and being young and mostly uneducated, any accusations the teen could make would be generally suspect. While the Cochrans would be highly concerned, their position in the community would surely trump an accusation from Prescott.

With Sally still young and attractive and Prescott living right in her household, some neighbors may have considered the possibility that she and Prescott might have been enjoying a relationship. Chauncey testified, "I had been absent several times two or three days each; a short time before the murder I was absent and left only Mrs. Cochran, two small children, and a girl of ten or twelve years old, with the prisoner."[9] This implies that Chauncey trusted Prescott and his wife alone together. Chauncey went on, "Don't know that prisoner ever accompanied wife in the evening; have known him to accompany her home from her father's. Had been below four or five weeks previous to winter occurrence; nothing said at that time of killing hogs; wife generally washed early Monday mornings; prisoner not generally required to make fire; when she washed he often got up; never knew anything in his conduct to induce me to suspect the winter affair to be an attempt at murder; know of no motive for his conduct."[10] Here—"washed early mornings"—Chauncey was not describing his wife rising early to bathe, with Prescott getting up too, but the day of the week that Sally would rise early, make the fire to heat the water, and then wash laundry. The reference to "killing hogs"—always done at the onset of winter—is intriguing. That work would likely have been done in the yard or perhaps in the barn cellar, connecting it to the reference to "been below." On small farms, hogs were generally struck on the head, perhaps with the blunt side of an ax, to stun them, before their throats were cut—eerily similar to Prescott's attack on the Cochrans.[11] It's unfortunate that most of the testimony from the trial was preserved in such a condensed form. Whatever the reference to killing hogs was in regard to, it was never mentioned again. Cochran portrayed Prescott as helpful, not devious, and also implied that the relationship between his wife and Prescott was a proper one.

The most likely reason that the Cochrans would overlook the attack is that they may have actually grown fond of Prescott, or at least very accustomed to him, in the three years he had lived with them. While no one described him as being a charming person, he does come across as at least steadfast and reliable. He may have appeared as a somewhat sympathetic character to the Cochrans, coming as he did from a poor and at times possibly even chaotic background, very different from the upbringing their children were experiencing.

But the winter attack had certainly gotten attention from those who had heard of it, an infamous event that may have left many disagreeing with the Cochrans' decision. This seems to be confirmed by the testimony of Abigail Calef: "I saw Mrs. Cochran a few weeks before her death and conversed with her about the January transaction. She remarked that her escape was truly wonderful; it was a great mercy that they both were not killed. I told her I would not keep such a boy. She said Prescott was a good boy; she had no doubt he was asleep, and did not intentionally hurt them."[12] It's easy to imagine that Sally might have responded quite assertively—maybe more enthusiastically than she truly felt—to Abigail's busybody-like (and wholly critical) comment that *she* would not keep such a boy. What Lettice Cochran thought of the whole thing is unknown. She was never called to testify and left no record of her thoughts even though she had probably observed Prescott nearly as much as her son had. Abigail Calef's testimony provided the only words that Sally is known to have said. The painful irony—that they were in kindly defense of her murderer—is especially tragic.

The Cochrans probably chose to forget the "January transaction" because they had affection for Prescott and ultimately, in their hearts, couldn't believe that he would deliberately hurt them or their children, and that the possibility of another sleepwalking assault was just too unlikely to even bear discussion. In spite of all the signs that Prescott was not a mild, placid young man, they may have been convinced that he shared their affectionate family bond. They were also, by this time, familiar with his work ethic; in most ways he seemed highly reliable. Just as Sally was beguiled by a beautiful early summer morning into thinking she was perfectly safe berry picking alone with Prescott, the Cochrans seem to have given little or no consideration to the apparently too-remote possibility that the boy in their midst could become a murderer, even with his past behavior. Whatever the reason, the choice they made was in error and Sally would pay the ultimate price for that tragic mistake.

⊰ 5 ⊱

THE PRESCOTT FAMILY

His brothers were not very pacific
—Mary Critchett

In the 1830 census, the last one before Cochran's murder, Abraham Prescott was recorded as aged ten to under fifteen but, since he was said to be eighteen at the time of her death, he must have been closer to the higher end of that age bracket when the census taker stopped in the Cochran farmyard on the first day of June to record their information for the fourth US Federal Census. Prescott had been hired shortly after Sally gave birth to her daughter, Sarah. Before that time, she'd been available to help Chauncey with some chores that were usually outside the female realm like shucking feed corn, helping stack hay or hoeing the garden, but once there was also a baby to tend, Chauncey needed—and could afford—additional male help. When Chauncey hired Prescott, he (and many others in Pembroke) were well aware of the boy's impoverished background and perhaps unrefined upbringing.

The Prescott family was already well established in New England by the time the Cochrans arrived in southeastern New Hampshire from Ireland. Some members of the family were highly successful, but the Prescott family was a late, and probably not altogether welcome, arrival into the tight-knit Pembroke community.[1] At the beginning of the eighteenth century, Abraham Prescott's forebears benefited from land grants that were offered to encourage inland settlement, with the population then gathered tightly against the coast, enjoying relative safety from Native American attacks. Prescott's great-great-grandfather became a major landowner, but in each successive generation that followed, there were numerous children. Since his particular forebear was always among the youngest in each subsequent generation, that man was cut out of the inheritance of land and farmstead by the typical rule of primogeniture, which meant the eldest son would inherit the real estate. The women those ancestors married would generally inherit a few textiles, occasional pieces of furniture, and sometimes small bequests of money, but none of Prescott's line enjoyed the wealth and stability that inheritance of land could provide.

Prescott's grandfather, also named Abraham Prescott, was born in 1717 in Kensington, New Hampshire. His reputation as a religious fanatic who was inattentive or abusive to his wife would feature large in his grandson's defense at his murder trials. Abraham's emotional difficulties and his position as one of the youngest children who inherited little may have kept him from acquiring much in life. When he died in 1789, he left a smattering of furniture, a couple of cows and a pig, and a good collection of farming tools to work his 33 acres of land. The average size of a farm in New England at that time varied from place to place and is very difficult to precisely quantify. However, starting in 1850, the federal census assembled agricultural schedules that collected detailed information on all individual farms in many states but not, unfortunately, for New Hampshire. In the nearby border town of Lebanon, Maine, in 1850 the average farm size was 94.75 acres, and almost none was less than 40 acres in size.[2] Although this statistic marks a place in time that is several decades later, considering the farm size was reportedly shrinking, Abraham's holding was quite small by comparison, barely enough to provide sustenance for his large family.

Chase Prescott, his tenth child, again one of the youngest, was born in 1761. Chase may have grown up in a fairly dysfunctional home with so many siblings and a mentally unstable father who didn't always provide well for his family. A few years before 1790, he married Betsy Thomas Otis, a widow, who was the mother of his first two children, Sally C. Prescott, who later married Caleb Hodgdon, and Chase Jr., who was born in 1793. Chase appeared in the 1790 Deerfield, New Hampshire, census with a household of four: himself, a male child, and two females.

One of these females might be his daughter, Sally; the other must be his wife, Betsy. The young boy could either be a son who didn't survive—Deerfield vital records are quite incomplete—or a young male relative or worker. Betsy died soon after, maybe of complications of childbirth, one of the most common reasons that women of that era died young; the next record for her widowed husband is his marriage to Mary "Polly" Lear of Epsom, New Hampshire, on July 2, 1795, in the Congregational Church of Deerfield, New Hampshire.[3] Polly's parentage is uncertain.

Polly Lear may have been the daughter of Samuel Lear and Mary Lucy, born in Portsmouth on May 9, 1773.[4] If that's the case, then she greatly exaggerated her age when she gave it at her son's trial, when she claimed to be seventy-four, but if she was Samuel's daughter, she would have been only sixty-one. Based on her age as Polly gave it at the trial, she would have been about thirty-five years old at the time of her marriage—late for a first marriage—so she may have been the widow of a Lear and quite likely related to the Lear sisters whom her sons Jonathan and Samuel later married.[5]

Polly and Chase had at least a further six children, some or all of whom were born in Deerfield. The most likely birth order of these offspring is: Benjamin, born about 1796, and married Martha Winslow in 1822; Jonathan, born in 1800, and married Eliza Lear in 1823; next was Samuel, who in 1819 married Lucy Salter Lear, the younger sister of his brother Jonathan's wife, Eliza. After Samuel's early death, Lucy maintained the interconnectedness of the Lear and Prescott families by marrying her husband's older stepbrother, Chase Jr., in 1824. A boy known as Otis may have been born next; he's the Alexander Otis Prescott who married Mary W. Ricker in Deerfield in 1823 and died soon afterward. Chase and Polly's next child was Betsy, who was born about 1808 and who married Francis Bickford; and finally, Abraham, who was probably born in the early spring of 1815, or possibly in 1816 if the dates in the medical records of a local doctor are forced to coincide with the recollections of Chase and Polly.

There are many hints that Chase Prescott's financial situation was far inferior to that of the Cochrans. Chase was an eighth son, again, inheriting little of what was a very small estate, at best. He reported that he "worked out," serving as a farm laborer between the ages of eighteen and twenty-two, and that he then left his father's home. As a laborer, his income would have been marginal, continuing into the next generation the poverty that his family would struggle with.[6]

A witness described the household he created with Polly in unkind terms that imply a sometimes chaotic situation. Mary Critchett, their neighbor, testified of young Abraham, "His brothers were not very pacific; used hard words, but did not come to blows; did not see any other boys so bad tempered, just the Prescotts." The very fact that Abraham, too, had been sent out to work as a farm laborer at about the age of twelve, especially taking into consideration that he was significantly younger than his surviving siblings and one of only a few mouths left at home to feed, reveals more about the Prescotts' financial situation. However, having Abraham go to work for a financially successful farmer could offer him better opportunities to get ahead in life than staying in his impoverished family home, so sending him out to work cannot be entirely attributed to the Prescotts' poverty.

Abraham Prescott was a sickly child. The physician whom the Prescotts called to treat his various illnesses, Dr. William Graves, reported that one of his visits to the Prescotts was at "the Widow French's." The Widow French is probably Miriam French with whom the Prescotts may have been boarding around the time of Abraham's birth, further evidence of their financial problems—that this late in their marriage they couldn't afford their own home.[7] Abraham's defense attorney also questioned whether the fact that Dr. Graves had visited the family only a few times might have been because they had a limited capability to pay, implying that their financial circumstances were rather dire.

When Mary "Polly" Prescott was called to testify at her son Abraham's trial on Tuesday, September 9, 1834, she gave her age as seventy-four years, so she would have been born about 1760 (if not lying or confused about her age) and would have been about fifty-five years old when he was born. Even given the standards of the era, with mothers giving birth right up until menopause made it impossible to conceive, Abraham would have been a very late-in-life child, and exposed to all the perils that an aged mother's pregnancy might present. Although no one mentioned birth problems at trial, "elderly" mothers even now tend to have more complications during labor and delivery than younger women, which can often result in harm to their infants.[8] Even more crucially, since many would testify that Abraham Prescott wasn't like others of his age, having a significantly older mother would expose him to a much greater risk of genetic abnormalities.[9]

However, a grown woman was recorded as living in the Chase Prescott household in the 1810, 1820, and 1830 censuses. While Chase's age bracket in each census matches with his known birth date, in the latter two censuses the female's age is younger than Polly would have been if she were telling the truth about her age at her son's trial, although it is correct for the 1810 census. She may have lied at the trial about her age to present herself as a more sympathetic character, or even may not have known her own age. In the 1810 census, the oldest female is greater than forty-five years in age (Polly would have been fifty at this time based on the age she gave at trial or thirty-seven if she was born in 1773). But in the 1820 census the eldest female is in the twenty-five to forty-four bracket (if she was the same person as in 1810, she has gotten quite a lot younger) and in 1830, the female in the census is listed as fifty to fifty-nine, but Polly should have been about seventy years of age. Although these types of age discrepancies are sometimes seen in early censuses, unfortunately, they're often the only records that exist for a person, especially for a woman. If Polly ever lied about her age, she might have been more likely to do that with a census taker (who would have been a member of her community and as such presented a situation where vanity was a factor) rather than in a courtroom before a judge and jury.[10] But with no definitive birth or death record for her, it does leave her age very uncertain. The other possibility is that Polly, who may have been illiterate, simply didn't keep good track of her age and wasn't particularly sure how old she was at any given time.

Polly and Chase Prescott described Abraham's early childhood as very difficult. He was a child wracked by illness, and given to long periods of fretful crying. Polly said, "When an infant, six weeks old, he began to falter, and his head to increase in size; sores broke out in his head; the doctors recommended showering."[11] When Polly talked about her son's increasing head size, she appears to have been describing macrocephaly, the medical term that simply means "big head." The disease process that many people associate with increasing, abnormal head size in an infant is hydrocephaly, a condition that causes problems with the drainage of cerebrospinal fluid from within the skull. In infants, this will result in an increase in head size, bulging of the fontanels (the soft parts of an infant's head that aren't yet covered by bone), and when untreated, most often leads to death, if not notable deformity of the head, and significant mental disabilities.[12] Since Prescott did not die from his enlarged head, or even seem to suffer extreme disability, hydrocephaly was almost certainly not the cause. Polly went on, "Dr. Graves called and said he did not know as any help could be given. He left some medicine, and it did relieve him some. The doctor said from the appearance of the child's head, he should think he might be crazy in after life; he had known such instances."

Physicians of the early nineteenth century had probably heard of hydrocephaly, but were not familiar with other, less common causes of an enlarged head. Standard treatments for hydrocephaly were limited and ineffective: head binding, bloodletting, administering calomel (mercury), purging, and, rarely, drilling holes in the skull to—hopefully— drain the excess fluid, a radical treatment that had an excellent chance of solving the problem by killing the child.[13]

A far more likely explanation for Prescott's macrocephaly was any one of many possible genetic mutations that can cause an infant's head to grow too rapidly, but not from the pressure of too much cerebrospinal fluid. Many of the syndromes associated with macrocephaly also are accompanied by varying degrees of autistic behaviors.[14] Among these could be failure to make eye contact, poor social skills, impulse-control problems, and decreased intellectual capabilities, all of which Prescott seemed to display. As noted previously, Polly's advanced maternal age would have made a spontaneous mutation much more likely, also fitting with this explanation for his issues.

Although Prescott didn't succumb to his early illness, he remained a sickly child. Polly recalled, "My son had a bad humor, which broke out in blisters on his feet and legs."[15] Polly, in describing Prescott's "bad humor," wasn't referring to his temperament, but explaining, in the common understanding of her time, that she believed the four critical substances that were thought to be in his body—blood, phlegm, yellow bile, and black bile—were out of balance. Physicians of the day would typically remove blood, often in remarkably copious amounts, or prescribe emetics to induce vomiting or purges to empty the bowels in their sick patients in order to restore the proper relationship between these four humors. Polly didn't mention the use of purges or bleeding for young Prescott, but instead the application of salt water. The water cure, hydrotherapy, had been in vogue for some years, and was at least not likely to cause further injury to the child.[16]

Prescott survived his early afflictions (and treatments) and was able to attend school, at least some of the time. In the 1820 census, Chase Prescott and his family were living in Allenstown, New Hampshire, the town just west of Deerfield. Five people were counted in the family, presumably Chase and Polly and their three youngest children, Betsy, Otis, and Abraham. Around 1828, when he was about twelve or thirteen, Abraham Prescott was sent out to work as a farmhand for a neighbor, John Kimball. While Kimball's description of him wasn't overly glowing, the boy worked there for about eighteen months, and apparently left that job to work for the Cochrans. Although it may have been hard to find good farm help, it seems unlikely that they would have hired Prescott if Kimball had spoken ill of the teen. With farmers sometimes sharing work, gathering to cut hay, for instance, Chauncey Cochran had almost certainly at least seen Prescott at work, so had some idea of what he was like.[17]

Prescott began working for the Cochrans in the spring of 1830, when he had just marked his fifteenth birthday. He had left school and had been working and boarding away from home for about a year and a half or more. Cochran testified that Prescott was working for him as an apprentice, but that he hadn't been bound out to him—there were no apprenticeship papers. Regarding establishing a formal apprenticeship, Cochran said, "I once applied to Esquire Cochran to make writings; he advised me to have nothing to do with the Prescotts," a warning he failed to heed, but further evidence of the Prescotts' status in the community.[18] Apprenticeship would have provided Prescott with certain legal protections.[19] Chauncey Cochran would have sworn to provide the teen with training, clothing, room and board, and possibly wages, and would have committed both the youth and Cochran to sustain the relationship for a set period of years. Clearly, the attorney thought a written, legal commitment would be risky for Cochran. Chauncey reported that he'd paid Prescott's father $10 for his son's services and that, at the end of his commitment to the Cochrans, Abraham would receive a further $100. Compared to the typical annual earnings of an adult farm laborer (about $102), Prescott, already fairly experienced, seems like a very good bargain, although he was receiving room and board as well as the $110 that his father would eventually realize.[20]

Prescott lived in a downstairs room of the Cochran household, at least in the colder months. He ate side by side with the Cochran children at the family table, and perhaps attended church with them. Sally would have washed and mended his few clothes along with her family's, nursed him if he was ill, and generally treated him as much as an older son as a hired hand. This impoverished boy had survived a destitute, possibly tempestuous childhood, and was now a member of the Cochran family.

⚜ 6 ⚜

INDICTMENT AND INCARCERATION

When about to return homeward, he made her a proposal
—John L. Fowler, coroner

For most New Englanders, steeped in a background of intense religious belief, Sunday was a day to lay aside all but the essential chores.[1] The Cochrans didn't attend church that morning. In the 1830s, religion had lost some of its previous firm control over New Englanders of a century earlier. Church attendance was no longer mandatory, and hadn't been for quite a while. More importantly, failure to attend church didn't indicate a sure path to damnation or even a severe lack of proper character, as it had not long before. Most people attended church on a regular basis.[2] But that the Cochrans weren't there that Sunday was no cause for comment. Later Cochran would become deeply involved in the Methodist church in his new town, Corinth, Maine, so it seems that he hadn't completely turned his back on religion. Although there was a Methodist congregation in Pembroke, it was small and still met in members' homes. No records of membership for that congregation exist for the time period that could confirm that the Cochran family had already joined that relatively new Protestant denomination.

Considering the rainy previous week, strawberry picking must have seemed to Sally Cochran to be an excellent way to enjoy some time outdoors without working quite as hard as usual. It might even have sounded like a fun distraction from her regular activities. The strawberries of the early nineteenth century were not even vaguely similar to the large, hybridized berries of today, but (not surprisingly) can still be found growing in the midst of grass if the plants haven't been destroyed by applications of weed killer. The berries were just a half inch or less in size and could be found only by pushing apart the already tall grass in the meadow. She would have needed to bend quite far over to spot the bright crimson berries and pick them, putting her, unsuspectingly, in a vulnerable position.

The trial record doesn't describe the path that she and Prescott took on their fateful walk. Her husband expected them to be picking berries in an area that was in clear view of the group of homes, including his and those of Timothy and Jonathan Robinson, all clustered together on the hilltop. But the pair wandered quite a bit further than that, down a steep hill and then over or around a brush fence. Eventually, they ended up in an area that Prescott had been to with Chauncey just a couple of weeks earlier. The two men had gone there to clear brush and work on the fence. Just the day before, Cochran had sent him there to get some bark, probably to be used to make dye. (Other versions of the trial record say that he was sent there "after dark" rather than "after bark.") Some of those who testified at the trial, including Cochran, said that berries were never found in that field. Other neighbors said it was a good place to search for berries. Prescott might have noticed strawberries while he was working there, although, clearly, Chauncey hadn't. Or the teen may have recalled that it was a secluded and very private spot and deliberately led Sally there with a tale of plentiful berries. That field was much too far down the hill to be seen from any house, including the Cochrans', which was the closest home.

Prescott provided more than one version of the story of what happened between him and Sally that morning. He told Chauncey the first version after being discovered wailing by the back of the barn. He and Sally had been peacefully picking berries when he was "seized with the toothache." He sat down on a tree stump while Sally, strangely unconcerned with his severe suffering, continued to amble along, picking berries, gradually moving further down into the isolated brook field. At some point, Prescott, lulled by birdsong and the buzzing of insects, dozed off, and while sleepwalking, found a fence post ("stake"), came quietly up behind Sally, beat her nearly to death, dragged her body about thirty feet into some underbrush, and then awoke, saw what he had done, and went back home to cry loudly, but not to actually fetch help for her. In this version Sally never saw him coming; surely she would have been alarmed to note him approaching, inexplicably carrying a fence post. Other versions of the event would follow, the next at the end of the summer.

The first legal proceeding after Sally Cochran's death was a coroner's inquest. According to coverage in the *New Hampshire Patriot and State Gazette,* a Concord newspaper, it was held that same day in the field by Cochran's body.[3] Although no record remains of who was there, the men in attendance were most likely some of the same ones who had gathered earlier in response to Chauncey's desperate screams. In rural New England, coroner's inquests were generally rather informal affairs, often held at the site of a crime while the event was still fresh in people's minds and the evidence could be viewed and, hopefully, preserved in participants' memories, a critical feature in the time before photography. With Prescott already apprehended in his bloody clothes, and since he had confessed to Cochran and to William Abbott Jr., there was little for the men to ponder. Sally Cochran was dead and Prescott was the perpetrator. He was kept under house arrest until the following day, when the next required legal event would take place.

On Monday, the day after Cochran's murder, Prescott was examined before justices Samuel Cochran, Samuel Sargent, and Winthrop Fowler in Pembroke and ordered to be held until the September term of the Merrimack County Court of Common Pleas, almost three months away.[4] Then he was packed into a wagon and taken for the long and bone-jarring ride on pitted dirt tracks to the county jail in the small village of Hopkinton, about twenty miles west of Pembroke, a very long distance from his parents' home. The rain poured down all that day, making the hours-long journey that much more unpleasant.[5]

During the time that Prescott was held there, the warden of the jail was Maj. Abner P. Stinson, but it was the live-in husband-and-wife team of Mary and Andrew Leach who directly oversaw the care of the prisoners.[6] Andrew held the post of "Jailer" for Merrimack County for many years, appearing on county records well into the 1840s, when he was in his sixties.

Nearly sixty years later, and long after the building had ceased being used as the county jail, local historian C. C. Lord described it: "The apartment of the edifice devoted to the purposes of a county prison was on the back part of the lower floor, and extended the whole length of the building, being divided mainly into two rough but strong apartments, which were reached by doors leading from a long, narrow hall. Near the partition was the small, square dungeon. Here, in one or all apartments, prisoners were confined until the year 1852."[7]

The house where the prison was located still stands on South Road in Hopkinton, although Lord believed the prison section had been renovated or reconstructed prior to his visit in 1890. Lord may have been describing an extension at the rear of the house. Today the home is a two-story Federal-style house with four rooms on the lower (first) floor. The extension, which currently is attached to the side of the house, was built long after the eighteenth-century period of the house's construction. The dry laid-stone cellar under the original house could have been the site of the jail, but it's small and only one room deep from front to back since it doesn't extend under the house's full width, so it would be unlikely to be described as "the back part of the lower floor." The house is small enough that both the household sounds and the smell of cooking food would reach the jail area, no matter where it had been located. Even though Prescott was locked away from it, he was constantly aware of the new household he had been thrust into.

From Andrew Leach's testimony, it's apparent that Prescott was mostly kept in heavy, uncomfortable leg-irons: "He once freed himself of his irons, and attempted it again, when I removed them on his complaining that they hurt his ankles."[8] Leach and a few others refer to Prescott having various cellmates during his incarceration. One of those, Amos D. Blaisdall, a shoemaker, testified that he had been imprisoned for his failure to pay a debt of fifty dollars. (Blaisdell would do a little better in coming years. He married in 1834, became the father of five children, and lived for the rest of his life in a modest house that he owned in Allenstown, New Hampshire.) It would have been typical of the time that Prescott, who had freely admitted to bludgeoning Cochran to death, was kept for two and a half years in a common cell with other prisoners, nearly all of them jailed for minor civil offenses. Murder was such a rare occurrence in rural New Hampshire that counties had no special prison cells to keep violent offenders separated from those who were jailed for civil crimes like debt. Prescott was apparently not kept in the dungeon that Lord described.

Blaisdall testified of an attempt by another cellmate, Carr, to mount an escape. (There were twenty Carr households in Merrimack County in the 1830 federal census. It's impossible to know who this Carr might have been.) Blaisdall said of Prescott, "The prisoner assisted in it, and talked of running to Canada." He went on, "Carr started the project of breaking jail; the prisoner seconded the design."[9] Mary Leach discovered the attempt before the prisoners ever had the opportunity to leave the jail. Andrew Leach described Carr as "a bad fellow" and said that after he finally permanently removed Prescott's leg-irons, he stopped trying to get away.

The Leaches were residents of Hopkinton for most of their lives, although Andrew had been born in Massachusetts. By the time of the murder, at least two of their young children were buried in the Old Hopkinton Cemetery, victims of one of the many lethal illnesses that shortened life expectancy. Just a couple of months before Prescott became their prisoner, their daughter, Clarissa Green, their only surviving child, had married Robert Follansbee Chase of Newburyport, Massachusetts.[10] She would likely have left for her new home before Prescott was incarcerated, but by some ill luck, she would return to play a minor but tragic role near the end of the whole sad business.

If the Hopkinton jail resembled other prisons of the era, it would have been an unpleasant place to spend the thirty months that Prescott passed there. Local jails remained catchall places that incarcerated those awaiting trial for all manner of crimes, the location where debtors were sent, and, increasingly, a place to house the mentally ill long-term, especially those who were disruptive.[11] By 1833, some states had built mental hospitals to sequester and perhaps even treat the mentally ill, but New Hampshire had none. In fact, the Hopkinton jail was the long-term home for a local man who suffered from a mental illness. Benjamin Rowell had accidentally shot, but not killed, a neighbor after having lost his senses while wandering in the woods, trying to select appropriate timber for a house frame, and was confined in the jail from 1832 until New Hampshire's first asylum for the insane was opened about eleven years later. Unlike Prescott, Rowell was occasionally allowed out to roam around the neighborhood and was a jovial enough man that he liked to play tricks on his jailors, mostly taunting them by staying just out of reach when they needed him to return to the cell.[12]

Jail played a key role in the management of crime in that era. In the years that immediately followed the American Revolution, the new United States repudiated many things British, and one of the first reform efforts in the new country, since extreme punishments appeared to contradict new republican ideology, was to scale back the severity of the criminal codes of most states, sharply limiting the variety of crimes that were punishable by execution.[13] At the time of the Revolution, the criminal code in England spelled out at least two hundred crimes that could be punished with death.[14] Pennsylvania was the first state to eliminate a mandatory death penalty for robbery and burglary in 1786, although in New England, burglars, especially repeat offenders, continued to be executed until the end of the eighteenth century.[15] However, by the time of Prescott's crime, most states authorized the death penalty only for first-degree murder, or just a few other severe crimes. It was believed that the threat of exceptionally long prison terms would be an effective deterrent against crime, or would at least prevent recidivism by keeping the troublesome offenders away from society.

This reasoned new approach, however, didn't work as miraculously as had been first hoped. Serious crime not only didn't conveniently disappear, it didn't even become less common.[16] The rational new approach, requiring the incarceration of criminals for extremely long periods of time, necessitated the construction of more houses of detention, and particularly prisons, where the offenders would be sent after conviction. As part of this evolving prison-focused movement, New Hampshire built a new state prison in Concord in 1812; if Prescott had been found guilty of some lesser crime (other than murder with New Hampshire's mandatory death penalty), he would have been sent there after conviction.[17] But both the jails and prisons of that era shared a common feature—they were brutal, grim, and often crowded places. While many American prisons operated on a rather misguided plan for reforming prisoners by instilling obedience in them through a remarkable system of isolation and abject silence, jails were more the catchall holding areas for a motley mix of minor offenders, debtors, the more raving (and potentially violent) variety of insane persons, and for those awaiting trial.[18] The structure of jails was less rigid and seemingly less organized. Since criminals were now much less likely to be executed, prisons were designed not just to detain prisoners but also to reform them; jails generally made less effort to improve their unwilling clientele.

There are just a few descriptions given by prisoners of jail life of the period. In not far away Salem, Massachusetts, an unlucky New Hampshire native, Timothy Joy, spent some time in the Salem jail and then in the new stone prison in Ipswich, not for fleeing from his New Hampshire creditors, as he did just prior to being arrested, but because, while he was drunk, he slandered a well-known local politician, apparently a far more egregious offense. Joy spent several months incarcerated and kept a diary. Of the Salem jail, he said, "The room in which I was confined was in the second story of the building & it was very open and cold & I thought I should have frozen before morning having only two blankets to cover me. My bed consisted of a sorry two cloth sacks stuffed with straw which made my bones ache."[19] He also described the food: "My allowance consisted only of a pint of coffe [sic] & a piece of coarse brown bread about as a cracker & this only twice every twenty four hours."[20] He complained of the "nauseous smell emitted from the vault [cesspool]" as well. Once he was moved to the stone prison, his situation improved somewhat. He was held in a cell that had large windows (although the prison also featured nine windowless dungeons) and he had more blankets, and access to books and writing materials. But the room was completely unheated and frigid in winter, and Joy seems to have quickly developed what may have been scurvy as a result of the poor diet, losing a number of his teeth before he was released.

Prescott had the misfortune to live in the Hopkinton jail during some of the coldest days in New England records, during January 1835. On the very coldest day of the frigid period, the mercury in Dartmouth, New Hampshire, not far to the north, managed to rise just to –7°F and the low for the day, recorded at dawn, was –32°F. The jail, if it was heated at all, would have been nearly unbearably cold.[21]

In 1848, Daniel Drayton was apprehended while using his Chesapeake Bay watercraft to ferry seventy-six slaves to freedom. He was incarcerated in the Washington, DC, jail to await trial, and after being sentenced to pay a steep fine, was returned there because he had no money to pay it. In 1853, his vivid and articulate description of his jail time was published: "One of the keepers threw me in two blankets, and I was left to sleep as I could. The accommodations were not of the most luxurious kind. The cell had a stone floor, which, with the help of a blanket, was to serve also for a bed. There was neither chair, table, stool, nor any individual piece of furniture of any kind, except a night-bucket and a water can."[22]

Many jailers received a stipend from the state for each prisoner's board.[23] The amount was generally only just barely sufficient to provide for the prisoner, yet jailers needed to also extract some profit from the sum, so food was generally poor and inadequate. "I should very soon have died on the prison allowance. The marshal is allowed by the United States thirty-three cents per day for feeding the prisoners. For this money they receive two meals; breakfast, consisting of one herring, corn-bread and a dish of molasses and water, very slightly flavored with coffee; and for dinner, corn-bread again with half a pound of the meanest sort of salted beef, and a soup made of corn-meal stirred into the pot liquor. This is the bill of fare day after day, all year round," Drayton reported.[24] Prescott's experience would have probably been very similar.

As in nearly all other jails, prisoners could receive food that visitors would bring them and those who had money were able to buy additional food from jailers. (This secondary food market offered jailors another lucrative way to make some money.) Prescott had no ready access to money, given his family's poverty. It's unlikely that many in Hopkinton felt any great sympathy for him either, so local visitors were probably few, if any. The significant distance between Hopkinton and his parents' home in Pembroke made frequent family visits impossible, so he was most likely dependent almost exclusively on the jail diet, however inadequate it might have been.

Because his "shirt, waistcoat and pantaloons" had been stained with Sally's blood and were taken for evidence by the coroner, Prescott had to depend on his jailer for clothing as well. Drayton was allowed to keep his clothes, except for his overcoat, which was taken away from him when he first reached the jail. He described prison clothes: "The allowance of clothing made to prisoners who were confined without any means of supporting themselves corresponded pretty well with the jail allowance of provisions. They received shirts, one at a time, made of the meanest cotton and of the smallest dimensions, trousers of equal quality, and shoes."[25] Since the Hopkinton jail was a much smaller operation than the Washington jail, they didn't have clothing that was specially made for the prisoners. Prescott was most likely furnished with cast-off clothing.

When the Court of Common Pleas met for the September 1833 term, Prescott was indicted for "feloniously, willfully and with malice afore thought having taken the life of Sally Cochran" and arraigned.[26] He pleaded "not guilty" and received as attorneys Hon. Ichabod Bartlett of Portsmouth and Charles H. Peaslee, Esquire, of Concord as his counsel. His case was continued to the next session of the court, scheduled for February 1834. On the same day, Ezra Straw, about twenty-seven, and William Jordan, about twenty-three, were arraigned for stealing money from Giles Tavern in Hookset.[27] They pleaded guilty and were sentenced to three years and four years respectively in the state prison. In later years Ezra would marry, father ten children, and run a farm in southern New Hampshire until his death in 1892, seemingly having put behind him his stint of crime. Jordan also married and found work as a shoemaker, later living with a married son until his death in 1865. If Prescott crossed paths with this pair of troublesome fellows, perhaps he envied their far less desperate situation.

Later testimony provides a glimpse of Prescott just after his arraignment in the autumn three months after the murder, creating a picture of a beleaguered young man who seemed to be trying hard to please his unfriendly visitors at the prison. On Thursday of that week, September 5, 1833, a rainy, then warm and muggy day, Prescott was visited at the prison in Concord, where he had been taken to be held for the arraignment, by Warden Abner Stinson, Deputy Warden George C. Thompson, and three Pembroke men, Norris Cochran, William Knox (a neighbor of Chauncey Cochran), and Coroner John Fowler, who were, no doubt, all in town for the court proceedings.[28] Chauncey Cochran wasn't there for this interview, and, notably, neither was Prescott's defense counsel. A prisoner named McDaniel was also in the cell with Prescott. (Concord Prison records identify him as Samuel McDaniel, a tall, twenty-two-year-old married man, blue-eyed with light brown hair. He was serving three years and ten days in prison for attempted murder.[29] He died poor in 1846, seeming never to have really succeeded in life.)

Fowler stated, "I went to the prison to see him [Prescott], and told him he had better confess the whole truth. At first he declined making any disclosure, but finally said he would before Major Stinson, warden of the prison, and myself, if Thompson, the deputy warden, would remove McDaniel, another prisoner who was present." It was at this point that Prescott provided, under pressure, a second explanation for why he'd attacked Cochran in the pasture.

Fowler took the lead after McDaniel was removed from the cell, leaving Prescott, now pale and thin from months in jail, surrounded by the self-assured officials and businessmen. He demanded to know why Prescott had killed his employer, a helpless young mother who had tenderly cared for the teen. Prescott gazed at the floor, weeping. Initially, he told them he'd fallen asleep and seen what he'd done only when he awoke later. Fowler objected. "That story will not do. We know that tale is a lie. Everyone knows you had a motive for killing her."[30] He demanded that Prescott tell the truth this time. "It will go easier for your immortal soul if you tell us the truth of what happened. I want to satisfy my own mind, and should like to have you state the whole truth to me, just as it is; your confession will make no difference to what happens to you." Major Stinson, the warden who was almost a stranger to Prescott, now spoke up, his voice adding significant weight of authority to what Fowler had just said. "You will stand a better chance of pardon if you confess," he lied reassuringly.

Prescott, already much smaller than any of the well-fed men confronting him, shrunk further into himself. He may not ever have considered that he might have a chance for a pardon. The last months had been very hard; the future looked bleaker still. Haltingly, he said that he and Sally Cochran went into the meadow together. Then they had picked berries all the way down to the "Brook field." Now they were nearly ready to return home. Prescott's voice faltered and then he sobbed. Stinson was losing patience. "What did you say to her, Prescott?" The teen cried harder. "Did you make a proposal to her? Did you touch her? What did you say to her before you struck her down?"

"I made her a proposal," Prescott whispered, echoing Stinson's words, as he perhaps imagined the pair of them down in that sunny, secluded field, just before everything had gone so terribly wrong. Perhaps, he thought, he'd asked to kiss her. Or maybe his "proposal" was even more explicit; he may have thought about how pretty and slender she was.

"Did you touch her then?" Fowler demanded.

In a barely audible voice, Prescott skirted the question and went on to say that Sally Cochran was very angry at his proposal. She, of course, would not like to hear of his feelings for her. He told the men gathered around him what Sally had responded: "You are a nasty, dirty rascal! I will tell Mr. Cochran what you have just said to me. He will punish you for daring to say such a thing. You belong in jail and he will see you put there forever."

At this point, the story Prescott told under the urging of the men became stranger: Since, after threatening him with prison, Cochran went placidly back to picking strawberries, he sat down upon a stump to consider his situation. He may have thought that the woman he had dreamed of being with had just rejected his passionate appeal. He felt shamed and he was also afraid. His employer would now send him to jail, he thought. He'd heard what that was like, locked up for months on end with no sight of the sky. He'd sooner die than be locked away. They could hang him instead, he resolved. She had, he probably thought, turned her back on his desire for her, dismissing his best manly effort to attract her. He was embarrassed but also angry.

He spotted the stake in the brush; the area was littered with them. Sally was still picking strawberries at a little distance away, and didn't even look up as he approached her, the long thick post in his hands. He struck her down. She never even tried to fight him off.[31]

Warden Stinson felt just a bit uncomfortable with the scene before him. Six men were crowded around Prescott, straining to hear his confession. He was well aware that Prescott was being pressured to come up with a story, and that he and Fowler had provided him with many of the details of one. He admitted later, "I think I either suggested then the motive the prisoner assigned for having killed Mrs. Cochran, or had done so previously."[32] The promise of a better chance for a pardon also embarrassed him slightly. But a confession was always very desirable and this one had fortuitously been given in front of numerous reliable witnesses. Although the Fifth Amendment to the Constitution, which protects defendants from being witnesses against themselves, and the Sixth Amendment, which guarantees the right to assistance of counsel, had been ratified on December 10, 1791, the concept of the Miranda warning was still almost two centuries in the future.[33] It was perfectly acceptable in 1833 for a defendant to be compelled or fooled into confessing. Not until Ernesto Miranda, a poorly educated twenty-four-year-old, was arrested for the kidnapping and rape of a young woman in 1963, and then tricked into confessing would this issue reach the Supreme Court and result in the creation of the warning now provided to each person upon arrest.[34] Whatever strategy the men employed to elicit a "confession" from Prescott was legal.

After the arraignment was over, Prescott was sent back to the jail in Hopkinton. When the time came for his trial, at the next session of the Superior Court, in February 1834, the defense requested a continuance as they said that they were having a difficult time getting witnesses to be available.[35] Wintertime travel could be challenging and several of the defense's witnesses were coming from a considerable distance. The continuance was granted and many more months passed, all of the spring and then the summer of 1834, a *very* long time between Cochran's death and trial in an era when just a matter of weeks could separate a crime, the trial, and conviction and execution of the criminal. Eventually, the appointed day arrived, Tuesday, September 9, 1834.[36]

With Prescott's coerced jail cell confession in hand, it appeared that there would be little for the defense to contest. Prescott had survived his challenging incarceration in the little Hopkinton jail, but now he would face the full force of the New Hampshire legal system, and the prosecution, with his multiple confessions recorded, was wholly prepared. Still, what would follow would be a very long and complex legal odyssey, spanning nearly eighteen full months.

PART II

ABRAHAM PRESCOTT'S TRIALS

Never betray your master's trust or from his laws depart

—ABR'M PRESCOTT'S CONFESSION,

of the murder of Mrs. Sally Cochran, of Pembroke, N.H.

—June 23, 1833. By a private individual at the Bar.

Period broadside

⅗ 7 ⅖

THE PROSECUTION

PRESENTS ITS CASE

The prisoner at the bar
—John Whipple, Esq.

Two prominent men would serve as the prosecutors for Prescott's capital murder trial: George Sullivan, Esq., and John Whipple, Esq. George Sullivan was nearing the end of his important career. Now sixty-three, he'd been born in in Durham, New Hampshire, not far from Portsmouth, the son of celebrated Revolutionary War General John Sullivan. He attended Phillips Academy in Andover, Massachusetts, and then Harvard College. After Harvard he returned to New Hampshire and read law, then was admitted to the bar and opened a law practice in Exeter, just a couple of towns south of his birthplace. In 1805, Sullivan began his political career, serving in quick succession in the New Hampshire House of Representatives, as state attorney general, in the US House of Representatives, then back to the New Hampshire House, then Senate. In 1816, he once again became attorney general, a position he then held uninterrupted until 1835. As Prescott's trial began, he was seemingly feeling his somewhat advanced age.[1] While Sullivan added gravitas and authority to the prosecution, John Whipple would end up doing most of the courtroom work. Only three years previously, Sullivan's eldest son and namesake had died at the age of twenty-two. He may have compared Prescott to that beloved young man. After his death a few years later, Sullivan was described: "As a professional lawyer, he had few equals in the country. His mind was of a high order, vigorous, discriminating, and

philosophical. He did not rely, however, on his native genius for emi-
nence in his profession, but upon unremitting application to the study
of law as a science."[2]

John Whipple was forty-five when the first trial began and had been
born in Hamilton, Massachusetts. After teaching school for a time in
Gloucester, Massachusetts, he relocated to Dunbarton, New Hampshire,
with two of his brothers. He graduated from Dartmouth College in 1812,
making him and both attorneys for the defense fellow alumni. In 1818, he
married Hannah R. Chase, the sister of Salmon P. Chase, who would go
on to serve as Abraham Lincoln's secretary of the treasury and was later
the chief justice of the Supreme Court, but all of that was still long in the
future.

Whipple read law with Baruch Chase of Hopkinton (Salmon's uncle) and then was admitted to the bar. He had practiced law in several
towns around southern New Hampshire and had just recently finished
up a term serving as the clerk of the New Hampshire Senate. Immediately after his term ended, he became the Merrimack County solicitor
starting in 1834.[3] New to the position, this was to be his first murder
trial. It was also the first murder trial to be held in Concord.

In fact, murder remained a rare crime in mostly rural New Hampshire.[4] The most recent conviction and execution for murder had been
that of Daniel Davis Farmer, who in 1821 severely beat the widow Anna
Ayer, who had previously accused him of being the father of her unborn
child. It was a claim the married man vehemently denied right up until
the time of his execution. Having already previously been jailed for a
time based upon her paternity accusation, Farmer was both angry and
drunk when he went to discuss it with her in front of her fourteen-
year-old daughter, Anna. Since the widow initially survived the attack,
she was later able to identify her assailant. The record of Farmer's trial
reveals that Anna identified Farmer with what is called a "dying declaration." She lingered, in fading consciousness, for a full eight days after
the attack. Every day when the doctor came to treat her gaping head
wound, neighbors were permitted to troop by the bedside to observe
the injury, only cautioned to move by briskly. The doctor estimated that
more than a hundred people would crowd in and pass by each time he
visited. If this wasn't enough to seal her doom, the physician also bled
her into a stupor twice during his treatment.

Farmer doesn't seem to have felt a great deal of remorse for his actions. He was convinced that Ayer had died only because she was a pauper and had been medically mistreated, relieving him of the guilt of murder, he thought. He was convicted with Anna's dying declaration and the testimony of her remarkably intrepid daughter, who first feigned death from his attack, then rose, severely wounded, after Farmer left and nailed the door shut, then put out the fire he'd lit to conceal the crime.[5] He was executed on January 3, 1822.

George Sullivan had shared prosecutorial duties with John Harris for that case, so Abraham Prescott was not his first capital trial. The next murder trial after Prescott's that would lead to imposition of the death penalty (a full decade after his) was that of Andrew Howard, who, on September 19, 1843, beat to death Phebe Hanson, the wife of a man whom he believed owed him money. Howard was executed on July 8, 1846. The *Journal of the American Temperance Union* would quickly seize onto the Howard case because he had been drinking heavily on the ten-mile, cross-country walk to Hansen's home, and then Phebe gave him a quart mug of cider—presumably hard cider—when he arrived.[6] Since Merrimack County, New Hampshire, hadn't been organized until 1823, when it was carved out of the oversized adjoining counties of Rockingham and Hillsborough, it didn't have much of a legal history of its own. Prescott's would be the first murder case for the still-young county.[7]

On a rainy, dreary Monday morning, September 8, 1834, a full year after his indictment, Prescott was taken from Hopkinton back to the prison in Concord, where he would stay for the duration of the courtroom proceedings.[8] The Superior Court convened the following morning, a windy, cooler day, in the Old North Meetinghouse on the corner of Main and Church Streets, a place chosen because it provided more seating than any local courtroom for the large number of people who were expected to observe the trial. Built in 1751, it was the site where the New Hampshire Convention ratified the US Constitution in 1788. It had been "improved" in 1783, enlarged in 1803, and may have been showing some wear by 1834. It burned to the ground in 1873 and was eventually replaced with a school.[9]

The wooden pews, worn smooth with use, were packed with people, mostly men, when the court was called to order at 9 A.M.[10] Some who personally knew the Cochrans had traveled from Pembroke, but the vast majority had come for the show and knew neither the accused murderer nor the victim. A murder trial was a rare event, and somewhat like having a circus come to town. The unpaved Concord streets, still a little muddy from the previous day, were crowded with wagons and carriages; many more people had arrived on foot. The church's windows were pushed open against the stuffiness the large crowd created, and the sounds of the small city drifted in even as the audience got settled and grew relatively quiet. In addition to the rumble of cartwheels and the occasional whinny of an impatient horse, children's shouts and the barking of dogs punctuated the morning. The murmur of those who had been turned away when the church was full and gathered outside around the windows at times threatened to drown out the quieter legal proceedings. Prescott's attorney described them as the "enraged populace even around the doors of the temple of justice, demanding the execution of the accused, and impatient even of the delay of the forms of a trial."[11] Throughout the trial, their occasional angry shouts would compete with the testimony from time to time. Large flies, drawn by the ever-present piles of manure on the city streets, buzzed in and out of the windows.

The first act of the court was the selection of jurors. There had already been a tussle over the jury pool. With the defense dissatisfied, the prosecution had agreed to have a further six men brought into the pool—three from Franklin and three from Salisbury—to provide some balance.[12] Fifty-three men altogether were called and interviewed, twenty-one challenged, and twelve were selected to decide Prescott's fate: Joseph C. Thompson of Andover was chosen foreman. Thompson was a thirty-nine-year-old farmer, landowner, and father of four (three were named George Washington, Walter Scott, and John Adams). Joseph A. Rowe was also from Andover and also thirty-nine years old, married, and the father of at least four children by 1834. Wyatt Boyden, from Boscawen, was forty-six years old, born in Greenfield, Massachusetts, and had become a widower the previous fall when his wife of twenty-seven years died. He would surely be very sympathetic to Chauncey Cochran in the loss of his wife. John Kimball of Bradford, New Hampshire, was aged thirty to thirty-nine in 1830. Early in the decade, his name appeared in the local newspaper as a satisfied owner of a newly invented Cylinder Cooking Stove. Jonathan Bagley, also from Bradford, owned the Cylinder Cooking Stove, too.[13] He was aged between fifty and fifty-nine in 1830, but was probably closer to fifty-nine. David S. Caldwell of Dunbarton was forty and by 1850 had relocated with his wife and seven children to Newbury, Massachusetts, a wealthy farmer with real estate of significant value. Nathaniel Webster, in his late forties, and a farmer comfortably well off, and Stephen Pingry were both from Salisbury. Pingry was a well-to-do farmer and dresser of wool. His first wife died in 1820, only three years after their marriage, so he, too, had lost a young wife. He would go on to father a dozen children with a second wife and remain civically active in his community for his entire life. Joseph Fifield, John Rowell, and James Colburn were all from Franklin. Rowell, aged forty-one, was married to Sally Fifield, who may have been related to fellow juror and Franklinite Joseph Fifield, a man who apparently didn't live too many years in Franklin since he appears in neither the 1830 nor the 1840 census there. Finally, there was William Gay of Wilmot, a forty-five-year-old married father of five whose oldest daughter wasn't much younger than Sally Cochran. He would live only another two years after the trial, but would play a secondary and surprising role in the Cochrans' lives.[14]

The jurors were a relatively homogeneous group of men (women could not vote and were not permitted to serve on juries) with an average age of about forty, all or nearly all married fathers, and although the census of 1830 didn't collect information about their occupations, New Hampshire inland demographics of the time indicate that most or all were Protestant farmers.[15] Most came from small towns that were almost thirty miles north and west of Concord, and so considerably distant from Pembroke and the scene of the crime. Only Caldwell, from Dunbarton, lived in any proximity to Pembroke, and he was still a couple of towns away and across the river. Rather than being a jury of Prescott's peers, they were very much the peers of Chauncey Cochran, which would further increase the challenge faced by the defense team. But several of them were old enough to have a son of Prescott's age. They would be likely to compare their own offspring to the defendant and might either feel sympathy for him, or perhaps disgust at his trajectory through life.

In the course of jury selection, twenty-one potential jurors were challenged. Of these, eleven were from towns that bordered Pembroke. Those jurors may have either had a substantial amount of prior knowledge of the case or even personally known some of those involved, and it was most likely that it was because of the size of this group that the defense had demanded additional jurors. Of the ten rejected jurors who were from more distant towns, five were either in the fifty to fifty-nine, or sixty to sixty-nine age bracket in the 1830 census, so they were also older than the average age of the chosen jurors. Whether they were rejected because of their potential opinions or if their age was a factor is not known. As was the law in 1834, because the jury was considering a case for which the potential punishment was death, they would be sequestered for the duration of the trial.

Once the jury had been selected and sworn in, a process that took up only part of the morning, Moses Eastman of Concord, clerk of the court, rose and read the indictment. He finished by intoning, "To this indictment the defendant has pleaded not guilty, and has put himself on the country for trial, which country you are; and you have been sworn to truly try the issue. May God send him a true deliverance. Good men and true, stand together and hearken to the evidence."[16] Maybe, initially, members of the jury were impressed by their critical role in this solemn process.

The trial commenced with the opening statement of the prosecution, as provided by John Whipple. "You are called upon, gentlemen of the jury, for the first time in this county—and I fervently hope an occasion of the like kind will never again occur—to pass sentence upon the guilt or innocence of a person who stands here, charged with the crime of murder," he said. "At the last September term of this court a bill of indictment was presented by the grand inquest of this county against Abraham Prescott, of Pembroke, for having feloniously, willfully, and with malice afore thought taken the life of the late Sally Cochran—a crime, gentlemen, revolting to the feelings of every humane and enlightened mind—a crime which, when committed deliberately, calls loudly for vengeance—a crime not only denounced by the laws of this state, but by the express commands of God—'Whoso sheddeth man's blood, by man shall his blood be shed. Moreover, ye shall take no satisfaction for the life of a murderer, which is guilty of death; for he shall surely be put to death.'"[17]

Whipple went on to remind the jurors of their civic duty to carefully listen to and weigh the evidence and warned them not to be swayed by Prescott's youth. "Your commiseration perhaps may be excited in favor of the prisoner at the bar, when you take into consideration his youth and his general appearance."[18] This statement leaves a tantalizing impression that Prescott's appearance, beyond his evident youth, was one that would elicit sympathy.

He may still have been clothed in cast-off attire provided by his jailors. He was certainly very pale, having been kept indoors for fifteen months. More importantly, he may not have appeared "normal." Over the course of the trial, many witnesses would have something to say about how he looked and acted. While some would call him as intelligent as others his age, many more would comment on his slow-moving, downcast eyes, and his unwillingness or inability to engage in conversations, which could have been due to shyness, subnormal intelligence, or mental illness—or a murky combination of all three.

Whipple described how Prescott had lived with the Cochrans for about three years, and then summarized the crime. "We shall show you that the prisoner, on the morning of the twenty-third of June, 1833, between the hours of nine and ten o'clock, proposed to the deceased to go into a field a few rods north of the house, and in full view of the road, for the purpose of picking strawberries—that he made this known to the husband of the deceased—that the prisoner and the deceased left the house together, and went into the field where he proposed to go—that this field was in full view of the road, and of three or four houses. We shall show that in this field there had been an abundance of strawberries, and that there were still plenty there. We shall also prove to you that the field in which the murder was committed had few or no strawberries; that it was about 70 rods distant from the house, and more than 100 feet lower than the field where they first went; and that the prisoner must have been fully aware of this, as but a few days previous he had been in this field in company with Mr. Cochran mending fence. It will also appear in evidence before you, that the pasture where the fatal deed was perpetrated was a retired and lonely spot, surrounded by woods on the north, east and west, and on the south there was no road or dwelling to be seen. In this place, so secluded and remote as to be beyond the reach of human voice, we shall show you that Mrs. Cochran was inhumanly murdered."[19]

Whipple went on, "It will appear in evidence before you, that on the spot where she was killed there appeared to have been a struggle—that the grass around the spot for a few feet appeared to be trodden down—that she was dragged from the spot where she was killed about two rods into the edge of the adjoining woods. It will further be proven to you that the prisoner, when arrested, had the marks of blood upon his garments; and still more, that he confessed the bloody deed." Periodically, as Whipple spoke, the brisk wind rattled the windows, providing a startling accent to his words.

Whipple surely had been sizing up the jury, probably wondering if he had their full attention and if he had connected all the dots of the case. Seemingly satisfied, he concluded, "When these facts shall have been clearly proven to you, as they will be, we apprehend all doubts will be removed that the prisoner at the bar is indeed guilty of the crime alleged against him."[20]

With that, Prosecutor Whipple called his first, and surely his most important witness, Chauncey Cochran. Cochran, by this time, had had more than a year to adjust to the loss of his wife, and to reflect at depressing length upon the events of that day. They surely must have occupied his thoughts almost continuously. Over the course of that time, his children, too young to understand the meaning of death, had grieved over the abrupt disappearance of their mother; given their very young ages, it must have felt to them like abandonment. Giles Newton, their younger child, by now scarcely remembered his mother, and for Chauncey that may have seemed almost as terrible as the pain and bewilderment of their first loss. No description survives as to how he presented his testimony; whether he seemed numbed to the tragedy, or if describing the events in detail tore open the wound of his sorrow. The testimony, as it survives in the record, seems dispassionate; that it was presented that way in court is unlikely.

Cochran described the events of that morning: Prescott approaching him as he was reading the record of Avery's trial; the request for him to accompany Sally to pick strawberries and the field that they would visit and he refusing to go; his mother hearing the strange noises and his discovery of Prescott moaning at the back of the barn and then telling his terrible news, that he believed he had killed Sally; the breathless run to the isolated meadow; Prescott refusing to go for help and Cochran's desperate screams for assistance as his wife slipped away; a description of the extreme isolation of the murder site and how his wife's still-living body had been dragged by Prescott under some bushes to conceal it.

According to the first newspaper coverage of the Cochran murder, which had appeared on July 1, 1833, in the weekly Concord, New Hampshire, *Patriot* (but was never mentioned again), Prescott enlarged upon his sleepwalking story by claiming that he knew nothing further after falling asleep "until he found himself standing by the side of Mrs. Cochran, who was wounded and almost dead, that he carried her into the shade and asked her to forgive him—that she could not speak, but made signs that she forgave him." The newspaper probably invented this further information since there was nothing later to corroborate it, and because the extreme severity of her head injury would have immediately rendered Cochran unconscious.[21]

Prescott's attorneys faced a significant hurdle in defending the teen since he had, on more than one occasion, admitted to killing Sally Cochran. Defense attorney Bartlett rose to question Cochran. He recognized the need to do this very carefully; there was no point in eliciting further sympathy from the jury for this bereft second victim of Prescott's attack. "Did the prisoner ever before make an assault upon you or your wife?"[22] This was a tricky topic. Bartlett hoped to show that Prescott demonstrated a pattern of insane behavior, but he didn't want to call attention to the fact that the Cochrans had so generously forgiven the boy for his first near-murderous attack.

Cochran answered, "On the night of the 6th of January, 1833, prisoner got up, built a fire, and afterwards struck myself and wife on the head with an ax. The account was given us by the prisoner himself. I and my wife were senseless for some hours. I was wounded on the temple and Mrs. Cochran on the cheek. Prisoner said he was unconscious of hurting us, and supposed he must have done it when asleep; first he knew of it, he saw me on my hands and knees, on the bed, bleeding; then called my mother and raised the neighbors."

"Had the prisoner been in the habit of getting up in his sleep?" Bartlett asked.

"This is the only time I ever knew of," Cochran responded.

"Did he make any attempt to escape?"

"No; he remained about home, as usual."[23]

After further questioning by Bartlett, Attorney General George Sullivan directed a few inquiries at Cochran, asking him if the field where

Sally had been attacked was a usual place to pick strawberries. Cochran denied it. The attorney general raised the topic of Prescott abusing the cattle, and Cochran confirmed that shortly before the murder, the beatings had become more frequent and more severe, but that he had reproved him more for that than any other thing over the past year. He added that when he chastised Prescott for beating the cattle, the young man "never made much reply, generally looked down and cross."[24]

Prescott's abuse of the cattle certainly demonstrates that he had a violent temper that he didn't control well under particular circumstances. He seems to have grown up in a family where violence happened and was accepted; the Prescott boys would be described as "passionate." However, Prescott apparently never abused the Cochran children; he no doubt knew that that behavior would not be tolerated under any circumstances. He was described as a boy who often got into fights with others, once again demonstrating a tendency for violent behavior, but in situations where it was more socially acceptable, if somewhat frowned upon. The observed escalation in Abraham's abuse of the cattle in the weeks before he killed Sally indicates that Prescott was either growing increasingly angry, or was giving in more frequently to whatever negative urges he had been feeling.

Understanding of mental illness in children and teens is far more sophisticated now than it was in Prescott's time. Certain behaviors have been identified as indicating a potential for violent behavior, including cruelty toward animals and signs of increasing anger and aggression, both of which Prescott showed in the months before the murder.[25] Prescott's reaction to criticism over his treatment of the cattle seems to reflect an angry rather than contrite response. Besides describing Prescott as seeming annoyed about being corrected on how he treated the cattle, Cochran also reported Prescott's lingering anger over Sally calling him to task for running with other boys and spoiling his clothes. Still, Cochran said that he had never beaten Prescott for any misbehavior.

After Cochran stepped down, Coroner John L. Fowler was called to testify. He was brought to the crime scene by Cochran's neighbor, Jonathan Robinson. Few people who visited the murder scene carried pocket watches (since they were still largely handmade and quite expensive) and the Cochran farm was too far away from town (about four to five miles "as the crow flies") for the sound of church bells to reach it, so many would guess at the time of the events of that day. Cochran's estimates of time may be the closest to accurate since he did have access to a clock and may even have glanced up at it when his mother came to the room to tell him about the strange sounds she was hearing. Fowler estimated that he arrived in the meadow between ten and eleven o'clock. Sally Cochran was already dead and Prescott was nowhere in sight.

Fowler went in search of the perpetrator. The coroner first went up the hill to Chauncey Cochran's house. When he didn't find Prescott there, he went toward James Cochran's house and found the boy, possibly by following his trail of matted grass, in a pasture between the two farms, near the lane that separated one farm from the other. William Abbott had also found Prescott in that field; perhaps he had remained there with him to make sure he didn't run away. Fowler took Prescott into custody, and with Cochran's neighbor, brought him to the Abbott farm, but then returned to the crime scene, where he observed that "The grass was trodden down very much; appeared as though there had been a scuffle at the place. A hair comb, one tooth broken out, basket of strawberries and calash, were within six or eight feet of the place ... The comb was a common large one, such as women wear on the back part of the head. There was no blood on the calash."[26]

Because the prosecution was attempting to show that Prescott's attack had followed Sally's rebuff of his improper proposal—the one he "confessed" to after his arraignment—they were also anxious to prove that there had been a struggle, which Prescott had denied in both of his descriptions of the attack. Since head wounds bleed profusely, the lack of blood on the victim's calash proved that she could not have been wearing it when she was struck with the fence post. But women didn't typically go out with uncovered heads. Cochran's delicate calash provided protection from the sun. Sun-darkened skin was regarded as a sign of commonness; proper ladies didn't need to work outside and their paler complexions served as proof of that. Bonnets also were an important fashion statement. Her outdoor attire was incomplete without her calash, and she would have worn it with the wide satin ribbons in a large, firmly tied bow beneath her chin; without tying the bow, the rigid, wire-framed calash would have fallen off her head when she bent to pick the berries.[27] Bonnets were also a sign of modesty. Matrons, married women, like Cochran, kept their heads covered with bonnets not only while outside; even for indoor use they had decorative light-weight cloth day caps, which they wore most of the time.[28] Since the fragile calash clearly was not on her head when she was struck, this alone provides evidence of a struggle.

Fowler described her wounds: "The blows were on the back part of the head of the deceased; there appeared to have been two blows; the wounds were deep; might lay in your three fingers; one was on the right and the other on the left side, running to the back part of the head."[29] Again, the condition of Cochran's tortoiseshell comb, observed by Fowler on the ground with just one of its delicate teeth snapped off, proves she was not wearing it when she was struck with such force that it created a pair of two-inch-deep gashes in her skull. Blows that brutally hard would have smashed the very brittle comb if she hadn't already lost it in a struggle for her life.

Fowler produced the murder weapon, the broken-in-half fence post, which he said was found near the area of trodden grass, and noted that there had been blood on it. He also identified the shirt, waistcoat, and pantaloons that Prescott had been wearing when he was arrested. He reported that he had seen these taken from Prescott and that he had had them ever since. Much later on, courts would require a chain of custody for evidence to demonstrate that it hadn't been tampered with, but that was not the case in 1834. It was enough for Fowler to just state that he'd kept the clothes and that they were stained with the victim's blood.[30]

Fowler described the long trail through the deep grass, two rods—thirty-three feet—to where Cochran's body had been concealed in some brush. When he saw her, she was lying on her back. Since she was still breathing when her husband reached her, some significant length of time after she'd been bludgeoned, Prescott hadn't dragged a lifeless body into the bushes, but that of a severely wounded woman in whose house he'd lived for the past three years.

Defense attorney Bartlett, during cross-examination, asked Fowler what Chauncey Cochran had said when he heard that Prescott had confessed to attacking Sally after she rejected his advance. The attorney general objected and the question was ruled inadmissible since the answer would constitute hearsay, literally something that Fowler had heard Cochran say. There is no evidence that anyone ever went back and asked Cochran about this directly, although he would testify for a second time later in the trial. Still, his attitude toward the supposed reason for the attack would later emerge.

Prescott showed ample evidence of what the FBI now associates with a "disorganized offender." The list of characteristics is lengthy and revealing: A disorganized offender typically has a low to average intelligence (IQ 80–100), is an unskilled worker, is socially immature, had a rough childhood and a father with an unstable work history, suffered from child abuse, was anxious during the crime, used alcohol or drugs only minimally, lived alone, lived or worked near the crime scene, exhibited a significant behavioral change before the crime, was nocturnal, had poor hygiene, wasn't dating, and had secret hiding places. Only a few of these characteristics don't apply (or aren't known to apply) to Prescott.[31] The implication of what the FBI learned a century and a half after Prescott's crime is that he almost certainly didn't plan ahead to kill her. A sudden furious response to an unexpected rebuff from Sally would fit with the FBI profile, but fails to explain why she would continue to pick berries after his proposition. Very likely, she did not.

The next witness for the prosecution was Jonathan Robinson. Robinson said he arrived at the scene at 9:45. His precise answer suggests that he had some access to a timepiece, but it also contradicted many other witnesses' estimates of the time. He thought that somewhere between five to eight people were already there; he couldn't remember exactly. This was probably because the number of people kept changing in the period of time he was there, the rest of the morning and into the afternoon. He noticed the trodden grass and thought it looked as if Sally Cochran had been knocked down there. Bartlett, in cross-examination, determined that Robinson lived just eighteen rods away from the Cochrans' (in a home that no longer stands, across the road and next door to William Abbott Jr.) and had never heard him speak a bad word about Prescott. Robinson clarified that the spot he had examined and where he had noted the trodden grass was where Cochran's calash, comb, and berry basket lay, and that he tried to keep people off that patch to preserve the evidence, recognizing immediately that if there were signs of a struggle, it might be an important piece of evidence.[32]

Next, Dr. Samuel Sargent was sworn in. He said that he arrived on the scene a little after eleven, and that he thought that Sally had been dead about fifteen minutes when he arrived. If he was accurate in his guess about the time, then Robinson must have been fairly far off the mark with his estimate. She was still lying in the brush where she had died when Sargent got there. He didn't examine her wounds until a jury of inquest and Dr. John Pillsbury arrived, which must have taken some significant period of time to accomplish.

Now he described her injuries: "There were two wounds on the back of the head; one on the right side, almost three inches in extent, the scalp cleaved from the skull from two to three inches in width; the skull fractured and compressed upon the brain; the wound on the left side two and a half inches long, and one and three-fourths to two inches wide; the skin broken, and skull fractured from the occipital to the temporal bone; there was a slight wound on the right side, near the temple; there were probably three blows; death must inevitably ensue from the wounds described." Sargent clarified the time: "I went from my house to the spot in about twelve minutes; she had been dead, as I was informed, about fifteen minutes."[33]

The severe nature of Sally's wounds indicates that Prescott had seemingly learned from his more tentative blows the previous January, which left the Cochrans unconscious and bloody, but alive. Two of these blows were lethally strong, and apparently struck one from each side, perhaps the first (likely the blow on the right side, which had also scraped away her scalp and which would have been the more glancing blow) as he came up behind her and the second while or after she fell to the ground, this one also breaking the post in half. But the third injury, the slight wound on the right side, raises questions. It seems unlikely that that much less grievous injury was also caused by the fence post. It's more probable that it was inflicted with less force and a smaller weapon, like Prescott's fist.

There is clear evidence both that there was a struggle and that Cochran was struck from behind. The most likely explanation for those seemingly conflicting events is that Prescott initially grabbed the young woman, maybe intending to sexually assault her, or perhaps in a rage. During that first violent contact as Cochran struggled to get out of his grasp, she would have lost her calash and comb. Then, knowing she couldn't hope to overpower him, and now remembering what he had done in January and recognizing that she was in mortal peril, she would have turned and tried to run. With the small field surrounded on three sides by thick woods, the only path to safety was up the very steep hill, through the deep grass, and over a brush fence, daunting enough, but she was also encumbered with a long skirt and heavy petticoats. She would have known that she couldn't outrun him. She may have made it a few paces since witnesses observed only a limited area of trodden grass. Prescott must have then struck her, first probably with his fist, causing the glancing blow that would have knocked her down. Then he took up the fence post and swung it.

In order to hit the back side of her head, Prescott, swinging the fence post, would have needed to be standing a few feet away and both behind and to the side of her. She may have been trying to get up out of the grass, with him standing to the side of her body, when he completed the first blow with the post. That could have had the effect of turning her head in the opposite direction as she fell back down so that the third blow hit on the opposite side. The extreme severity of the blows and the fact that the final one was unnecessary to kill her provides evidence of "overkill," which forensic profilers associate with crimes that are both personal and include anger. In fact, although he didn't hit the Cochrans hard enough in January to kill them, that attack also apparently consisted of multiple blows.

Sargent's description of Cochran's wounds is carefully detailed. Whether he examined her again more fully later is unknown. Sarah Cornell, the victim of Reverend Avery, was examined by physicians after her murder, but not until after she had been buried and then exhumed.[34] Cornell was also in an urban area, Fall River, so standards—and the situation—may have differed. Cornell was an all but anonymous woman discovered far from her boardinghouse residence. Cochran's body was surrounded by relatives and friends and located in her own back field. A more careful postmortem examination of her body by the male doctors would likely have been viewed as highly intrusive. While it was never specifically mentioned in testimony at this trial, there must have been concern that Cochran had been sexually assaulted by Prescott, given the viciousness of the attack and the age and gender of her assailant, and hints of that worry are noticeable in the language used by the men who questioned Prescott in his prison cell. (Cornell may have also been sexually assaulted, but the women who prepared her body for burial by stripping and washing her, and who noticed her injuries, at trial were too modest to fully describe her condition, and no doctors—who could have testified—actually observed her body prior to her first internment. Attorneys and the judge tried in vain to force one of the witnesses to either confirm or deny evidence of rape. She would only report that Cornell had been "severely abused."[35])

A sense of the need to protect Cochran, even after her death, from an immodest examination probably kept the two male physicians from looking for signs of a sexual assault, or even for injuries other than her very obvious head wounds, which could have proven whether or not she and Prescott had struggled. In fact, members of the coroner's jury objected when physicians, in their search for evidence of sexual assault or pregnancy, began to strip the exhumed body of Sarah Cornell, who was a complete stranger to them.[36] Other female murder victims of the period underwent autopsies, but quite possibly the rural setting and the presence of a perpetrator who had already confessed to the killing may have resulted in a more conservative treatment of Cochran's remains. There is no evidence that an autopsy was conducted, except, possibly, Sargent's comment on the extent of her partially hidden skull fracture. However, Comfort Abbott (neighbor William Abbott's wife) and Mary French (Sally's maternal aunt), mature women who understood what they should look for, both later testified that they carefully examined her body and found no other injuries, and that her dress "was in no way torn or disordered." Although tragedy had forced the male world into Sally's life and death, caring women performed this final, most private of examinations and kept it firmly in the female sphere, just as society and culture demanded. The maiden Robinson sisters helped prepare Sally's body for burial by washing her, redressing her, and wrapping her in her shroud.[37] They, however, were not asked to testify regarding evidence of sexual assault because they were much younger ladies, and may have been viewed as too modest to respond, and also most likely quite properly ignorant of the whole concept of sexual assault.

But a lack of disorder of Sally's dress was not convincing evidence. Women of the early 1830s always wore several petticoats to give their dresses a nice fullness, but, surprisingly, no undergarments. Bloomers (which wouldn't even be named for another couple of decades) or drawers didn't come into common use by grown women until the late 1850s, when steel hoopskirts—given to exposing too much skin in a strong breeze—were introduced as a lighter alternative to layers of petticoats.[38] Prescott would have been able to sexually assault Cochran without interfering much with her clothing. If he had pulled up her skirts to assault her, they would have been restored to a proper position when he grabbed her by her hands or armpits and dragged her into the brush. However, since murder itself required the death penalty for punishment, even if Cochran had been raped, it was essentially immaterial to the legal outcome.

Defense attorney Bartlett cross-examined Sargent about the event of January 6 and he responded by describing the Cochrans' injuries. Bartlett presumably drew attention to the previous attack because he wanted to show a pattern of Prescott's insanity or sleepwalking. Sargent helpfully conceded, "I thought it probable he got up in his sleep; knew of no difficulty in the family."[39]

The attorney general then asked, "Did you state in the presence of the prisoner that the wounds of the 6th of January, if on the back of the head, would have been mortal?" In effect, the actual question asked might have been, "Did Abraham Prescott learn in January what it would actually take to kill a person by striking him or her on the head?" Sargent agreed that Prescott was present when he said that. The chief justice then inquired about whether Cochran's lethal wounds were more on the back or the side of her head. Sargent replied, "The wounds extended from each side of the head to within about three-fourths of an inch of each other on the back of the head. There was about three-fourths of an inch not separated or cut."[40]

Finally, Dr. John Pillsbury was called and he agreed with Sargent's testimony, but added, "I well recollect stating to Cochran that if the blows of the 6th of January had been on the back of his head, they must have been fatal. The prisoner was within hearing."[41] This was further corroboration of Prescott learning of the art of murder. Both doctors had told him. Neither Sally's sister, Mary Jane, who must have been a regular visitor in the home, nor Chauncey's mother, Lettice, was ever called to testify at this trial. Since both could have provided valuable information regarding Prescott's behavior, this seems like a surprising oversight, but also reflects society's view that courtroom testimony was not included within the female sphere.[42] While women could and did provide testimony, it's likely that neither the defense nor the prosecution was willing to put these two most-affected ladies through that trying experience if it was not necessary.

The case was simple from the point of view of the prosecution. Abraham Prescott had a previous history of attacking the Cochrans, although his behavior after the fact had convinced some that he had attacked them unintentionally. He had a violent and often uncontrolled temper, as evidenced by his mistreatment of the cattle. He initiated the strawberry-picking foray, escorted the defenseless young woman to an isolated place far from where he ought to have taken her, picked up a fence post and bludgeoned her to death, even though she may have tried to fight him off—an issue that was barely explored. The murder weapon, a fence post he may have even cut himself a couple of weeks earlier and that he would have known would be available in that field, and his bloody clothes were produced. He had admitted his guilt to Chauncey Cochran and then to the coroner on the day of the crime. Later, he confessed to others of his improper, rebuffed advances. He had full knowledge of precisely how to strike Cochran in order to kill her. The evidence appeared ample for the jury to convict him of first-degree murder. It was well past noon when the prosecution confidently rested its case.

It was time for the midday break. The jury was released, and the sheriff was told to provide them with refreshments and make sure that they were "kept by themselves," fulfilling the requirement of being sequestered, until 2:30, when the defense would begin its presentation. Later, it would become clear that the sheriff didn't always follow these instructions as precisely as he should have. As the crowd exited the front door, most with plans to enjoy the picnic lunches they'd packed, the jury was led out the back door and up the street to a local tavern, where their lunch would be provided free of charge. The group settled at public tables in the dimly lit and already-crowded dining room. Around the table there was much to talk about.

⚜ 8 ⚜

THE DEFENSE'S OPENING

ARGUMENT

Like the ancients producing their weeping wives and children
—Charles Hazen Peaslee

Prescott was being represented by two relatively experienced attorneys who were appointed at his indictment, Ichabod Bartlett and Charles Hazen Peaslee. At the time of his trial, judges made the decision about whether or not to appoint counsel in cases—like Prescott's—when the defendant was unlikely to be able to hire counsel. It was also typical in New Hampshire (and many other places) at that time to appoint counsel for cases that might result in capital punishment. Although the Sixth Amendment guaranteed, among other things, the right to counsel, it was generally interpreted to mean that a defendant who could afford to hire and had chosen to have counsel would not be *denied* representation. In England, it was often the practice to deny access to counsel even for defendants who wished to be represented. It was this issue that the Sixth Amendment was written to correct.[1] It did not become the law of the land that there was an actual right to be represented—even in capital cases—whether or not the defendant could afford it until the US Supreme Court decided *Powell v. Alabama* (the "Scottsboro boys" case) in 1933.[2] The Scottsboro boys were nine unemployed African American teens who illegally rode a train in Alabama. After they were arrested for that crime, two white females accused them of rape. All nine were quickly tried, with almost no legal representation, before an all-white jury. All but the youngest one, a twelve-year-old, were sentenced to death. A thirteen-year-old's case was overturned in the Alabama Supreme Court, but it took a ruling from the US Supreme Court on the right to legal representation to ensure new trials for the others.[3]

It's not known whether Prescott's two counselors were paid, or performed their work pro bono, which was typical in many jurisdictions. An able representation of even a despised defendant could generate public admiration and new business, a good reason to participate, even without the promise of a paycheck. However, Ichabod Bartlett and Charles H. Peaslee gave every evidence that, however much they were paid, they were deeply committed to Prescott's defense.

Ichabod Bartlett was born in Salisbury, New Hampshire, in 1786. After his graduation from Dartmouth College, he first studied law in the office of Moses Eastman, also a Dartmouth graduate, in Salisbury, and then in the law office of yet another Dartmouth graduate, Parker Noyes. At this time, a legal apprenticeship was the typical method of studying law; in fact, there were only a few law schools in the entire country, even by the time of Prescott's trial.[4] In 1811, Bartlett was admitted to the bar of the Court of Common Pleas and opened a law practice in Durham, New Hampshire. He relocated to the thriving town of Portsmouth in 1816.[5] Since Parker Noyes had been one of the two counselors for the defense in the murder trial of Daniel Davis Farmer, which George Sullivan prosecuted, it's probable that Bartlett consulted with him regarding Prescott's defense. Both cases featured apparent perpetrators who had done little or nothing to cover their tracks, so the cases had much in common. In Farmer's case, he also brutally assaulted his victim's young teenage daughter, who, along with the murder victim, survived to identify him. Farmer claimed that his crime amounted to no more than manslaughter, and witnesses to his previously good character were called to try to prove that point.

By 1817, Bartlett's career was soaring, as he became clerk of the State Senate. In 1819, he was elected to the New Hampshire House of Representatives, followed by election to the US House of Representatives, where he served for six years. He then returned to the New Hampshire House of Representatives, where he served from 1830 to 1832. In 1831, the Whig Party nominated him as their candidate for New Hampshire governor, but he lost the election. When Bartlett was appointed as Prescott's attorney, he was a very well-known and highly regarded politician who also continued to practice both civil and criminal law, although given his busy political career, law must not have been his primary focus. His thick, dark hair was often a little wild, rising off his head in a prominent wave, many years before that became the prevailing style for men. He had full lips that appeared permanently pursed into a look of mild disdainfulness.

Charles Hazen Peaslee was born in 1804 in Gilmanton, New Hampshire, the third of thirteen children. He attended Gilmanton Academy, and then graduated from Dartmouth College in 1824. He read law in Gilmanton and was admitted to the bar in 1828, starting a practice in Concord.[6] He had just been elected for the first of three terms to the New Hampshire House of Representatives as Prescott went to trial. His contemporaries would later judge him (not altogether enthusiastically) a "safe counselor and good business lawyer," as well as "a pleasing speaker," but the best years of his career were still before him as he went to work defending the teen.[7] He and Bartlett would almost certainly have known each other prior to the trial, but there is no indication that they previously collaborated on a criminal case. This was most likely the first murder trial either of them had ever participated in, but given the infrequency of the commission of murder in New Hampshire in that period, few others in Merrimack County would have had more experience.[8] While Peaslee was still early in his legal career, aged twenty-nine when he was appointed as one of Prescott's attorneys, and also a local lawyer, Bartlett was an experienced politician, well established professionally, and had his offices in much more distant Portsmouth, making his selection a less obvious one. Peaslee was slightly overweight, with dark receding hair and a pleasantly round, even childlike, beardless face.

From the beginning, Peaslee and Bartlett faced a difficult battle. No one, including Prescott, seemed to dispute that he had bludgeoned Cochran to death. If, as the State of New Hampshire asserted, he had deliberately planned her murder, then he would face a certain death penalty, a sentence that had been carried out in New Hampshire a total of only six times since 1739, when widow Sarah Simpson and young servant Penelope Henry were both executed on December 27 for "feloniously concealing the death of an infant bastard child" with the implication that each had caused her child's death, or at least had concealed the natural death of an infant.[9] With murder so uncommon, especially in rural New Hampshire, a death sentence was an unusual occurrence, but mostly because the crime was rare rather than that most accused murderers were either acquitted or sentenced to lesser punishment. In order to save him, Prescott's defense team would have to prove that he was not in full possession of his senses at the time he killed Cochran either because, as he said, he was asleep, or because he was insane.

Neither of these two defenses had much in the way of legal precedent, but of the two, sleepwalking had almost no record of success, although fantastical sleepwalking stories were abundant, whereas insanity was just beginning to be recognized as a possible explanation for a seemingly inexplicable and murderous act. Accompanying the Industrial Revolution was a new popularization of science. Science-based lectures became common and even newspapers often included stories that related to scientific study, encouraging a new emphasis on analytical thinking. Most educated people no longer viewed insanity as a possession by the devil, as an earlier generation would have described it, but as an actual recognizable, perhaps even treatable, disease process. Since Chauncey Cochran, in fact, accused Prescott, at the time of the murder, of being possessed by the devil, he may not have fully shared this more enlightened viewpoint. As was typical even just a few years earlier, Daniel Davis Farmer's murder charge actually described him as "being moved and seduced by the instigation of the devil."[10]

If Prescott had acted insane all or most of the time, this defense could have, even in 1834, potentially resulted in acquittal or at least in a show of clemency. There was a very recent precedent. Just the previous year, John Barnum, about seventeen, of Danbury, Connecticut, was told by his father during dinner that he should go to his married sister's house on an errand. Moments after the teen left, someone fired a shot through the window that struck and killed John's father. John was arrested and tried. His teacher testified that he was far behind his peers in his ability to understand things, but John was quickly convicted and sentenced to hang. Many who knew him petitioned the General Assembly to show clemency. Some reported that he had previously been insane and looked wild on the day of the crime. Based on a concern for his youth (less than a year younger than Prescott) and his previous insanity, which the Assembly believed must have been affecting him at the time of the crime, his sentence was commuted to life in prison.[11]

Unfortunately for Prescott, most of the time he appeared to be in possession of his senses. Many people would find it unlikely that a person could be insane enough for one brief period in time to commit a heinous crime, and yet, just minutes later, appear to be nearly normal. More important, it would be extremely challenging to convince a jury of pragmatic, middle-aged farmers of such a possibility, especially taking into consideration the sympathetic nature of the victim, a young mother. Judging by the tack they took, Peaslee and Bartlett considered the sleepwalking defense a very challenging one, although they would frequently reference it; there was no point in rejecting that line of defense if anyone might accept it. But they chose instead to focus more on the issue of Prescott's sanity. From time to time, they would even attempt to convince the jury that somnambulism and insanity were nearly the same thing.

Peaslee and Bartlett would have been familiar with a case that had gone to trial in October 1824 in the not-distant town of Knox, Maine, where an insanity plea had been attempted. Seth Elliot, a successful farmer and businessman in Knox, was described at trial as "the wealthiest man in town."[12] He was the married father of seven and employed four workers. He was also a heavy drinker, and when he was drunk, he was often angry.[13] He developed an apparently unfounded conviction that his wife had had an affair and that his two-year-old son, John Wilson Elliot, had been fathered by some other man.[14] For weeks before the crime, Elliot had viciously insulted his wife and pushed the hapless toddler away.

On Sunday morning, July 25, 1824, Elliot got up and insisted that nearly all of his children and his four employees attend church.[15] Elliot took the toddler, John, into a bedroom, where he cut his throat.[16] He then made three superficial cuts across his own throat. When the neighbors (who thought he'd been drinking) and then a doctor arrived, he was treated for his wounds, then taken off to jail. Later, while sober, he admitted to killing John and said that the child was his own property, so he could do with him as he saw fit, a horrifying defense if ever there was one.

At trial, his two attorneys argued strenuously that Elliot had shown numerous signs of insanity, and brought forward a number of witnesses who described his erratic behavior and thought that it occurred even when Elliot hadn't consumed alcohol. They believed that Elliot's excessive alcohol consumption had caused his insanity, but that the loss of blood from his self-inflicted neck wounds after he killed his child had resulted in a temporary restoration of clear thought, since physicians who saw him just after the crime judged him to be sane.[17]

In their closing argument, the prosecution would cite the then current "knowing right from wrong" test for insanity, but also emphasized a single, much more restrictive definition of insanity, one of many that were in existence, but the only one they authoritatively named: "There must be an absolute dispossession of the force and natural agency of the human mind."[18] Elliot's insanity, if it existed, never reached that level. When the judges instructed the jury, they concurred with the legal standard of knowing right from wrong, but never contradicted the prosecution's additional, much more narrow definition of insanity. Elliot was quickly convicted. On February 3, 1825, a huge crowd gathered in Castine to witness his execution. Before he was hanged, Elliot satisfyingly provided them with an impassioned, hour-long lecture on the dangers of intemperance.[19]

Perhaps that unhappy outcome was on Mr. Peaslee's mind when he rose to begin the case for the defense. The morning had gone briskly for the jury. One witness had quickly followed another, each briefly presenting evidence that would have been fascinating, maybe even slightly titillating to the jurors, confirming whatever gossip they'd heard about this case. They'd gotten their first look at all the participants, although surely Abraham Prescott and Chauncey Cochran must have been most interesting. The bloody clothing and the broken fence post captivated their attention. They had had ample opportunity to observe Prescott as the damning evidence was presented, each new detail of the case hammering home his guilt, very much like nails being driven into his coffin. There was no time for their attention to wander, or for them to doze or even daydream.

By afternoon, the building had grown warm, crowded as it was with spectators. The jury had enjoyed a satiating—and delightfully free—lunch, or "dinner" as they called it, and with the midday meal the largest of the day, their stomachs were comfortably full. As Mr. Peaslee began to speak—then rambled on and on in his opening statement—and as the fast-paced novelty of the morning wore off, perhaps the jurors grew drowsy. Very long speeches were more the order of the day than an aberration, and Mr. Peaslee already had a reputation as a skillful public speaker, so the length of his opening statement must not have come as a surprise to his captive audience. In fact, the *Patriot* said of him, "Let Peaselee only get before the jury, and he can draw tears, if need be, every time."[20] The man who transcribed Peaslee's speech added only rare punctuation. Whether that was just his style or if it reflected the fact that Peaslee seemed to speak in one uninterrupted, long stream of consciousness sentence is unknown. He began:

> Gentlemen of the Jury: The prisoner before the bar is charged with the crime of murder, and you are to determine in calm deliberation, in sober judgment and cold blood, whether he is guilty of an offense punishable by death. If then, as Jewish teachers inculcated, places of devotion, the vases and everything connected with our church establishment, should be deemed holy and sacred, never could this house be appropriated to more solemn and legitimate purposes than on the present occasion, viz., the administration of justice, and the exercise of the highest earthly power over our fellow-man. The vast number who have assembled, taking cognizance of our proceedings, desirous that impartiality and equity should be administered,—constantly reminding us by their presence that the life of a fellow-being is at stake, and who will retire with increased or diminished respect and attachment to our institutions, confident of a fair trial, however monstrous and unnatural may have been the crime of which they in turn may be accused—and secure of the protections the laws afford them against an ignominious death, so long as their motives are pure, although they may not be secure of a ray of reason to guide, or of consciousness to bind their actions; or else with feelings of insecurity and distrust—the momentous consequences of the matter now pending upon the prisoner at the bar, and with all our duty to ourselves (else reflection may come when reflection is too late)—these considerations should indeed characterize our proceedings with candor and solemnity, should hinder you, gentlemen of the jury, in particular, from being influenced by the thousand rumors which have been circulated, and some have no doubt reached your ears; should restrain witnesses

from saying anything lightly, heedlessly or from prejudice—and all of us from doing aught unbecoming a court of law and justice in a civilized and enlightened community.[21]

Not only was there just a single period in that long sentence, there didn't seem to be a place to insert another. Mr. Peaslee went on: he told the jury that even though the prisoner was a poor man, he lived in a country where he would receive a fair trial. He described Prescott as "only the helpless youth whose life, whose all, is in your hands," and then reminded the jury that the teen had been confined "to an dungeon," making it difficult to prepare his defense, a description of the jail that Andrew Leach, Prescott's jailer, may have resented. With respect to Prescott's confession, he spoke of the witnesses "who, whether from a feverish ambition to make themselves conspicuous, or from a more culpable motive, have lurked about the prisoner's cell to get the sayings of an insane man."[22]

Peaslee argued that, taking into consideration Prescott's past and character, it would have been impossible for him to murder Cochran *and* then readily admit to the crime unless he was a "real lunatic." He warned the jury to clear their thoughts of all they had heard of the crime, and of prejudicial evidence like the "bloody garments and instruments of death" they had been shown just that morning. He described those as "like the ancients producing their weeping wives and children in courts, baring their arms and showing the scars they had received in their country's defense," produced by the prosecution in order to "influence the jury and get a verdict."[23] This may have rung a little out of tune for the jury, aware as they were of the brutality of the murder and Sally Cochran's total innocence and pathetic trust in Prescott. The prosecution would be expected to produce the murder weapon and the few pieces of physical evidence—his bloody clothing—that connected Prescott to Cochran's murder. There was nothing inflammatory in doing so.

After continuing his warnings at length, Peaslee then turned to various definitions of murder, "the necessary ingredients in order to constitute the crime."[24] Each one he read, four in all, emphasized the important criteria that the perpetrator must be of sound mind, and that the crime must include "malice, either express or implied" that preceded the killing, but then added five more that spelled that the accused must be of sound mind.[25] He concluded that part of his opening statement: "It is clearly then recognized by the law that whenever there is a defect of understanding as in case of injuries committed by persons in a state of lunacy, somnambulism, or idiocy, no offense has been committed. Idiots, madmen, persons not at the time in full possession of their reason, such as somnambulists, are excused, whatever injuries they may commit. A madman, as the law says, is punished enough by his madness alone, for should you bring in the prisoner not guilty, by reason of insanity, he must be consigned to the prison walls in effect for life."[26] Peaslee may have put particular emphasis on the words "a madman is punished by his madness alone."

This was a concept that was beginning to change at the time of Prescott's trial: that the insane were already being punished by their unfortunate conditions and didn't then deserve further unpleasant consequences from the courts. Typically, in the eighteenth century, those rare individuals who had been acquitted because of their insanity had been released back to their families for safekeeping, rather than housed in either the few existing mental hospitals or locked up in jails.

That changed with the trial of James Hadfield, who was accused of trying to assassinate King George III on May 15, 1800.[27] At that time in English courts, an insane person was defined as "lost to all sense" and "incapable of forming a judgment upon the consequences of the act he is about to do," a legal standard that had existed for more than half a century at that point (and was quite similar to the standard cited by the prosecution in the Maine murder case of Elliot in 1824). Since Hadfield had engaged in planning for his attack, that seemed to contradict the standard—he clearly had some kind of sense. His defense attorney instead argued that delusion "unaccompanied by frenzy or raving madness, was the true character of insanity."[28] Under a new law, he was tried for treason rather than attempted murder.

Hadfield's case concluded when the two judges halted it, stating that there was ample evidence for acquittal based on the man's insanity, even in the absence of the previously required frenzy.[29] He was found to be not guilty since he was believed to be insane. There was concern that, given his mental state, he was likely to make another attempt on the king's life. This resulted in the introduction, just four days later, of the Criminal Lunatics Act of 1800, which made it a requirement that those who committed certain crimes while insane would be held indefinitely, not leaving the choice to judge and jury. Hadfield was incarcerated at the Bethlehem Royal Hospital for the rest of his life, dying in 1841.[30]

Peaslee next turned to the case of Captain Paddock of Valparaiso and the "inhuman judicial murder of the amiable man." Capt. Henry Paddock was the ill-fated master of the whale ship *Catherine,* sailing out of Nantucket, Massachusetts.[31] Late in 1832, shortly before Prescott attacked the Cochrans, Paddock, a man who was regarded as a mild and temperate person, according to one of his crew, either had too much to drink (perhaps not quite so temperate as he'd been thought to be) or suffered a loss of sanity, and shot or stabbed and killed one to three people—reports varied—in the port of Valparaiso, Chile. According to a brief reference to him in the *American Railroad Journal,* "The packet of the 9th contains a paragraph stating that Captain Paddock of the whale ship Catherine, who had killed three people and wounded several others in Valparaiso, was shot at that place of the 10th of January last. On his way to the place of execution he exhibited unequivocal marks of insanity."[32] While Peaslee would later cite numerous other case histories of insanity, the pertinence of Paddock was that he had been executed—on foreign soil by a government that was obviously ignorant of the proper and fair legal treatment of a man who could not possibly be held responsible for his murderous act. It was a not-so-subtle reminder that American citizens—like the gentlemen of the jury—must be wiser and more careful in their handling of the current case, or risk comparison to Chileans.

Peaslee then moved on to the topic of reasonable doubt, reading numerous definitions of that concept, but at one point he read a passage that counseled the jury to hold themselves to an even higher standard—that they should be without any doubt at all—certain of Prescott's guilt in order to convict.[33] He went on for a long time, reviewing biblical concepts of guilt, responsibility, and appropriate punishment.

Having thoroughly covered the lengthy history of both Christian and Jewish law, he told the jurors that the death penalty did not serve as an effective deterrent to murder. He noted that in England, where many less lethal offenses still carried the death penalty, the crime rate had risen much more rapidly than the population, even though nearly all the men who were awaiting the punishment of death had witnessed executions sometime previous to committing the crimes they were sentenced for.[34] Thus, even if a judgment of guilty was appropriate, it would not prevent further crime so should be rejected for that reason, if none other.

He also commented, with evident distaste, on the nature of executions. "Many persons are to be sure collected to witness public executions—but some to pick pockets—some to gamble and fight—some for noisy festivity, and but few for better purposes than to got drunk with the excitement— and the horrid pleasure of witnessing the last agonies of a fellow-being, swung between the heavens and earth. If witnessing such a scene is not sufficient to deter men from the commission of smaller offenses on the spot, nay, more, if it rather invites them—and even murders have been committed under the very gallows—who will believe that it will operate to deter them at a remote point?"[35] His description of the nature of a public execution would prove to be remarkably prescient.

He turned back to the topic of Prescott's youth and innocence:

Can you believe that the young man before you has the hellish disposition which would have led, while in possession of his senses, to the
commission of this crime? Such is the constitution of our natures, fash-
ioned and made after the likeness and image of God and partaking of
some of His attributes—that no man, however abandoned, aspires to
commit the least wicked action but from a hope to gain some profit,
much less a crime so black and detestable, so horrid, that it would seem
to be a complication of all guilt. Where is the evidence, that the accused
has been from his infancy an object of dread and detestation—that his
life has been a continued series of idleness, cruelty, vicious indulgence
and violence—where in the thousand kind attentions to the children,
in the alacrity with which he performed every service and anticipated
the wants of every member of the family—where, in the confidence and
esteem he inspired, was the countenance beaming with rage, the fierce,
bold and headstrong demeanor, that caused all around first to tremble,
then to hate, and which would indicate a readiness, upon provocation,
to fly, regardless of consequences, in the face of all laws, human and
divine?[36]

Considering that Prescott had previously viciously attacked the Co-chrans, this was a bold and risky strategy for Peaslee.

He reminded the jury that Prescott was the salt of the earth: "We shall prove to you that he was brought up and has always lived among people than which their lives not on earth a more uncorrupted, substantial population. He was educated in the school of honest integrity, his only associates our farmers, who respect and esteem men for their virtue and integrity."[37] It had not escaped his attention that the jury was comprised solely of farmers.

Peaslee then returned to the previous January's attack: "The confidence reposed in the prisoner after the winter occurrence, by those who thoroughly knew and were best able to judge, is confirmation strong of his innocence, for facts will not lie. Why, it shows in that case he was not only innocent but above all suspicion; and if he was innocent then, he was the June following."[38] This was a point that the defense would repeat, but seems not to have been based on any kind of legal or psychiatric evidence. Even given that Prescott could have committed the first attack while sleepwalking, the obvious possibility existed that he remembered in June how well the claim of somnambulism—real or pretend—had protected him from punishment after the first assault.

Peaslee now turned his attention to insanity and somnambulism, "which is allied to insanity, and frequently, as it were, runs into it." He said:

> We know that the virtuous and vicious, the idle and industrious, the weak and strong, the rich and poor, are all liable to be precipitated without a moment's warning into the gulch of madness. In that horrid state, as well as somnambulism, the mind may be indeed considered as a city without walls, open to every insult, and paying homage to every invader, every idea that then starts, however absurd, however criminal or foolish, however untrue, becomes a reality; and reason and judgment, being dethroned, can make no resistance against the tyrannical invasion.[39]

It was even possible, he said, that "the presence of a superabundant acid in the stomach, dyspepsia, however produced, may disturb its exquisite attunement and prostrate the reason." He went on a bit later: "Slender is the tenure by which all of us hold our moral and intellectual existence."[40]

Defense counsel Peaslee had, by now, discoursed at length on the need for the jurors to understand the pathos of the defendant, provided

multiple, complex definitions of murder, described in detail a few remarkable cases, explained the history of Christian and Jewish jurisprudence, described the distasteful nature of executions, and thoroughly
explained the close relationship between somnambulism and insanity.
There was much more for him to tell.

⚜ 9 ⚜

THE DEFENSE DISCUSSES
SLEEPWALKING

Somnambulism, or sleepwalking, forms, as it were,
the connecting link between dreaming and insanity
—Dr. L. W. Belden

Four justices presided over the courtroom: Chief Justice William M. Richardson, who had also officiated over the murder trials of Daniel Davis Farmer in 1821 and Daniel H. Corey in 1829; Associate Justice Joel Parker; and two Court of Common Pleas justices, Benjamin Wadleigh and Aaron Whittemore. Neither Richardson nor Parker was a novice when it came to capital cases and both were highly respected.

Richardson, born in 1774 in Pelham, New Hampshire, had fully planned to be a farmer, as his father was, until he suffered a severe injury to his hand as a teenager. Although he eventually recovered, during the time he was disabled he had the opportunity to take academics more seriously. He attended Harvard College, and after two stints of teaching, began to read law in Groton, Massachusetts, and was admitted to the Massachusetts Bar in 1804. He was appointed to fill a vacancy in the US House of Representatives in 1811, then was elected to another term, but resigned in 1814 to return to New Hampshire, where he opened a law practice in Portsmouth. He was appointed chief justice of the newly reorganized New Hampshire Superior Court system in 1816.[1] He had a fair complexion with dark, short hair that sometimes spilled in a wave over his forehead but did little to disguise his oversized ears. He married Elizabeth Smith and became the father of seven children. In 1829, he was one of three justices to hear the capital case of Daniel H. Corey, who was accused of murdering, while he was insane, an elderly widow, Mrs. Matilda Nash, while he was insane.

Associate Justice Joel Parker's presence on the court was significant because he was one of the two attorneys for the defense in Daniel Corey's case. Daniel Haseltine Corey was born in 1790 and farmed family land in Sullivan, New Hampshire. Around 1823, Corey began to have spells of mania and delusions that, among other things, involved beliefs that there was buried treasure in the woods near his home, which he spent quite a lot of time digging for while neglecting farm and family, and that black cats were possessed by the devil and should be killed, both beliefs fueled by alcohol consumption.

By 1829, Corey was threatening (and likely physically abusing) his beleaguered wife.[2] On June 13, his wife, mother-in-law, sister (who also was disabled by a mental illness) and three of his children fled to the home of neighbor Daniel Nash. The eldest son was sent to have the Sullivan selectman swear out a warrant to arrest Corey. Nash was away that morning, but his seventy-year-old mother, widow Matilda Nash, either volunteered or was talked into visiting Corey to try to settle him down. She took with her a bundle of flax as an excuse to visit, and was accompanied by Nash's twelve-year-old daughter, Elizabeth.

When they got to Corey's, Nash called in through the open door to him, "How do you do, Mr. Corey?" He grabbed a musket that had been hanging nearby on a hook. Nash and her granddaughter turned and ran, but Corey caught up to Nash, and struck a blow across the back of her head with the musket and then another after she fell. He then ran after Elizabeth, who had witnessed this attack and was fleeing, she knew, for her life. After she scrambled over a rail fence, he gave up the chase and went back to Nash. He then beat her so viciously that her body was later identified only by her clothing. Corey, now calm and seemingly unaware of his crime, was arrested and when asked if he would try to escape, said, "Oh, no. I was crazy." He was put on trial. There were many neighbors available and willing to testify that he had been intermittently afflicted in very obvious ways for many years. Although the state was able to find a few who would testify that they had never seen or heard of his spells, their statements paled against the vivid commentary of the defense's many believable witnesses.

Corey's defense counsel, Joel Parker, cited numerous previous cases (mostly English) that had dealt with insane perpetrators. Parker, practically a child prodigy since he began in the sophomore class at Dartmouth College in 1809 at the tender age of thirteen and graduated at sixteen, was an experienced attorney by the time of the trial in 1829.[3] His full dark hair framed a youthful face. He wore a fringe of ragged beard, but no moustache. His calm, direct stare could be disconcerting to witnesses. The jury considered Corey's case only briefly and returned a verdict of not guilty by reason of insanity.[4]

Benjamin Wadleigh and Aaron Whittemore were among the many justices who served locally in the Courts of Common Pleas; they joined Richardson and Parker on the bench. Both of them were fifty-one years old in 1834. Wadleigh, a farmer from Sutton, town clerk, state representative, and justice of the peace, had just been appointed to the bench in 1833. Whittemore was from Pembroke and thus knew personally both the Cochrans and Abraham Prescott. He was a merchant, tavern keeper, town clerk, and former state representative. Although their presence added gravitas to the proceedings, they were little more than observers, since neither was even an attorney.

Still, two of the four justices presiding over the trial were experienced in capital cases, making them among a small minority of New Hampshire justices with that capability. They were fully prepared to handle the Prescott trial, manage the crowds that gathered, and provide the guidance to the jury that would aid them in their verdict.

Now defense attorney, Peaslee, continuing his opening statement, launched into the meat of his defense. He said he planned to describe a series of remarkable cases of sleepwalking that had been reported recently in various medical journals and newspapers, episodes that were, he said, "familiar to everyone," although this was surely the first case of murder supposedly committed while sleeping that most of the jurors had heard of.[5] The cases shine a light on both a growing awareness that human behavior was governed by sometimes inscrutable internal complexities rather than demonic possession, and that even the educated public remained surprisingly credulous in their acceptance of most of what they perceived, whether or not it flew in the face of apparent logic, common sense, or everyday experience.

First, however, even though it didn't relate to sleepwalking, Peaslee described in greater detail than earlier in his opening statement, the groundbreaking case of James Hadfield, who had unsuccessfully attempted to assassinate King George III. Peaslee "read at length" from Hadfield's attorney's courtroom speeches—so much so that the record of trial doesn't include all of what he said. Hadfield had not been asleep when he made the murder attempt. In fact, he was at the theater when he fired a shot at the king. He had, however, apparently been insane, so that may have seemed a good enough reason to include his case now.

Peaslee then began to read a very long passage from a work of Dr. John Abercrombie. Dr. Abercrombie, a Scottish physician (1780–1844), had made the study of "the mental aspects of medical science" a focus of his work. Abercrombie spoke of degrees of somnambulism. The first degree was talking in one's sleep.[6] Sleepwalking was the next degree. He illustrated this by describing the case of a European nobleman who got up in his sleep, wrapped himself in a cloak, climbed out onto a roof, stole a baby bird from its nest, and returned to bed. In the morning, the nobleman described the events as being a vivid dream—disproven when he found the baby bird in his cloak.[7] Abercrombie cited a case of sleepwalking that was described in the impressively titled *A Manual of Pathology Containing the Symptoms, Diagnosis, and Morbid Characters of Diseases, Together with an Exposition of the Different Methods of Examination Applicable to the Affections of the Head, Chest and Abdomen* by Louis Martinet of France. (At the time, France was widely regarded as being the epicenter of medical knowledge.)[8]

Having documented several vivid cases of sleepwalking, Abercrombie—still being quoted by Prescott's attorney—now went on to describe a condition he felt was related:

coming on in daytime in paroxysms, during which the person is affected in the same manner as in the state of somnambulism, particularly with insensibility to external impressions; this presents some singular phenomena. These attacks in some cases come on without any warning; in others they are preceded by a noise or sense of confusion in the head. The individuals then become more or less abstracted and are either unconscious of any external impression, or very confused in their notions of external things. They are frequently able to talk in an intelligible and consistent manner, but always in reference to the impression which is present in their own minds.[9]

Peaslee hoped the jury would make the obvious connection that Prescott was similarly afflicted. As an example of this daytime sleepwalking state, Abercrombie discussed a young woman who could not play certain challenging pieces on the piano. When affected by daytime somnambulism, however, she could play them fluently.[10] More interesting was the case of a young woman who was under the care of Dr. William Dyce (1770–1835) of Aberdeen, Scotland. This woman, a servant, first became hard to awaken in the morning. Later she experienced periods of an hour or more when she would go about her work setting the table, dressing her employers' children, and other duties, "her eyes remaining shut the whole time." Abercrombie reported that while afflicted she could recall things that happened during previous paroxysms. She "read distinctly a portion of a book that was presented to her; and she sang both sacred and common pieces, incomparably better, Dr. Dyce affirms, than she could do in the waking state."[11]

Quoting from Dr. Benjamin Rush (1746–1813), a well-known and respected Philadelphia physician, Peaslee intoned, "Somnambulism bears a closer analogy than a common dream to madness. Like madness, it is accompanied with muscular action, with coherent and incoherent conduct, and with that complete oblivion (in most cases) of both, which takes places in the worst grade of madness."[12] As an example, perhaps, he next cited the case of young John, who worked at Cardrew in England in the sump house of a mine. Getting up in his sleep, he descended a narrow ladder into the mine about twenty fathoms—120 feet—where other workers eventually found him. They were forced to shake him quite hard to awaken him. Fortunately, he managed to cling to the ladder in spite of the shaking.[13]

Peaslee described the case of "Lord Culpepper's brother," who, he said, in 1686 was put on trial for shooting "one of the Guards, and his horse to boot."[14] He was acquitted when more than fifty witnesses testified to him doing "extraordinary things" while he was asleep, perhaps representing a precedent for what Peaslee hoped would be the verdict in Prescott's case. Peaslee, however, here inadvertently took some liberty with the truth. Although he told the jury that Colonel Culpepper was acquitted, in fact he was found guilty of "manslaughter while in-sane."[15] He'd found this case and quite a few others he cited in a book called *Philosophy of Sleep* by Dr. Robert MacNish, a Glasgow physi-cian, with the second edition having just come out earlier in 1834. It was MacNish who reported Culpepper's case incorrectly.[16]

Peaslee listed further sleepwalking cases: no lesser personage than Benjamin Franklin, who reportedly slept for an hour while floating in a salt-water hot bath. (Franklin reported this incident of sleep-floating in his diary: "I went at noon to bathe in Martin's salt-water hot-bath, and, floating on my back, fell asleep, and slept near an hour by my watch, without sinking or turning. A thing I never did before and should have thought impossible. Water is the easiest bed that can be.")[17] Peaslee listed more cases: a young man who left his home asleep at midnight, walked a distance of two miles on a "difficult and dangerous road," then swam along the coast of Ireland a mile and a half before he was spotted and rescued by a night watchman; a young French boy found fishing in a boat in the middle of the night; and a man who got out of bed, and dreaming his house was being robbed, climbed out of his window, and was walking to the police station when discovered.[18]

He went on to describe both a minister and a student who composed sermons while asleep; a miller who was habitually discovered "attending to his usual avocations at the mill" while asleep; a doctor who arose and conversed and sang with his family while sleeping; soldiers marching in their sleep; and a boy who dreamed he scaled a precipice and stole from there an eagle's nest, which he imagined he brought home and placed under his bed, only to discover it there when he awoke, an adventure surprisingly similar to that of the European nobleman who found the baby bird in his cloak.[19]

Another case he mentioned was at least as interesting for the treat-ment the sleepwalker received as for the problem itself. Peaslee read the tale to the jury, once again, from *The Philosophy of Sleep*. The book described a sixteen-year-old boy who got up, asleep, in the night. He fetched his spurs and whip, went to the stable, and when not able to find his saddle, went back to the house to ask for it. Not finding it there, he then mounted his horse without a saddle. Two other apprentices in the household got him down off the horse and brought him inside. There the boy stood for about fifteen minutes, seeming to believe that he was stopped at a toll gate but didn't have enough money to pay. Meanwhile, his employer had sent for a physician. After finally believing he'd paid the toll, the boy spurred and whipped his imaginary horse.

> His pulse at this time was 136, full and hard; no change of countenance could be observed, nor any spasmodic affection of the muscles, the eyes remaining closed the whole of the time. His coat was taken off his arm, shirt sleeves tucked up, and Mr. Ridge bled him to 32 ounces; no alteration had taken place in him during the first part of the time the blood was flowing; at about 24 ounces, the pulse began to decrease; and when the full quantity named above had been taken it was at 80—a slight perspiration on his forehead. After the arm was tied up, he unlaced one boot and said he would go to bed; in three minutes from this time, he awoke, got up, and asked what was the matter (having then been one hour in the trance), not having the slightest recollection of anything that had passed, and wondered at his arm being tied up, and at the blood, &c.[20]

He was then administered a strong laxative to complete the cure. The next day, not surprisingly since he had been bled almost one quarter of his body's blood, he was somewhat weak. Fortunately, he was said to have made a good recovery.

By this time, the afternoon was well advanced. Perhaps, now that Peaslee had turned to these fairly amusing, even astonishing anecdotes, if the jury's attention had wandered, now they were reengaged in his very long monologue, and not in danger of nodding off in the warm church. There is no record of their response. Prescott sat impassively, appearing to pay little attention to the proceedings.

However, defense attorney Peaslee wasn't done with his unusual tales. He added a couple with tragic conclusions: "The case of Mr. Little, of New York, who rose in his sleep, gained the roof of his house, three stories high, and walked off the gable-end."[21] This man's case was reported in a small entry in the February 1, 1834, issue of *Thomsonian Botanic Watchman,* a serial that, beneath its masthead, portrayed itself as "The Sun of Science arising upon the Flora of North America." Mr. Little survived his fall, although he broke both his back and feet, and told his doctor he had dreamt that his wife was just falling off table rock at Niagara Falls and that he had stepped out to help her when he fell instead.[22] Peaslee had another tragic one:

> The case of a young girl, ten years of age, who was discovered early in the morning, walking on the top of one of the loftiest houses in the city of Dresden, apparently occupied in preparing some ornaments, as a Christmas present. She continued her terrific promenade for hours; sometimes sitting on the parapet, and dressing her hair; at others, gazing towards the moon, and singing or talking to herself. Once she approached the very verge of the parapet, leaning forward, looking upon the nets suspended from the balcony of the first floor, the thickly strewn straw, in the street beneath, and the multitude expecting her fall; she rose up, however, and returned carelessly to the window, by which she had got out; when she saw there were lights in the room, she uttered a piercing shriek, which was re-echoed by thousands below, and fell dead into the street.[23]

Then Peaslee turned to "the astonishing case of Jane C. Rider of Springfield, of which you have all heard."[24] He proceeded to describe her case at some length, perhaps in case they had not heard, although her remarkable story had appeared in some newspapers and had attracted a great deal of attention in New England. Rider was known as "the Springfield Somnambulist." While her troubles began in the spring of 1833, just as Prescott's were too, a full account of her strange tale didn't appear in print until shortly after her case was presented by Dr. L. W. Belden "as a lecture before the Springfield Lyceum, January 22, 1834," and then printed in book form by the Springfield publisher, G. and C. Merriam, more famous for publishing their dictionaries. Prescott's attorneys must have read the account with some satisfaction, since it began "Somnambulism, or sleepwalking, forms, as it were, the connecting link between dreaming and insanity; and, in order to a full understanding of its nature, it will be necessary to offer a few remarks relative to these two seemingly different, but really analogous states."[25] Here was a full confirmation of their claim, scientific, recent, and close to home.

Rider was said to be the daughter of an "ingenious and respectable mechanic" from Brattleboro, Vermont.[26] In April 1833, at the age of seventeen, Rider moved to Springfield, Massachusetts, where "she became an inmate of the house of Mr. Festus Stebbins," employed as a house-maid. Although she was in good health, if "of a full habit"—possibly a bit plump—she was well educated and "her intelligence and uniformly mild and obliging disposition soon secured the confidence and love of all with whom she was connected."[27]

Over the past few years, Rider had complained of frequent headaches, and she also had a slight tenderness in the region of her head that phrenologists—pseudoscientists of the nineteenth century who attached great significance to the shape of people's heads—connected to "the organ of marvelousness," and she had experienced that for as long as she could recall.[28] Notably, the severe headaches that would be a part of her new symptoms always originated precisely in that spot.

On the night of June 24, she was found struggling to get out of bed, and presumed to be deranged. Dr. Belden was called. Her eyes were closed, her face hot, and her pulse was rapid. Believing her to be suffering from a stomach ailment, Belden gave her a powerful emetic that worked well; he even helpfully described her stomach contents. A very large number of green currents apparently were responsible for her misery. She fell back to a sounder sleep and in the morning couldn't remember any of the night's events.

Almost a month passed before the next event: one night she arose, got dressed, and began her work, again presumably while asleep. While members of the family watched in amazement, she did it all in near total darkness—and with her eyes shut. After this remarkable event, she began to get up two or three times a week and complete work while supposedly asleep. Belden pointed out that her movements were regulated by her senses—that is, she wasn't readily tricked.

As her disease advanced—or her audience grew, as she became quite a popular local attraction—she began to have a daytime version of her nightly rambles, more convenient for audiences.[29] Eventually, Festus Stebbins and his large family began to tire of the sideshow their servant had become. "As it was very apparent that her disease was aggravated by the daily trial of her peculiar powers to which she was subjected by a constant stream of visitors," a decision was made in December to send her to the relatively new (and surely viewed as cutting-edge) state insane asylum in Worcester, Massachusetts. Her first "paroxysm" there occurred the following day. When she lapsed into one of her states, a few people repeatedly asked her to read. "With an air of impatience," she refused.[30] Without her large enthusiastic audience, the show was over. After extensive, unpleasant, months-long treatment, Rider was judged to be recovered and was discharged from the hospital in early spring, perhaps lucky to have survived the staff's harsh ministrations and certainly weary of them.[31]

Peaslee wasn't quite done. He pointed out, "You will perceive, Gentlemen, that there is an endless variety of wild and inconsistent conduct in insane and somnambulating individuals, and that these diseases are confined to no rules or limits, either in the duration or mode of attack." He went on:

> These may be inexplicable phenomena, and the case now under consideration may appear to you mysterious. Well, if any one should undertake to explain why any of the cases cited, so happen, it would be only undertaking to explain a very great obscurity, by being somewhat more obscure; it is sufficient for us to know they are facts, and corresponding with one now on trial and the Government having, it is believed, completely failed to prove the felonious intent, every idea of malice being in fact negative by their own witnesses—every act of the prisoner, before, at the time, and after the homicide, being contrary to any known conduct of a sane man (either before or since the flood), who had intended such a crime—all the probabilities, surely are in favor of the prisoner's innocence, and the case falls short, far short, of being made out as law requires, beyond a reasonable doubt.[32]

In essence, Peaslee argued that the common thread linking the eighteen sleepwalking cases he'd described in such detail was that they were strange, and so was Prescott's case. And since Prescott had not been obviously murderous before killing Cochran—if one chose to overlook the January attack as Peaslee did here—and he had not come up with a rational explanation for his crime, and hadn't fled like a wiser man might have after committing it, then he must be insane. Either Prescott was sleepwalking, just as all of the remarkable people Peaslee had described—so many, in fact, that extreme cases of sleepwalking might come to be seen as commonplace—or he was insane, or both.

⚜ 10 ⚜

THE AVERY CONNECTION

Enquire of the Mr. Rev. Avery of Bristol
—Sarah Marie Cornell

If that explanation hadn't covered it all, with the afternoon wearing on, defense attorney Peaslee now changed his direction a bit. After a little more verbose explanation, he played his next card. "We shall prove that the grandparents, sister and cousin of the prisoner were subject to sudden attacks of insanity, which lasted for a short time and went off, and that these diseases, as well as numerous others, are transmissible from one generation to another."

Gregor Mendel, whose experiments with plants would lay the groundwork for a modern understanding of genetics, was born in 1822 and was just twelve years old at the time of Prescott's trial. His experiments with pea plants, which would begin to explain the mysteries of heritability, were still years off in the future.[1] But even before Mendel's groundbreaking work, people commonly understood that traits could pass down in families and that careful breeding of farm animals could result in better livestock. However, nobody really knew much about the specifics.

Intermarriage between cousins was fully accepted in the Federal era; marriage within families was not unusual and offered some advantages.[2] Both Sally Cochran and her younger sister had married their first cousins, and her parents were second cousins. Marriage between cousins cemented kinship ties and effectively kept property within families, so it served a highly practical purpose. (Even in 2018, marriage between first cousins is legal in twenty-one states.) Taking into account the societal acceptance of in-family marriage in 1834, the comments Peaslee quoted, from physician George Man Burrows's *Commentaries on Insanity* (1828), are interesting. "It is of little real importance whether it be a predisposition, or the malady itself, which descends and becomes hereditary; but no fact is more incontrovertibly established than that insanity is susceptible of being propagated; or in other words, that a specific morbid condition sometimes exists in the human constitution, which by intermarriage or according to the vulgar but expressive language of cattle breeders, 'by breeding *in and in*,' may be perpetuated ad infinitum."[3]

Although Peaslee would then go on to document the other cases of supposed insanity in Prescott's family, he made no attempt to prove that they had practiced "breeding in and in." In fact, even experts of the day weren't convinced that it represented a problem, at least in animals. A contemporaneous animal breeder, Sir John Sebright, who made a study of the process of inbreeding, stated that breeding animal siblings or parent to child—the two most common forms of "breeding in and in"—would produce lines that bred true, and certain bad traits could be completely eliminated with this practice.[4]

After quoting several other pertinent passages from Burrows's recent book, Peaslee listed four proofs that Prescott was insane: that his grandparents were insane, that his "collaterals" were similarly afflicted, that he exhibited an early problem with his head, and that he had "actual early somnambulism." He commented that each of these factors alone would have been enough to cause "a breaking out," and that it was a wonder he had maintained his equilibrium for so long. The fact that the teen was well fed, well cared for, had few worries, and "lived in perfect harmony" in the Cochran household all protected him from the time bomb that had been, since his birth, apparently ticking within him. Given that nasty combination of inheritance and defect that he described, Peaslee then asked, "Do you inquire, Gentleman, what was that mental irritant, that excitement of the imagination, which helped to throw him off his balance?"[5]

This must have felt like an aha! moment to Prescott's attorney. "Why, it was the Avery trial, by which Cochran was reading at the time they left the house. A subject, which so intensely, at that period, engaged the thoughts of the whole community, but at that particular time of every member of this family, and concerning which, very probably, he and Mrs. Cochran conversed, as they passed along."[6] No record exists of Prescott reporting that he and Sally might have discussed it as they searched for strawberries. In fact, given other descriptions of the teen, they may have not conversed at all; he was not known to have been a boy of many words. It is improbable that Prescott could read fluently so he would have had to be dependent on someone else, presumably Sally, for providing the details of the case. Since Avery's victim was pregnant but unmarried when she was murdered, it would constitute quite an unseemly topic of conversation for a gentlewoman like Cochran.

Recently, murder trial records were quickly published after the conclusion of the courtroom drama and had a wide, enthusiastic audience. The urban penny press, beginning in late 1833 with the *Sun* and soon followed by the competing *Transcript* in New York, would initiate graphic and very popular newspaper coverage of crimes. However, Avery's trial was one of the very first to receive extensive press coverage as it was occurring.

The trial of Rev. Ephraim Avery had captivated readers all over the country. On December 21, 1832, a farmer's son discovered the cold body of thirty-year-old Sarah Marie Cornell hanging by the neck from a cord attached to a five-foot-tall haystack post in an isolated field in rural Tiverton, Rhode Island.[7] It was at first assumed that the young mill operative had committed suicide—although she'd surely gone to great lengths to do so, having hiked several miles beforehand on a cold evening to get to this particular field—but the later discovery of a note in her handwriting among her possessions completely changed that assumption and did little for the reputation of Avery. It said, "If I should be missing, enquire of the Rev. Mr. Avery of Bristol, he will know where I am."[8]

A postmortem exam later revealed that she was about four months pregnant. Other incriminating evidence seemed to confirm that Avery had had a role in her death. During his murder trial, which dragged on for nearly a month, his attorneys used every opportunity to impugn the victim's character, which was not difficult since she had been somewhat less constrained and more forthright than other young women of the era. Cornell had been living on her own for several years, working at one mill and then another, and although there were many young women similarly engaged, she was especially emancipated—running her own life—at a time when it was viewed as less than proper for a young woman not to be under the supervision of some male, or at the very least a matronly woman.

Birth and marriage records prove that children conceived out of wedlock were not at all unusual in the 1800s.[9] The issue with Cornell was that the presumed father of her child was both married and a minister. While the scandalous case had been highly titillating and the topic of much discussion throughout New England for many months before the courtroom drama even began, and the trial was covered by a crowd of reporters, the verdict—acquittal on all charges—announced on June 2, 1833, surprised no one, but, happily, displeased many.[10] Seemingly, Cornell's pregnant condition provided wagging tongues (and jurors) with plentiful evidence of her inadequate morality; compared to the more pristine reputation of a minister—any minister—she would be found lacking. With an all-male jury, there was little hope that any would show her the sympathy and mercy she surely deserved. However, public opinion was another matter altogether. Many believed that Avery's acquittal was a miscarriage of justice. His scintillating case never quite slipped from public notice; it has been the topic of several nonfictional and even some fictional works in recent years.[11]

Unfortunately, no one testified at this trial that Prescott had heard the Cochrans discuss the case, making Peaslee's remarks appear conjectural. Nonetheless, although he was defective both by inheritance and form, ultimately the blame for Prescott's crime could be, according to Peaslee, laid at the doorstep of his employers; it was their discussion of the Avery crime that fired Prescott's murderous passion. Oddly, this theory doesn't differ much from the blame placed on Sarah Marie Cornell for Reverend Avery's behavior.

Peaslee wasn't quite done citing cases. Now, having established that Prescott could have inherited insanity, he enumerated a few recent homicides seemingly committed by people similarly afflicted, not settling for mere sleepwalking. All of these cases had occurred in France, even though there had been a handful of other murders in New Hampshire in recent decades that had been attributed to insanity, and that the jurors were surely familiar with. He had mined medical books rather than legal tomes for his information. He described a case of a twenty-four-year-old woman, who, having lost a first infant, became fixated on murdering her second one. She was hospitalized before she could act on her urge.[12]

He told of a second woman who wanted to murder all of her children. A third woman, a young mother of two, was shown the site of a recent murder, and then developed an uncontrollable urge to kill her mother. She gradually overcame this, but "it was some time before she could bear the sight of her mother."[13] Yet another lady heard of an assassination and then had a strong desire to kill her seven-year-old child, even finding a weapon to use. Peaslee explained that all these cases were linked by "a change in sensibility—in short, on the principle of morbid sensibility."[14]

His listeners would have understood his reference to sensibility in a way that modern readers do not. They would have known that emotional life was driven by sense (rational thought) and sensibility (passionate urges), not all of which were negative, of course. A man who fell in love, for example, would likely be surrendering to his sensibilities, especially if the object of his affection had little in the way of dowry to bring to a marriage. Jane Austen's 1811 novel, *Sense and Sensibility,* describes the vicissitudes of two sisters, one of whom lets emotion—sensibility—run her life and who falls in love with a dashing but ultimately unreliable man, who then abandons her; thus sensibility perhaps shouldn't be allowed to run one's life. Peaslee characterized Prescott's sensibility as "morbid." It was bad enough to let sensibility run one's life; morbid sensibility would be much, much worse.

Peaslee also opined that farmers, like Prescott, were "more liable to be deranged than any other class of people of the same grade of intellect." He attributed this to the greater solitude of their lives, especially in winter (although Prescott in particular had probably had little experience with solitude) and that they were more exposed to "its corporeal causes" by labor and accident.[15] Since Prescott had first attacked the Cochrans in the winter, Peaslee felt this confirmed his thesis that being a farmer was a cause of the teen's problem. That the second event happened in summer, "immediately after great bodily effort," further proved his case, he believed.[16] There is no record of Prescott having engaged in any previous significant physical exertion that morning, although he surely would have participated in normal daily chores like animal care and fetching firewood, even on a Sunday. Peaslee may have been referring to the strawberry picking itself, although that seems unusual given that Sally Cochran could perform this while wearing a heavy long dress, several petticoats, and a restrictive corset. It's surprising that he wasn't a little concerned about insulting his all-farmer jury with this line of speculation.

Peaslee was finally winding down his opening argument. He'd been talking for a couple of hours, but he had one more point to make. He asked the jury if they needed one final key proof of Prescott's insanity: "something standing aloof from everything else, and standing on the front of the whole transaction'—these letters, 'he is insane.'" Peaslee thought it was providential that the government had, in fact, produced such evidence, "making his innocence still more clear." Peaslee played the last card of his opening statement:

> It has been proved to you that he was, at the time, violently seized with the toothache, so much so, that he was obliged to sit down. We shall prove to you that this affection is nervous, and caused by the state of the stomach, and that so is somnambulism and insanity. This, then, is a most important and conclusive fact, taken in connection with his insensibility, his insanity; to show that an adequate physical cause existed at the time to produce insanity, unless you believe the prisoner to have feigned it, knowing its connection, which is the most unlikely of any thing [sic] that can possibly be imagined.[17]

Peaslee's remarkable statement deserves further examination. First, he commented that it had been proved that Prescott had suffered from a sudden, violent toothache so severe that he was forced to sit down. Chauncey Cochran, in his previous morning's testimony, had stated that Abraham reported the toothache to him as they ran down the hill to where he had attacked Sally. Prescott may well have been trying for an excuse at that point that would exonerate him, lying about the toothache.

Dental care in the nineteenth century was limited and rudimentary.[18] Decayed teeth were more often extracted than treated. But tooth loss in Prescott's age group was relatively uncommon compared to that of those in middle age. Still, the teen would have known many people who had suffered from violent toothaches, even if he hadn't had one yet. There is no mention in the trial record of Prescott reporting previous (or further) dental problems that would add credibility to his claim. Since that toothache constituted the key first part of his explanation of the crime, it seems at least probable that if his teeth required further treatment, it would have been mentioned. Of course, the jury hadn't heard any proof that Prescott had actually had a toothache, only that he told Chauncey he'd had one.

However, Peaslee stated that the toothache was evidence of Prescott's insanity, and apparently not of tooth decay, so he would have been disinclined to offer evidence of a physical cause for his claim of dental pain anyway. While Peaslee's connection of the two—toothache and insanity—now appears ridiculous, it is unfair to judge him based on modern knowledge; it's more critical to confirm that contemporaneous sources linked the two. George Man Burrows described in great detail symptoms he connected with the onset of insanity. While, not surprisingly, most of these were psychological in nature, he included a brief summary of physical changes, not including a toothache: "Usually the first physical signs of mental derangement are broken sleep and troublesome dreams, slight cephalgia [headache], palpitation, a sensation of blood rushing to the head, or pulsation at the temples, occasional heat or flushing of the face, slight giddiness, and buzzing noise in the ears. The digestive functions are altered; the appetite is precarious, sometimes increased, sometimes diminished; the complexion changes and the patient grows thin."[19]

Benjamin Rush, to whom Peaslee earlier referred, but who was also of the previous generation and not "cutting-edge," mentioned toothache when he attempted to describe the causes of insanity. He attributed insanity primarily to disease of the blood vessels, emphatically denied that it was caused by gastrointestinal disease, but in a very long list of potential other causes of mental illness (for example, fever, intense study, and hysteria) he conceded he was aware that "It has been brought on in one instance by decayed teeth, which were not accompanied by pain."[20] The smoking gun that Peaslee implied was certainly lacking in these two preeminent resources with which he was clearly familiar.

The final part of Peaslee's statement—"unless you believe the prisoner to have feigned it, knowing its connection, which is the most unlikely of any thing that can possibly be imagined"—is particularly troubling. Peaslee clearly implied that if Prescott feigned the toothache, it would be because he was aware of the supposed connection between insanity and dental pain. The attorney's deliberately disingenuous statement completely ignores the far simpler explanation: that the teen was using the complaint of a toothache to justify why he had first come to sit down on the tree stump that led to his supposed murderous nap. To ask the jurors to assume a train of thought like this instead—(1) Prescott recognizes that he needs to set up an insanity defense for the murder he has just committed; (2) Prescott is familiar with some obscure academic source that links toothache and onset of insanity; (3) Prescott thus pretends that he had a toothache that could have caused his period of insanity—is, as Peaslee stated, "most unlikely of any thing that could be imagined." However, the young man's life was in very grave danger; Peaslee would employ all the hyperbole he could to defend it.

Peaslee offered the jury one final conclusion: "Lastly, we refer you to the act itself, as evidence strong of its being the act of a maniac, towards one, for whom he never entertained any unkind sentiment, or unfriendly feeling. The verdict of innocence has been pronounced on the winter transaction by those best able to judge; who were thoroughly acquainted with his motives, his feelings and his character, and if he was innocent then, he must have been the June following."[21]

Peaslee had, in the last portion of his long opening statement, attributed Prescott's murderous act to somnambulism, insanity that ran in his family or in farmers, his becoming impassioned by discussing the Avery trial with his victim, and by a toothache. Finally, Peaslee had concluded that the Cochrans' willingness to keep him after the winter assault was somehow proof of his innocence.

Prescott's defense attorneys had worked hard to establish the concept that an insane person should not be held responsible for his acts. Although Peaslee's two-hour-long commentary had been delivered in a loud, clear voice that had filled the crowded sanctuary, his thorough examination of the topic may also have been tedious for some of those gathered to listen. However, the *Patriot* characterized it as "very powerful, ingenious and eloquent."[22] It certainly had been erudite, but that may have made it intellectually challenging for those who lacked sufficient education. With all of these issues now thoroughly covered, Mr. Peaslee finally called his first witness.

₳ 11 ₰

MENTAL ILLNESS IN THE
PRESCOTT FAMILY

He was crazy at times and difficult in his family
—Hezekiah Blake

It seems likely that Peaslee had several points that he needed to prove with his witnesses, but all of them eventually devolved down to Prescott's sanity or lack thereof. The five points he had drawn attention to a half hour or so earlier established the crux of his argument. He hoped to use the witnesses to show that (1) insanity ran very strongly in Prescott's family so he had inherited the tendency to become insane himself; (2) he had a history from early childhood of being abnormal, especially with regard to his head; (3) he had a history of sleepwalking, which was akin to insanity; (4) Prescott's case resembled other recognized cases of insanity closely enough that it was impossible not to conclude that he was also insane; (5) insanity need not always be present; it might well occur in paroxysms followed by periods of normalcy.

Many of these issues were evident in a case Prescott's defense attorneys were aware of, that of Caleb Adams, another youthful offender who came from a troubled background. According to a sermon Moses C. Welch, a Mansfield, Connecticut, minister, delivered at Caleb's execution, the young man was born in Leyden, Massachusetts, in 1785. Several months before his birth, Caleb's father had taken in a young woman of ill repute and her "idiotic" child. Driven to despair by this situation, Caleb's mother died only months after his birth and his father then married the other woman, who died soon after, probably when Adams was still in early childhood. (There was an implication in this that Adams himself may have been "marked" or negatively influenced before his birth by the presence in the house of the defective child.) Accounts report that Caleb's father became insane. He was unable or unwilling to raise his son, so Adams was sent out to live with various relatives. Since he was (according to what he told the minster while awaiting execution) given to lying, stealing, and torturing small animals from a very tender age, he didn't fare well in school and tended not to last long in any one household.

At the age of fifteen he went to live with Elisha Chapman and his wife, a benevolent couple in Pomfret, Connecticut. Later, the Chapmans took in another child who was an orphan, Oliver Woodward. Woodward, being younger, had far fewer work expectations placed on him. On September 13, 1803, while Adams was picking beans, Woodward dragged a sled out into the field and wanted the older boy to play. Adams refused, but the boy persisted repeatedly. This enraged Adams, who resolved to murder the child.[1] He went back to the barn and sharpened, with his hapless intended victim's help, a knife and an ax. They then went into the woods, where Adams quickly dispatched the child. He fled miles away, but later confessed, saying, "The devil had led me on until I had done it, then left me."[2] He was arrested, tried, and convicted.

There were two problems. One was his age, just eighteen at the time of the murder. The other was the matter of his sanity. It was said, after Adams was sentenced, that he did not appear to be of normal intellect. Others wondered if his total lack of conscience might actually represent some form of insanity. One of the ministers at his execution felt that his slow behavior was a deliberate ploy, encouraged by some other older prisoner at the jail, and that Adams believed he would be saved from execution if he could manage to convince people that he wasn't normal.[3] A petition begging for clemency was signed by many and brought to the General Assembly, but that body declined to act. As was typical, a helpful publication that included his particulars, the sermon, and details of both the crime and the execution was published right away, and available for Prescott's attorneys to review.

Although Adams had been executed thirty-one years earlier in another state, there was nothing in his tale to encourage Prescott's defense counsel. The strong similarities between the cases—insanity in the family, an impoverished upbringing, the cruelty to animals, the spontaneous nature of the two murders, the potential intellectual deficits or insanity of the perpetrators, their near identical ages, and the unhappy outcome of Adams's trial—must have felt ominous. Perhaps with some real diligence they could overcome the issues that the two young men shared and achieve a better result for their client.

Attorney Peaslee called five witnesses in a row to try to establish, in their brief testimony, that many members of Prescott's family were seemingly insane. Hezekiah Blake, born in 1753, lived his entire long life in Kensington, New Hampshire, dying in 1841 at the age of eighty-eight.[4] Since he had married Lucy Prescott, a distant cousin of Abraham's grandfather, Abraham Prescott Sr., he had extensive contact with the Prescott family over the years. He testified that he had lived about a mile and a half from Abraham Prescott Sr. and had known him well. He said, "He was crazy at times and difficult in his family," that he acted strange and "would disregard his wife." He felt that Abraham Sr. was also clever and religious. According to Hezekiah, Abraham's nephew Marston was also a troubled person who would "go about, house to house, making all sorts of fun, and would sometimes use very bad and wicked language."[5] Marston's son, Moses, he also felt was troubled: "He is not in his right mind, but not so crazy as his father." Moses, he reported, was under guardianship and could only sometimes manage to work. Under cross-examination, Hezekiah then denied that he had ever personally seen the elder Abraham deranged, but only knew of it because others had mentioned it. He also described Marston's situation in greater detail, and although he reported that Marston "generally wanted cider," which was an alcoholic beverage, he didn't think that drunkenness was the entire cause of his problems, both comments discrediting his judgment that the pair were insane.

Next, Mary Poor was called to the stand. She was born in Kensington in about 1775 and lived there, she said, until she was twenty-seven years old. She reported that she was about fifteen when old Abraham Sr. died. She described Abraham Sr.: "Saw him sometimes before his death, at his daughter's opposite my father's.[6] Friends then called him an insane person. He was sometimes very talkative and lively, at others more sad and mute; heard folks say he dwelt very much on religious subjects."[7] Mary also knew Marston Prescott. She agreed that he was considered deranged. She had sometimes seen him going about in wet and dirty clothes that made her think he had slept out in bad weather. Like Blake, when she was cross-examined, Mary conceded that she had personally never noticed that Abraham Sr. had difficulties, but just had heard folks say that he was "unsteady." She also confirmed that Marston was "intemperate" and made a habit of going from house to house to beg for cider, again providing more support for the prosecution.

Next to testify was Abraham Prescott Jr. His identity is slightly confusing; he was most likely actually born Abraham Prescott III.[8] This Abraham described the errant behavior of his brother, Benjamin. The confusion arises in that the names Abraham and Benjamin occur repeatedly in the Prescott family. Apparently, even Prescott Jr. wasn't quite certain of his connection to the Abraham on trial; he testified that he believed Benjamin (and thus he) must have been a cousin of the defendant. Benjamin, he said, "was subject to hypochondriac affection for a number of years, which entirely disqualified him from business. He would sometimes appear almost destitute of reason; refused to take off his clothes for fear he should die in the act; labored under the belief that he did not breathe; would often run across the room to the looking glass, and sometimes keep his hand to his mouth nearly all day, to be sure he actually breathed."[9]

Hannah Huntoon was the next witness called.[10] (It could not be determined if she was related to the Nathaniel Huntoon who was challenged and not selected as a juror.) Her testimony was about Abraham Prescott Sr.'s youngest child, Sally (aunt of the defendant), who was born in 1766 and married Jeremiah Blake of Candia. (Jeremiah was the son of tavern keeper John Blake and his delightfully named wife, Love Sleeper, and also operated a tavern and took in work as a tailor.) Sally had died quite recently, in 1832, so she wasn't available to describe her own affliction. Hannah testified that she had worked for Sally about forty years ago. Her description of Sally portrays a woman who seemingly was profoundly depressed: "She appeared dull and melancholy; everything went wrong with her; she said she was of no use, could not plan her work, and wished she might die. She seemed discontented with everything; folks said she was crazy. Her husband told me not to mind anything about it, as she was occasionally a little out."[11] On cross-examination Hannah said that Sally appeared, while she worked for her, to be so different from what she had previously been that she supposed her to be crazy and that some people had said that "her cra-ziness was caused by violent passions," but she hadn't noticed Sally to be particularly passionate. Abraham Sr. provided Sally with the same small inheritance he gave one of his other daughters. But he also men-tioned his daughter Abigail, whom he described as being "non compos mentis" in his will, and charged two of his sons with her care for the rest of her life. This daughter, who clearly had some mental affliction, wasn't mentioned at the trial, an interesting distinction.

Next called to testify was Mary Blake Rowe, the sister of Jeremiah Blake, Sally Prescott's husband. She was probably born in 1775, and re-ported that she had lived, off and on, with her brother and Sally for about twelve years, during Sally's active childbearing time. She thought Sally had spells that lasted sometimes for as long as three months when "she appeared very dull," and didn't enjoy her work. They would try to take her mind off her troubles by having other people around to distract her. Mary found her to be "cheerful and lively" when not having a spell, however. She also found Sally was not as nice to her husband as some women might be, but since this man was also Mary's brother, she might have been a little biased.

Mary also knew old Abraham Prescott: "very odd at times"; Marston Prescott: "seen him often when he appeared crazy"; and Moses Prescott: "when he talked and acted like a crazy man." More telling, Peaslee felt for jurors, was her statement regarding old Abraham: [the] "reason of thinking him crazy was his getting up of nights; folks said he got up; did not know it, but thought he looked and acted very odd."[12] Perhaps he was a somnambulist as well. Each of these witnesses had, Peaslee hoped, reinforced the idea for the jury that insanity ran strongly in the Prescott family. It certainly appears true that many of them would have been regarded as odd. But in almost every case, the prosecution had been able to whittle away at their evidence.

Next, Mary Prescott, known as Polly, was called to the stand. She said, "Am the mother of the prisoner, and am now seventy-four years old."[13] Surely she was an object of some sympathy—elderly and terribly pathetic. Although no images of her are known to exist, she, no doubt, looked very old. If she resembled most elderly New England women, she had lost most of her teeth and her mouth would have been sunken in, adding to her aged appearance. Her testimony captures the efforts of impoverished and bewildered parents as they tried to care for their diseased and seemingly doomed youngest child. While she had surely been encouraged by the defense attorneys to not minimize her son's childhood suffering, her description of those times has a sad ring of truth.

First, she was called upon to describe their efforts at caring for Abraham when he was very young. "When an infant, six weeks old, he began to falter, and his head to increase in size; sores broke in his head; the doctors recommended showering. Dr. Graves called and said he did not know as any help could be given. He left some medicine, and it did relieve him some. The doctor said from the appearance of the child's head he should think he might be crazy in after life; he had known such instances. My son had a bad humor, which broke out in blisters on his feet and legs; we carried him to the sea when two years old, but the salt water did him no good. He used to have dreadful spells of crying, when I could scarcely hold him. These spells lasted sometimes half the night. I was poor, and did the best I could to keep him dry and warm. When he grew older he used to get up in his sleep, and many a time I have had to watch him for fear he would stray away. He always acted different from other children. I don't think he had his senses as other children."[14]

Polly described her irritable baby and trying toddler. Recent studies show that some hard-to-nurture infants have subtle neurological deficits that predispose them to later behavioral problems. In addition, as it turns out, according to recent research, there may be a genetic element in antisocial behavior. The parents of these children may have their own psychological problems and are often lacking in the types of skills that would result in best parenting for difficult children. With Abraham's grandfather's recognized psychiatric issues, it's doubtful that his father, Chase, received a normal upbringing in a calm, stable family, putting him at greater risk of repeating parenting problems with his children. Terrie Moffitt noted in an article in *Psychological Review* that "the juxtaposition of a vulnerable and difficult infant with an adverse rearing context initiates risk for the life-course-persistent pattern of anti-social behavior. The ensuing process is a transactional one in which the challenge of coping with a difficult child evokes a chain of failed parent-child encounters."[15] In essence, irritable babies are harder to care for and their mothers are more inclined to respond negatively than they might with happier children. These children are also more likely to resist parental discipline even in their toddler years, extending this negative loop.

Polly, with her attention divided by her brood of unruly offspring, would not have been able to give Abraham the one-on-one attention he needed or the consistent discipline that would have been essential to rein in his challenging behavior. Although she was an experienced mother by the time he was born, and she probably did her best to comfort Abraham, she was busy with all the demands on her time and he would have often been left to soothe himself if he could.

If Abraham were to be found not responsible for Cochran's murder, Polly had a vested interest in portraying her son as being as disabled as possible, but her summation—that he didn't have his senses as other children—depicts a child who was of subnormal intelligence. With contemporary sources reporting that Abraham provided a variety of different reasons for the murder he committed, the teen's explanations for the crime seem to demonstrate weak understanding of planning and what the outcome for him might be. This might have been a result of his purported insanity, but just as likely could come from a boy who wasn't as intelligent as others. In more modern times, Abraham would have been subjected to a battery of psychological tests, and if he were found to have a mental age far below his chronological age, that would presumably have been taken into consideration during his trial.

The defense then questioned Polly about some other members of the family. She agreed with Mary Blake Rowe that Sally Blake had some mental problems. She reported that Sally "once came to our house deranged," and that her husband had to come and take her home the next day, but that had occurred over thirty years earlier. She also reported that Mrs. Hodgdon, a half sister of the prisoner (this would be Sally Prescott, Chase Prescott's eldest child by his first wife, who married Caleb Hodgdon), "was always deranged when sick [pregnant or menstruating]; was once taken suddenly ill [went into labor, perhaps?] at our house; physician was sent for, she was out two or three days, and was carried home. Refused to ride with her husband in returning or to nurse her child; took several to hold her; she used medicine at Raymond for the disorder in her head and grew better."[16] After the cross-examination, which focused only on Sally Prescott Hodgdon's mental status, sad, careworn Polly stepped down from the stand and disappeared into history.

Chase Prescott, Abraham's father, was called next to the stand. He reported that he began working away from home at the age of eighteen and was twenty-two when he left his father's home. He noted that his father was "occasionally deranged" and described trying to divert the man during one of his spells by bringing him out into a field to "cut stalks" and that his father didn't cut them well—he cut off the ears of corn along with the stalks. Chase said that his son Abraham had often walked in his sleep, and that Polly "a great many times got out of bed to take care of him." He went on, "His head was diseased, and he appeared crazy when quite small. He had terrible fits of screaming. At three years old his head was nearly as large as mine. I know it because we used to try on hats. Dr. Graves said he would put something on his head to stop it growing until his body came up. We used to shower him with cold water three mornings, and then miss three, and when we put the water on he would look scared and wild. We dipped him in the sea, but it didn't do good."[17]

That poor young Abraham Prescott would look "scared and wild" as the icy water rained down on him is hardly very surprising. This suggested hydrotherapy may have been based on the work of a Scottish physician, James Currie, who had, he claimed, successfully treated a contagious fever in Liverpool in 1797 with cold water.[18] He energetically promoted this treatment, which led to an enthusiasm for cold-water applications and bathing in the sea as a treatment for a variety of illnesses. The hydrotherapy would not actually have been at all helpful, but may have appeared so compared to more common and harmful treatments like bleeding, the administration of strong emetics and laxatives, and dosing with mercury.

At the time that Chase talked about hydrotherapy for his young son, bathing was still regarded with suspicion by many people, especially those who weren't well educated. Water, while ubiquitous, could easily be viewed as having special therapeutic properties because many people—believing that bathing had a significant potential to cause harm—consequently bathed very infrequently, if at all. Hands and faces would be washed daily, but any part of the body that was clothed rarely got a serious cleaning.[19] Body odor was an ever-present fact of life, although some studies have shown that just daily vigorous dry rubbing with cloth, and a change of underwear can do quite a lot to control that problem. Personal cleanliness would gradually take on some importance around mid-century. Until then, water continued to hold the potential for near-magical therapy.[20]

Chase then agreed that his daughter Sally (Caleb Hodgdon's wife) was "out of her head if anything ailed her." He reported that she would strike her children during those situations. He also agreed that Marston Prescott was "crazy a number of years" and that Benjamin Prescott was "crazy or hypochondriacal" and that "he had to be shut up and was a part of the time chained." On cross-examination, he was asked about the frequency of his father's derangement and reported that it happened once every year or two. Interestingly, he said, "He could easily be put out, and kept traveling around the neighborhood."[21]

In the eighteenth century, many victims of severe mental illness simply wandered, and weren't confined. Only as towns became much larger and the mentally ill gravitated to population centers and became, consequently, too troublesome to be ignored were they likely to be locked away either in jails or later in mental hospitals. From Chase Prescott's comment about his father, it seems that he may even have been deliberately turned out by the family to wander when his illness flared up.

Benjamin Prescott must have been far more difficult to deal with, for whatever reason, since he was sometimes chained up rather than sent to roam the neighborhood. His treatment mirrors that of murderer Daniel Corey, who, years after his trial for murder, spent more than a decade caged in his home. The prosecution, once again, avoided asking Abraham's parents about his childhood, even though that had been the largest portion of their testimony. Chase was merely questioned again about his father's difficulties and confirmed that the man was "always deranged at intervals, while I lived with him." With his brief testimony ended, Chase stepped down.

A variety of witnesses had now testified that Prescott had several insane relatives and that their mental illnesses had been seen by many of their neighbors. Prescott's parents had done their best to establish his personal history of mental problems, documented his oversized head, fits of uncontrollable crying, and other illnesses. His mother had confirmed that he lacked the sense of other boys. But the prosecution had scored significant points as well, undermining the effectiveness of the defense's witnesses.

12

THE PHYSICIANS BEGIN
THEIR TESTIMONY

Close attention to important cases
—Dr. William Graves

Now the defense would bring on the testimony of medical profession-als, from local Dr. Graves whom Polly Prescott had described treat-ing her youngest son, to some of the preeminent psychiatric experts of the age, often called alienists. Although the jurors were all probably familiar with members of their communities who behaved oddly, those situations generally never resulted in murder. The professionals could describe cases that had ended tragically, and would also bring to bear the new modern weight of scientific evidence.

Dr. William Graves, who was apparently the only fully trained phy-sician who treated Abraham Prescott's childhood illnesses, took the stand next. When called to testify, he was a man who had a somewhat unsavory reputation. Born in Brentwood, New Hampshire, in 1782, in about 1807 he had relocated to Deerfield, New Hampshire, and opened a medical practice. Like virtually all physicians of his day, he had appren-ticed with another doctor, and may have studied some science at a col-lege. He isn't known to have attended a medical school, although by the time he began practicing, there were some established medical schools in the United States. The University of Pennsylvania was first, but Har-vard and Dartmouth also had medical schools that were even closer to home.[1] In nearby Maine, The Medical School at Bowdoin advertised that it provided a series of three months of lectures, followed by graduation, but was open only to men of good character.

Dr. Graves trained novice doctors himself; at least four or five young men, including his own son John, are known to have studied under him between 1810 and 1825. Most likely there were others. Graves, like other medical educators of his day, needed to provide instruction in anatomy and physiology but, especially in rural New England, suitable corpses to be dissected by his students were in short supply. Dr. Graves seems to have had a plan for that.

On September 28, 1820, Josiah Prescott, forty-four, of Candia died from a fever. Early the next winter, suspicion arose that his body may have been removed from his grave in North Road Cemetery. The following May, with the ground now thawed and dried out, his grave was opened and found to be empty. Grave robbing to provide cadavers for dissection was an unfortunately common practice. Locals were highly suspicious of two of Dr. Graves's students, Dr. Isiah Lane and Dr. Noah Martin, but it was Graves who was prosecuted.[2] The young men were his apprentices and under his supervision. It would be highly unlikely that they could dissect the corpse of someone from the neighborhood and that Graves wouldn't know where it had come from. More likely was that Graves played a key role in obtaining the corpse.

Just as was described in *The Adventures of Tom Sawyer* half a century later, Graves would probably have hired someone to procure a body, although he would have been fully aware that it would be stolen from a local grave. The horror of the Prescott family when they discovered their son, husband, and father's fresh grave disturbed is beyond imagining. Whatever the case, Graves was eventually acquitted of the charge, largely because Prescott's body was never found. Graves's respected and necessary position in the community and his use of a go-between would have helped protect him from conviction. That the disinterred man was a distant cousin of Chase and Polly Prescott doesn't seem to have discouraged them from consulting Graves when they needed professional medical care. He was one of the very few doctors available in tiny Deerfield.

Around 1823, Dr. Graves ran into trouble with authorities a second time when he was accused by the state medical society of treating a fellow doctor's patient, and of attempting to lure away a second patient from another area physician. This type of infringement on other physicians' business was not to be tolerated, and, in fact, resulted in a harsher response than the supposed grave robbing. He was investigated and censured by the society at the next meeting.[3] In 1837, he ran afoul of the law one last time when he was accused of murdering young widow Mary Anne Wilson of Greenfield, New Hampshire, by attempting to induce an abortion.[4] She told a Greenfield physician that she knew of a doctor in Lowell who could perform the operation to relieve her, so Graves's willingness to perform abortions must have been relatively well known since Lowell was nearly sixty miles away. He seems to have suffered little damage to his reputation since an 1868 history of Lowell characterized Graves as "one of the most prominent among the physicians and surgeons of the early days of Lowell."[5] Dr. Graves was described as a genial sort of fellow, but was also noted as being immensely obese, weighing well over three hundred pounds by the time of Prescott's trial.[6] Clean-shaven, with a prominent double chin, Graves exuded an aura of well-fed self-satisfaction.[7] The contrast between him and teenaged Prescott, slight and pale, must have been stark. He began his testimony by confirming that he had treated *some* child of Chase's.

"The statement of Mrs. Prescott is, in part, confirmed by my books. By them it appears that I prescribed for her child several times about eighteen years since. Have several charges for medicine and advice for a boy of Chase Prescott, but whether it was for the prisoner at the bar, or one of his brothers, have no means of knowing." It's notable that Graves's records named only the person responsible for paying the account, not the patient. These were business accounts, not medical records. Graves then read from a copy of his account book the relevant visits:

March 15, 1816 Medicine and advice for son.
April 16 Visit and medicine by Dr. Merrill, a pupil, for child.
August 29 Call at Widow French's, and advice for son.
October 15, Medicine sent by Dr. Goodhue to child.
October 19 Visit and medicine for child and grandchild.[8]

Dr. Merrill and Dr. Goodhue were Graves's students. Graves went on to explain that, although he had other charges for Chase's family in his

books, they all named specific other patients. He said, "[I] have no recollection of any unusual enlargement of the child's head neither have I
any recollection of making such remarks respecting the disease of the
child as have been stated by his parents. Neither can I persuade myself
to believe that the disease was of that serious character which has been
described. Knowing as I do, my uniform method of close attention to
important cases, it appears to me that if I had considered the case so
alarming and interesting as has been stated, that my visits would have
been more numerous and not so far from each other."[9]

Defense attorney Ichabod Bartlett responded suggestively, "Would
that not depend, doctor, a little upon the ability of the party to pay?" Prosecutor Sullivan jumped to his feet and objected, "This I protest against
as a reflection upon the humanity of the witness!" After the justices over-
ruled the objection, Dr. Graves replied with irritation, "I never measured
the extent of my professional services by the ability of my patients." However, whatever the Prescotts' financial situation, on at least two of the five
visits, Graves sent one of his young, inexperienced students to tend their
sick infant rather than traveling there himself.

Dr. Graves was also questioned about Mrs. Blake's mental state. He
reported that he not only treated her for the entire nineteen years that
he lived in Deerfield, but that after she was widowed, she moved to Lowell and he took up her care again. He said, "I never saw her deranged,
and never heard it intimated to," certainly not the kind of testimony that
the defense would have wished from their witness. Perhaps Peaslee violated that sacrosanct bit of attorney wisdom to never ask a question if
he didn't already know the answer. It's hard to imagine he would have
wanted Graves to reply in this way.

Graves went on to deny ever knowing Marston Prescott, but had
known Moses Prescott for many years and agreed that he "was given
to intoxication," and was troublesome to his family and neighbors. On
cross-examination Graves stated that prior to becoming "excessively fond
of intoxicating liquors," Moses was a "correct and industrious man."[10]
The prosecution also asked him again about Sally Prescott and he confirmed that he'd never seen her insane. After those telling and unwelcome
(by the defense) comments, Graves then stepped down, and returned to
Lowell. He would live on until 1843, eventually dying of complications
from his obesity.[11]

With the sun setting and the church growing dimmer by the minute, the court was adjourned for the evening. Over the course of the day, Prescott's defense attorneys had described a series of cases that, they believed, bore similarities to his. They'd brought to the stand a long list of Prescott's neighbors and relatives who had reported apparent evidence of insanity in his forebears, and his parents had related their woeful tale of his difficult upbringing.

The jury was escorted back to the inn, where they enjoyed supper and settled into their shared rooms. Some of them didn't remain there, but returned to the tavern to drink and discuss the case, not just among themselves, but with others gathered there who were perfectly willing to share their opinions of the testimony and the gossip they'd heard.

The court reconvened at 9 A.M. the following morning, Wednesday. It was fair and windy that day, the nice weather and the now drier roads making it possible for lots of out-of-towners to travel to Concord.[12] The church was, once again, completely full with a crowd of spectators, and many more gathered noisily outside, hoping to get a seat when others left.

Dr. Rufus Wyman was called to testify first. He had been the superintendent of the highly regarded McLean Asylum for the Insane in Charlestown, Massachusetts, since 1818, when it had opened. For several years, he managed the facility practically alone, treating upwards of a hundred or more inpatients at a time, but around the period that John McLean provided ample funding in the early 1820s (which led to the hospital being renamed after him), a second physician was hired to dispense drugs and then a steward to oversee day-to-day operations.[13] Wyman eschewed restraint and punishment and steered treatment toward that of moral reformers: patients were assigned tasks and given rewards for normal behavior; they were expected to use their own inner morality to control abnormal behavior.

By the early nineteenth century, larger metropolitan areas were plagued by people, like Chase Prescott's wandering and mentally ill father, suffering from mental illnesses but having no one to care for them. Old ways of dealing with the problem—letting the mentally ill wander freely; either forcibly sheltering and sometimes physically restraining afflicted people in homes; locking them in jails or almshouses; or forcing the mentally ill back to their original towns if they had left them—were no longer effective when there were so many people to deal with. This, combined with a period when alcohol consumption had reached an impressive all-time high, made for a motley and large collection of needy people burdening urban resources.[14]

While that overabundance of mentally ill on Boston streets was the primary reason for establishing the McLean Hospital, the problem was complicated by the fact that most of the homeless mentally ill had no resources to pay for their own care. If the McLean Hospital was to succeed, it either would require significant fund-raising efforts, the indigent mentally ill would have to be turned away, or rich patients who could pay their own way would have to be attracted in spite of the distasteful presence of the mostly impoverished patients.

The solution came in two parts. One was the generous influx of funds from John McLean. The other arrived later with the opening of the Worcester State Hospital in 1833. Once the indigent mentally ill began to be shunted toward the state hospital, the McLean Hospital was able to evolve into a more desirable place for the well-off mentally ill to receive treatment. Wyman, in failing health due to an unspecified lung disease, possibly tuberculosis, briefly stepped down from the management of McLean the year before he testified at Abraham's trial, but then returned for three more years. He retired sometime shortly after 1835, and died in 1842.[15]

Defense attorney Peaslee had read to the jury at great length about various cases of sleepwalking and causes of insanity, but he now called Wyman as an expert witness on the topic. At the time of his testimony Wyman was among the foremost psychiatric doctors of the era and his testimony would be credible and likely to carry significant weight. If Peaslee called Dr. Graves as a preemptive strike against the prosecution, Wyman was a different story entirely. He would have been carefully vetted prior to testifying, and may well have been paid for his testimony.

Wyman, a thin man, had a long, narrow, clean-shaven face and a Roman nose. He kept his straight thin hair combed forward in an attempt to conceal his receding hairline.[16] Dr. Wyman began by saying that he had listened to Peaslee's reading of the various medical cases and that all of them were well authenticated and "received medical facts." He confirmed that "it is now a medical fact everywhere" that people could inherit a predisposition to mental illness. He then cited statistics—that of the 1,015 patients he had treated, 122 had insane ancestors and another 59 had "insane collaterals." In England, however, the rate was more like 50 percent. He (unhelpfully) said that he hadn't known of any cases where the first evidence of an inherited mental illness was "a disposition to kill," but he had known of cases where the first symptom was a sudden act of violence. He also felt that most inherited cases came on gradually. He was familiar with many cases that exhibited "monomania," with the patient apparently fully sane on all topics but one.[17]

While he distinguished somnambulism from insanity—"a different affection"—he then cited the case of a very young teen who was plagued by episodes of sleepwalking. Although she recovered after several weeks from that, "she afterwards became deranged, and so remained until she died," so perhaps they weren't fully different affections. Referring, tangentially, to Prescott's claim of being "seized with the toothache," he said,

"A paroxysm of insanity may be induced by excessive mental or bodily exertion; by any labor or posture of the body which would cause a great flow of blood to the brain. Severe muscular exertion in this way might bring on the attack in persons predisposed to the disease. Pain in a carious or sound tooth may be produced by indigested food in the stomach, by worms, and other causes of irritation in the bowels, and in females by a state of pregnancy or nursing. Insanity is often caused by similar irritations. Somnambulism and dreaming are also produced by similar states of the stomach and intestines."[18]

In essence, a toothache could be caused by a variety of different things, including worms, pregnancy, nursing, or indigestion. Additionally, pregnancy, nursing, indigestion, a toothache, or even bending over to pick strawberries could all bring on insanity, if the person was predisposed.

Wyman described yet more of the wondrous sleepwalking adventures that permeated the trial. One story was of a man who had been afflicted with sleepwalking since he was a young child. He got up in the middle of the night, dressed himself, then picked up the bed in which his wife was lying (terrified, to be sure) and carried it to the big hearth in the next room, where he set it down. He then went to the home of a servant and ordered him to deliver produce from his farm to the next town (which the frightened servant did), and then the man quietly returned home and went back to bed—in the fireplace. In the morning he was greatly surprised to find himself looking up the chimney when he awoke.[19]

On cross-examination, prosecutor Sullivan asked, "I understand, doctor, that insanity is in some cases hereditary. Now if an insane man had a grandchild who commits a homicide, would you infer from the fact of his ancestor's infirmity that the murderer was himself insane? The act might be connected with circumstances going to show the existence of insanity. If no act of violence precede or follow the fatal deed, and no apparent motive can be found for the murder, should one believe a homicide to be insane merely because he had insane ancestors?"[20] This, at first glance, seems like an odd question for the prosecution to ask, unless Sullivan expected that Wyman would, in fact, not consider the act of murder proof enough of insanity.

The defense must have been concerned about Wyman's possible answer. Bartlett objected to the question as improper. "To suppose a case, and to ask the opinions of medical men on such a case is stepping out of the province of the jury."[21]

Sullivan countered that he couldn't perceive any grounds for an objection. The prisoner was setting up an insanity plea based on the mental condition of his forbears. He just wanted to get Wyman's opinion, but he would be happy to withdraw the question if the judges thought it to be out of line. The court found that since Wyman's response could only be based on supposition, it was indeed inappropriate. Wyman did not answer Sullivan's question, but the next witness would do so in his opening comments and Bartlett, surprisingly, found no reason to object.

Wyman's testimony was calm and self-assured. There was little to be gained by cross-examining him, but to let his words go without challenge seemed like a mistake. The prosecution raised a question. Unfortunately for the state, it just gave the physician the opportunity to reiterate his already damaging statements. He repeated that insanity could pass off as quickly and unexpectedly as it had appeared. He added, "New varieties of the disease are constantly occurring, every case is unique."[22] Wyman said that insanity could come on suddenly, whether or not it was inherited. But he also added that even in cases of sudden insanity, those who knew the victim would afterward be likely to recall previous little incidents that were evidence of the developing disease. (Prescott, of course, during the January attack, had exhibited rather large evidence of previous violence.) Wyman conveniently cited the case of a farmer who unmercifully beat his animals; this behavior escalated to other violence, so that now the victim was locked away in the Worcester hospital.[23] Prescott had been known for his violent treatment of farm animals as well. With that last key connection still hanging in the air for the jury's consideration, Wyman stepped down.

Although Dr. Graves's comments had done little to advance Prescott's defense, Wyman's testimony was a completely different situation. It must have been clear to those in the courtroom that he was an expert and that he was quite sure that the teen was not responsible for his murderous act. The prosecution could do little but brace for the next expert witness.

⚛ 13 ⚛

MORE PHYSICIANS FOR
THE DEFENSE

The motion of his eye is idiotic
—Dr. Nehemiah Cutter

Dr. George Parkman was called to testify for the defense. In another remarkable twist in the Abraham Prescott case, Dr. Parkman was, unfortunately, destined to become a murder victim himself in a highly notorious case. Parkman was a Boston native, born into a wealthy Beacon Hill family in 1790, and had been a sickly child. He began attending Harvard at the age of fifteen, where he was a fine student and emerged as salutatorian of the class of 1809. He studied medicine in Scotland for two years, where he was particularly interested in the treatment of mental illness, appalled by the horrifying conditions in which many of the insane of the era were housed. He then studied under well-known doctors in Paris. After returning to the United States in 1813, he attempted to jump-start the creation of a mental hospital in Massachusetts, and offered a donation of $16,000 to begin the effort.[1] His generosity led to the creation of the McLean Hospital, but he was not chosen as the head physician since some apparently believed his donation and subsequent appointment might seem inappropriate.

While he opened his own home and treated people from time to time, by the early 1820s, after his father's death, his primary focus was in real estate. A rather thrifty man at best, Parkman, right up until his death in November 1849, would stride very rapidly about town, thin and appearing much taller than his five feet nine or ten in his stovepipe

hat, collecting rents on his numerous properties. Many people felt that
he was just too cheap to use a horse and carriage, as might have been
expected for his station in life. He was also regarded as an impatient
man when it came to overdue debts. None of his debtors seemed to feel
that he was warm and pleasant.[2]

Dr. Parkman, now forty-five, was just starting to develop gray hair.
He was clean-shaven with a jutting chin, well-dressed, and very brisk
in his movements. He rarely slowed down. He must have been taking
notes on Wyman's testimony since he now read back to the court the
question that prosecutor Sullivan had asked a short while ago and Bartlett had objected to. Parkman reported that, prior to the opening of a
mental hospital near Boston (McLean), he had operated one himself,
and that he had "continued to attend insanity" ever since. In response
to Sullivan's question, he said, "The fact [of the insanity of a murderer's
grandfather] would suggest a strict review and inquiry should be made
into the course of the life of the grandchild, in search of an explanation
of the homicide, by comparison of it with his other acts."[3] He went on to
say that even though it was hereditary, insanity might not appear in all
who had inherited the tendency "if they escape exposure to the causes
which seem to excite the actions in which it consists." He continued,
"Many facts seem to point to the conclusion that the knowledge of deeds
of enormity leads to repetition of them. In certain vacant, ill-regulated
minds they seem to induce a sort of state of temptation, of headlong,
almost irresistible propensity or impulse to like deeds and excesses."[4]
Perhaps when Parkman spoke of "Knowledge of deeds of enormity"
leading to repetition, he was harkening back to the defense claim that
discussion of the Avery trial had incited Abraham to commit murder,
especially given his inherited predisposition. Or the deed of enormity
might well have been the January assault.

He noted that insanity typically appeared in people between the ages
of twenty and thirty, and that digestive disturbances, including "severe
pains about the teeth," were often a forerunner. On cross-examination,
Parkman also became even more of an asset to the defense when he
stated that "Insanity takes every variety of form, and every length of
continuance. Hence it has been termed a "multiform monster."[5]

It's unclear why Wyman was then called back to the stand. He offered another brief anecdote of a young man who came to Boston, was

suddenly seized with a "paroxysm of derangement," ran into a shop and attempted to stab the woman who worked there. He was brought to McLean, where he remained just a week, and was then released to his father and remained perfectly normal.[6] This offered a very good example of a case of homicidal mental illness of extremely brief duration. He then mentioned in closing that some people were reluctant to admit that insanity ran in their families, preferring to keep that damaging information concealed.

Dr. Thomas Chadbourne provided another anecdote. He was born in 1790, educated at Dartmouth, and opened a medical practice in Concord, New Hampshire, in about 1814.[7] Unlike the previous experts, he didn't limit his practice to the mentally ill. He also concurred that Peaslee's readings of the previous day had come from well-recognized and respected medical sources and agreed that insanity was an inheritable condition. He noted that insanity and sleepwalking were essentially different processes, and unhappily for the defense, he had not heard of any cases where a sleepwalker had shown a tendency to hurt someone.

Like all the other physicians, however, he had another little story to add. His occurred in nearby Maine a few years before. The sleepwalker tried to kill himself and had to be guarded every night in case one of the frequent attacks overcame him. One night he escaped and was later discovered in a nearby field, hanging—by his feet rather than his neck—from the high branch of a tree. It was necessary to fetch a tall ladder to rescue him. In a similar case, he mentioned in passing, a patient tried to commit suicide whenever he had "indigestible food" in his stomach.[8] On cross-examination he was asked whether cruelty to animals was a precursor to insanity, but he didn't know. Not surprisingly, he was also asked what had become of the man who hung by his feet. He hadn't heard about that either. He noted that this man was the brother of the deceased Dr. Chandler "of this town." He was referring to Dr. Moses Chandler, who was born in Fryeburg, Maine, in 1786 but had had a medical practice in Concord.[9] Moses had twelve younger siblings who survived to adulthood and eight of them were males. Which of the late Dr. Chandler's brothers was a sleepwalker is lost to history.

Next, the defense called Dr. Nehemiah Cutter, who stated that he had operated a "private asylum for lunatics" in his home in Pepperell, Massachusetts, for the past fifteen years.[10] He brought several anecdotes to court, which he offered after confirming that Peaslee's sources of the previous day were up to date and reliable and that insanity was hereditary, although he thought it most likely to appear between the ages of twenty to twenty-five, a narrower window than Parkman had provided. The main point that Cutter wanted to make was that "delirium may come on suddenly and go off just as suddenly. It is sometimes accompanied by an irresistible disposition to do violence and kill."[11] He proceeded to illustrate that with the cases of several of his patients.

He'd treated a twenty-one-year-old man who had had epilepsy for about eight years and was suddenly seized with a delirium in which he would attack his parents. While afflicted, he was cunning in his planning of attacks on caregivers, but between episodes, was perfectly normal. He was not yet cured.[12] Another recent patient, a fifty-year-old woman, began having brief episodes of a few minutes when she was irrational and profane. Seemingly cured of this, she stayed well for a few months, and then made a couple of suicide attempts, which she later couldn't recall.[13] He listed the short case histories of five more patients, none of whom seemed to have had a predilection toward violence, so it's not clear why they were pertinent.

Finally, defense attorney Bartlett asked, "Have you observed the manner and appearance of the prisoner at the bar?" perhaps hoping for a quick diagnosis. Sullivan objected. The court ruled, "As a question of skill it is admissible; the jury will weigh its propriety."[14]

Cutter was ready with his answer. "I noticed the appearance of the prisoner at the bar yesterday. The motion of his eye is idiotic, dull, lazy, indifferent; no appearance of fear or anxiety in his countenance: no signs of any attempt at feigning; could not deceive one practiced in examining idiots. In general, cases of this kind of insanity settled down into confirmed idiocy. Noticed no agitation or anxiety in the prisoner during the examination of the first two witnesses on the part of the government; paid particular attention when Cochran testified." The prosecution raised a question about Prescott's eyes. Cutter replied, "Dullness of the eye no certain mark, for instances are known of persons of dull and inanimate countenances possessing minds of a high order; but in the appearance of the prisoner's eyes I should think there was evidence of idiocy rather than insanity. In insane persons, the motion of the eye is quick and brilliant; in that of the idiot, dull, motionless and heavy."[15]

Cutter's observations are telling. He, a professional, thought that Prescott was not mentally ill, but suffering from a mental deficiency. It's an opinion that Prescott's attorneys may have shared. While there's no proof that he suffered from a genetic defect, his mother's apparent advanced age at his conception would have put him at high risk of that type of problem. Cutter was the only witness to provide a relatively detailed description of Prescott as he sat at the bar. To his professional mind, the teen was not of normal intellect.

At the time, *idiot* was a word generally used to describe a person of subnormal intelligence. It would, by the very early twentieth century, become a scientific term, meaning a person whose intelligence fell into the very lowest bracket, with a mental age of less than three years, as compared to an *imbecile* whose mental age was three to seven years, and a *moron,* with a mental age of seven to ten years.[16] The term *idiot* remained in legal use in some states until into the current century.[17] Although Cutter didn't think that Prescott had an appearance of normal intellect, he had not spoken to the youth; in fact, none of the medical professionals reported that they had personally examined him.

Dr. William Perry was called to the stand next. Born in Norton, Massachusetts, in about 1789, he had relocated to Exeter, New Hampshire, by 1814 and remained there for the rest of his life. He seems to have run a general medical practice, and although he said that he had "given the subject of insanity considerable attention for several years, and have been frequently required to testify in cases where persons were supposed to be affected,"[18] he doesn't seem to have been the author of any works on the topic. Perry, when questioned about Prescott's early development of an oversized head, thought that it alone was not a sure sign of insanity, but that early brain enlargement could be accompanied by "early mental developments, attended with unusual development of intellect" and that was sometimes a dangerous situation.

None of the medical professionals seems to have thought that Prescott exhibited signs of being too intelligent; in fact, the dull affect that Dr. Cutter observed would surely have implied the contrary. While Perry joined the other physicians in agreeing that defense attorney Peaslee had read from standard medical texts, and that insanity was often hereditary, he added on cross-examination—most unhelpfully for the defense—"I never knew a case of insanity of shorter duration than four days or five days."[19] This was another instance where the defense was seemingly taken by surprise by their witness's damaging testimony. Perry's comments contributed nothing to their case, and his last opinion directly contradicted one half of their two-pronged plan of either proving that Prescott committed the murder while sleepwalking, or that he had suffered from an inherited but ever-so-brief form of insanity. He followed that up by stating that when the insane commit violent acts, they are likely to do so again unless "extraordinary circumstances may prevent this." Again, this comment seems highly damaging to the defense.

Although their case was far from done, the defense now called just one last witness, Abigail Calef. Abigail either may have been the wife, aged sixty to sixty-nine, or the daughter, aged thirty to thirty-nine, of John Calef, who was enumerated on the 1830 Pembroke federal census.[20] Abigail described a conversation she had with Sally Cochran some time that spring of 1833. She must have asked Cochran about Prescott's January attack, and raised a question about the boy. She reported that Mrs. Cochran replied, "That her escape was truly wonderful; it was a great mercy that they both were not killed." Calef responded, "I told her I would not keep such a boy." Cochran replied that, "Prescott was a good boy; I have no doubt that he was asleep, and did not intentionally hurt us."[21]

The attorney general, Sullivan, objected to "this kind of conversation." The judge responded that it was not at all clear what the point of the testimony was, but that the jury could evaluate its worth. The attorney general replied that it merely showed Mrs. Cochran's belief about Prescott, and that they could just as well offer testimony from someone else of his belief that the young man was awake at the time of the attack. The court allowed the testimony to stand, saying, "Yes, if you put in the winter transaction as evidence of malice."[22]

Having provided ample evidence of current medical understanding of mental illness, the defense then rested its case "for the present." The defense had brought a pair of the foremost American experts in the field of mental illness to testify and backed up their weighty opinions with those of a few lesser lights in the field, and finally capped that off with the pathetic but remarkably contradictory opinion of the victim herself.

⚜ 14 ⚜

THE PROSECUTION REBUTS

He did not stop to think of the consequences
—Norris Cochran

Now it was time for the prosecution to call rebuttal witnesses. The defense had tried to offer several themes with the testimony of the people they had presented. The most oft-repeated idea was that strange manifestations of mental illness were *everywhere.* Prescott's case fit nicely into that spectrum of disease, either by way of insanity or sleepwalking, which were closely related anyway. The second major theme was that many neighbors were aware that insanity was relatively common in the Prescott family, spanning generations, and that it was well known by medical science that it was hereditary, so likely to appear in Abraham. The final major theme was that Prescott had been abnormal from birth, and consequently prone to insanity. The prosecution would now try to undermine that testimony.

The first witness called by the prosecution was Norris Cochran, one of the men who had visited Abraham in his cell at the state prison in Concord in September 1833, whom John Fowler, the coroner, had described for the prosecution a couple of days previously. Norris was a cousin of both Sally and Chauncey. He was a cattle drover in Pembroke and moderately well-to-do.

He reported, "I asked him how he could do such a deed without provocation, as he had nothing against her. He said he was put out for what she said to him. He thought from what she said that he should have to go to prison, and therefore killed her. I asked him if he didn't know that his fate must be far worse than going to prison, if he killed her. He said he did not stop to think of the consequences."[1] On cross-examination, Norris Cochran continued, "William Knox was present when I saw Prescott at the prison. Chauncey Cochran went in, and a number of others. Prisoner did not say what Mrs. Cochran said, but he was offended at what she did say."[2] He added that Prescott did not say that Sally had reprimanded him for ruining his clothes. The prosecution then asked Norris if he had ever heard Chase Prescott say that his father was not insane. The defense objected that the prosecution could have asked Chase that directly, but Norris was allowed to answer. He went on to report that he had been a neighbor of Chase Prescott and that he went to see Abraham's parents shortly after the murder. Norris said, "The old lady, his mother, said he must have been crazy when he did it. His father said he was not crazy, any more than the devil was. He said the devil was in him; he never knew one of the Prescotts who was crazy."[3] Chase's supposed comment oddly echoed that of Chauncey Cochran's previous testimony: "I told him I believed the devil had got full possession of him." But it also neatly brought into evidence the comment of Chase Prescott that the defense had just tried to exclude. Norris then provided a description that matched what many others described of the scene of the crime when he arrived there at about noon. Even then, Sally's body still lay where Prescott had dragged her. Norris was the only person who stated that Chauncey Cochran had been present at the interview with Prescott, which occurred at the Concord Prison just prior to his indictment. It seems likely that he was mistaken.

The prosecution next called a series of witnesses whose primary purpose was to comment on the trodden grass. Brothers Timothy and Henry Robinson (who lived across the lane), Dr. Samuel Sargent, and William Knox all testified that there was an area of trodden grass with the comb, calash, and spilled basket of strawberries in its center. Knox summed up the prosecution's intended point: "[I] should suppose there had been a scuffle."[4] But perhaps the prosecution had two points to make here, one more obvious than the other. The most pertinent is that Cochran had fought for her life; she was an innocent who had been in terror, struck down during what was surely more than a mere "scuffle." The more subtle point may have been that, even if Prescott had been asleep when he murdered her, wouldn't this violent struggle have awakened him? (If the prosecution did, however, intend to make this point, it was never specifically stated.) In fact, the trodden grass, broken comb, and fallen calash were all evidence not just of a violent attack but of Cochran's desperate attempt to fend him off, and that contradicted both of Prescott's stories, the sleepwalking story and the second version from the prison interview. Of course, there had been so many curious visitors to the site. Only those who had arrived first, like the Robinson brothers, could have seen the crime scene in its most pristine state. Everyone else must have seen quite a lot of grass tramped down by the visitors who continued to arrive.

Next, the prosecution called a series of residents of Deerfield in order to negate the various defense witnesses who had testified to the insanity that supposedly ran in the Prescott family. Benning W. Sanborn, Jeremiah Batchelder, Dr. John Pillsbury, Andrew O. Evans, and Hall Burgin, all of whom had known Prescott's aunt, Mrs. Blake, each briefly testified that although they knew of trouble in the Blake family, none had heard that she was insane. Evans and Burgin had both also known Abraham since he was a child. Evans stated that he had lived in Allenstown for many years, and that Abraham had attended "our school" since his parents had lived only about four miles away. He added that Abraham "lived sometimes at Mr. Kimball's," and that he had never heard of the boy being insane prior to the trial.[5] Allenstown was a very small village on the eastern edge of Pembroke, between Deerfield, where the Prescotts often lived, and Pembroke, where the Cochrans resided and where the Prescotts eventually moved as well.

Hall Burgin, whose testimony may have carried special weight since he had previously served as a state senator, said that he had known Abraham Prescott since he was a small child and that the boy used to work for him since he lived nearby. He, too, confirmed that he had never heard of Prescott being insane. At this point, one of the judges spoke up and told the prosecution that there was no need to present evidence that Prescott was sane prior to the crime as "the counsel for the prisoner do not pretend that he was insane previous to the time of the killing."[6] The defense didn't appreciate this and requested that the prosecution go ahead and present whatever evidence they had, but the judge ruled, "It must be presumed that up to the time of the killing the prisoner was sane." And then Hall Burgin confirmed that: "Never saw anything like derangement in the boy, discover no difference in the motion of his eyes since quite young. He is naturally downcast, has always been so and has a dull look."[7] On cross-examination, he testified that he could see no difference at all in Abraham from when he had known him—his "cast of eye" and looks were unchanged except that he was very pale from his imprisonment.

The next few witnesses were called by the prosecution because they had known Prescott at some time during his brief life. First was John Johnson. Although—remarkably—there were thirteen John Johnsons enumerated by the 1820 federal census just in southern New Hampshire, the correct one is probably John Johnson of Allenstown, who was middle-aged at that time. He, too, knew that Prescott had attended school there, and agreed that he had seen the boy a lot, sometimes every day, and that although there was no change in "the appearance of his eye" from childhood, he had never thought him to be deranged.[8]

Chauncey Cochran was recalled and said that after the winter attack, Prescott's parents had assured him that they had never known Abraham to walk in his sleep, which contradicted Polly Prescott's earlier testimony.[9] Perhaps anxious to have the Cochrans keep their youngest employed, Abraham's parents lied about his previous history of sleepwalking, or maybe Polly perjured herself in court to try to save her son. After January's violent assault, it wouldn't be surprising if the Cochrans would want to make sure Prescott wasn't a habitual sleepwalker. Cochran described Prescott's eyes: "No difference in his eyes; he always had a dull look and a down look; motion in his eye slow; scarce ever looked any man in the face."[10]

On cross-examination, Cochran reported that at one point he had decided to codify his relationship with Prescott by having apprenticeship papers drawn up by his cousin. The attorney advised him to have "nothing to do with the Prescotts." Cochran followed that advice and kept Prescott on as a farmhand, but didn't formalize the agreement into an apprenticeship, which would have provided the boy with financial security and the guarantee of training, clothing, and perhaps some parting rewards at the end of the indenture, usually a full set of new clothes and possibly some tools. (The advantage for the Cochrans of formal apprenticeship would be that Abraham would be required to remain in their employ for a set number of years.) He stated that he paid Abraham's father ten dollars for the boy's labor and that Abraham himself would have received one hundred dollars when he had finished his service to him. Probably to deflect the earlier testimony that hard labor could bring on insanity, he said that Prescott had worked with him only two days recently on building stone walls and another day working off the Cochrans' tax commitment to repair the town's roads.[11]

Samuel Cochran Jr. testified next, agreeing that when he arrived between noon and one o'clock, the grass was well trodden at the crime scene, and he, too, had noticed Sally Cochran's comb there with a single tooth broken out of it. Her body was still there and he noticed that one of her earrings was dangling unfastened from her ear. He said Prescott's eyes were "always dull, downcast and heavy, slow in their motion."

Now John Kimball was called to the stand. There were nine John Kimballs on the 1830 census in Merrimack County, New Hampshire. Because Kimball testified that he employed Abraham before the boy went to work for the Cochrans, he must have been one of the two John Kimballs who lived in Pembroke at that time. Kimball bluntly reported, "Am acquainted with the prisoner. He lived with me eighteen months before he went to Mr. Cochran's. Same motion of the eyes then as now; never insane; intelligent; showed no bad temper while with me. Afterwards he told me he would as soon kill his brother or not, if he got mad with him; then about fourteen years of age; good boy to work."[12] Given the timeline of Prescott's work record—that he was probably about eighteen years and four months of age at the time of the murder, and had worked for the Cochrans for three years—he was employed by Kimball until he was about fifteen.

Now Mary Critchett was called. She didn't mince words. "Have known the prisoner since four or five years old; passionate, ugly-tempered boy always; never bad to me. He would get in a passion with his relatives. Once he got mad and told his brother Jonathan he would soon as kill him as a snake. Don't suppose he intended to do so. No difference in his eyes; always had dull, heavy eyes, slow in motion."[13] On cross-examination she conceded that all the Prescott boys had always treated her kindly enough, and that she'd never actually seen Abraham or his brothers fight with anyone else.

Francis Bickford, Prescott's much older brother-in-law, married to Abraham's sister Betsy, next testified for the prosecution. "I have been acquainted with the prisoner about twenty years; never insane; always dull-eyed, passionate; when six years old, threw an ax at me for threatening to whip him. Never heard of any of the Prescotts being crazy until this trial. He was a boy of good understanding, intelligent as other boys."[14] He went on to explain that the ax didn't actually strike him.[15]

William Abbott Jr. had been one of the first to arrive at the murder scene that June morning; he said that there were four others (besides Chauncey) when he arrived: Jonathan Robinson, his next-door neighbor, accompanied by two of his daughters, and Mrs. James Cochran, who was, in fact, Sally's younger sister and was also Abbott's next-door neighbor on the other side. She was pregnant at the time. Abbott noticed the trodden grass, broken comb, and fallen calash. But he also checked that Sally's pulse had stopped—somewhat surprisingly given the fact that she had by now not been breathing for some significant period of time, and given the obvious extreme severity of her head injury. With her family gathered around her corpse and neighbors clustered about the crime scene, his move to check her pulse seems remarkably officious and condescending.

Abbott then left to find Prescott, a boy he had known for seven or eight years, now a murderer. He said, "His natural abilities I have always considered good. He was rather passionate. Knew of his whipping Mr. Cochran's cattle once or twice, had spoken of it to Mr. Cochran."[16] Like everyone else, he'd noticed Prescott's failure to make eye contact, and the slow, dull look of his eyes. However, he also felt that "He is a boy of good understanding, as to work, as any other." Of course, Prescott would have needed few skills to do the kind of work that farming required of him. Abbott noted that not only had Abraham and Sally had to climb a fence to get into the pasture where she died, which was certainly not an easy feat for her in her cumbersome clothing, but that there weren't even any strawberries growing there. Since Prescott had quite recently helped Chauncey build fences there, he was likely to have known whether or not strawberries could be found in that field. Sally was far less likely to have recently ventured down there. Prescott would presumably thus have been the one to suggest it. Since Abbott had felt the need to confirm that Sally really was dead, it wouldn't be surprising if he also checked for the presence of strawberries in that field.

On cross-examination, the defense asked Abbott about Prescott's previous demeanor. Abbott repeated that he had worked with Abraham upwards of a hundred days over the past few years, evidence of the way farmers shared hard tasks that required heavy labor. He had never seen the teen angry—a surprising statement considering that he had told Chauncey about seeing him abusing the cattle. He said that he went to find Prescott after the attack. He located him in a field, with his shirt off, crying loudly but without any tears. Abbott paraphrased Abraham's words: "He had killed Sally. He sat down by a root, having the toothache; there he supposed he got asleep, for he was conscious of nothing until he found he had killed her."[17] When Abbott asked him why he had taken off his shirt, which was stained with her blood, he replied that he had "thought to hang himself with it as he supposed they would hang him for killing her." (Earlier in the trial, coroner John Fowler also reported that he had found Abraham in the field after the murder.)

Samuel Martin, the local blacksmith from Allenstown, stated that he had known Abraham since his childhood and found him "a person of sound mind, as intelligent as boys in general," but that he "always had a dull, slow-motioned downcast eye."[18] Martin found him to be passionate and violent with other boys around his shop. "He scuffled in earnest," he said.[19]

Samuel Tuck and Jonathan Fellows, both elderly men from Kensington, New Hampshire, each testified that they had known "old" Abraham Prescott and his son Marston. They had not found the elder Abraham to be deranged, but neither of them thought much of Marston, whom they found to be an intemperate man.[20]

Next, Hopkinton jailors Mary Leach and then her husband Andrew were briefly recalled to the stand. Although Mary found Abraham to be a quiet boy, she judged him to be honest as he "paid a strict regard to the truth," but she also said that he wasn't as intelligent as other boys. Her husband believed him to be sane. Once the teenager had taken off his leg-irons since he said they hurt his ankles. Leach solved this problem by leaving them off. He, too, thought Prescott was less intelligent than average.[21]

Although Leach said that Abraham had never made any attempt to escape from the jail, presumably proven by the fact that he trusted him without the leg-irons. Amos P. Blaisdell, aged twenty-nine, of Deerfield contradicted that for a second time, having testified on the first day of the trial. He reported again that Carr, whom Andrew Leach had described as a "bad fellow" and who was also incarcerated, began a plan to break out and escape to Canada and Prescott participated in the plan, later blaming Carr when Mary Leach discovered their plot.[22] Since Andrew Leach had left off Prescott's leg-irons, it may have seemed to Leach to be in his own best interest to say that Prescott had never tried to escape. Perhaps the purpose in recalling the Leaches and Blaisdell was to help bolster the state's contention that Prescott was not only sane, but capable of planning.

Now the defense called in rebuttal four witnesses in quick succession: Jonathan Robinson (Chauncey's next-door neighbor) and then his daughters, Lucy and Belinda, and finally Abner P. Stinson, who was the county warden. Jonathan said that he had gotten to the scene of the murder shortly after his daughters. All three of the Robinsons agreed that strawberries could be found in that field, and Jonathan reported that there was no need to climb a fence to get there if one went "by the usual way."[23] It's difficult to imagine Cochran hiking up her skirts and clambering over a fence so perhaps this rings more true. Neither of the Robinson daughters thought that there was any particular sign of a struggle; Lucy thought that Sally's clothes were only as much out of place as dragging her would have caused. It's hard to know if, in caring for his dying wife, Chauncey Cochran wouldn't also have rearranged her dress either by accident or on purpose to protect her modesty, so Lucy may not have seen the crime scene as it originally appeared. She didn't find the field to be especially lonely, or hadn't before the crime anyway. She said, however, "It looks lonely now."[24]

It was to Lucy's home that Prescott had been sent for help on the night he attacked the Cochrans with the ax. She went directly to the Cochran home that night and found Chauncey still unconscious but Sally able to speak, contradicting Dr. Sargeant's previous testimony that the couple had been unconscious for hours after the attack. She said that afterward Sally always defended Prescott, saying, "If he had been awake he would have hurt himself as quick as them."[25] That night, too, Prescott was loudly lamenting, she noticed. Whether there were tears on his face she didn't say.

Abner Stinson noticed that during his several visits to Prescott's cell when he was brought to Concord for his indictment, that whatever he was asked, the teen "answered in the affirmative" and that he "seemed disposed to sooth the feelings of the questioners." He thought that he had suggested to Prescott that he had killed Sally after she rebuffed his indecent proposal, not that Abraham had spontaneously reported it that way.[26]

Now the prosecution was given one more opportunity to rebut the testimony of the defense's recent witnesses. They called only one man to the stand, George C. Thompson, deputy warden at the state prison in Concord, who had been present for most of the interrogation that Stinson had just described. Stinson had clearly come to believe that the beleaguered prisoner had been talked into confessing. Thompson reported his version of the interview.

> I was present at the time of the confession spoken of by Mr. Fowler and Major Stinson. I removed McDaniel and then stood at the door." [His summary of Prescott's confession agreed with the others who had described the events after Abraham had approached Sally with his proposition.] "He retired and sat down by a stump. He then thought she would inform Mr. Cochran, and he would have to go to the State Prison, to avoid which he would kill her. She had started for home, and was stooping to pick strawberries by the way. He seized the stake, came up behind her unperceived, and struck her on the head just as she was about to look up. When asked by Mr. Fowler as to the motive for the winter transaction, he said Mrs. Cochran once reprimanded him for running about Sundays and nights, wearing out his clothes, and said if he didn't stop he would be no more respectable than his brothers; and he never liked her for that, and always remembered it.[27]

Not long before, Norris Cochran, also present at that jail cell meeting, had specifically denied that he had heard Prescott tell of Sally's reprimand. On cross-examination, Thompson confirmed that he had missed the first part of the interview, but maybe was gone for only about two minutes. He also said that Stinson had noticed that Prescott's various stories didn't agree very well with each other. Thompson was the last witness called in the trial.

The prosecution had made a thorough (if sometimes uneven) effort to prove there was evidence that Sally Cochran had struggled for her life, that the Prescott family was generally perceived to be sane, and that the defendant had always been believed to be sane prior to the crime, and seemed to remain sane afterward. With closing arguments, the next step in the trial, likely to be lengthy, and since the day was drawing to a close, the counsel for both sides agreed that an adjournment to Thursday was in order.

15

THE DEFENSE BEGINS ITS CLOSING ARGUMENT

Has his whole appearance before you been mere acting?
—Ichabod Bartlett

Unlike modern murder trials, which are often lengthy affairs, nearly everyone expected that the Prescott trial would be concluded within two or three days, although the Avery trial had lasted much longer—twenty-seven days.[1] Since it was September, most of the crops had already been harvested, but there was still much to do on the farms to prepare for the long, bitter northern New England winter. The jury members still needed to bring in the root crops that would carry hungry families through to the next harvest, cut and husk the corn that would be used for animal feed, pick apples and make cider, and slaughter the farm animals.[2] The jury of farmers just didn't have time to dedicate to a long, drawn-out trial.

The jurors, refreshed from a night's rest, returned. Some of the spectators must have spent the night in Concord and come back for a third day of the show. There were, no doubt, also new faces in the crowd, replacing those who had had to go back to the grind of their daily lives. As interesting as some of the testimony was, not everyone could dedicate a full three days to the event. Mr. Peaslee, Prescott's defense attorney, rose, probably feeling a bit daunted and very weary after the previous day's proceedings. Although Ichabod Bartlett would deliver most of the closing argument, Peaslee hoped to make a few more points first. For about a half hour, he read to the assembly further cases from his collection of medical books. When he took his seat, it was Bartlett's turn.

If Abraham was found guilty of murder, then the *only* sentencing option, by New Hampshire law, was death by hanging. Now, in the face of almost insurmountable evidence presented against Prescott, Bartlett knew the young man's life hung in the balance, separated from a death sentence by only whatever profound arguments he could marshal. He seems to have believed that a flood of words might be what it would take to save the teen. He cleared his throat and began. According to the *Patriot,* the attorney spoke for a full four hours. They described his speech as "exceedingly happy, logical, learned and eloquent." If the witnesses had been interesting, ever changing, and their testimony even somewhat exciting, that wasn't true of Mr. Bartlett's summation. It was a fair, cool day outside, but the crowded meetinghouse quickly became warm. Some of the listeners must have grown bored, restless, and then sleepy. Flies flew in through the open windows and buzzed among the spectators, providing a little distraction. Street noises—shouts, animal noises, and the sounds of wagon wheels—intruded and probably provided a little stimulation. Some jurors may have dozed from time to time. One of them occasionally took a drink of gin from a flask he kept concealed, but would later state that it was for his health.[3]

Bartlett began by describing the prisoner at the bar: his youth, his inoffensive appearance, "the indelible marks of blood-stained guilt" that all who were present in the courtroom attributed to him since there was no question but that he had struck down Sally Cochran. He mentioned how friendless the boy was, standing before the might of the government with not even relatives to represent him, since they lacked the capacity and the means to do so. Bartlett noted that Prescott, before the crime, had had two good friends, but that now he had killed one of them, and the other stood as his accuser.[4]

Prescott's case was further complicated by the onerousness of his crime, striking down an innocent woman who was in all but name his mother. Bartlett told of how this act had been a frequent topic of discussion throughout the area, and how biased against him people had become. In addition to that trouble, how hard, Bartlett wondered, would it be for people to accept that Prescott had been insane when he committed the crime since he currently didn't appear insane. Bartlett asked the jury to cast off their preconceived prejudices against his client.

Then he began a rather long but well-thought-out commentary on the nature of the death penalty. He noted how, until recently, many crimes had merited capital punishment, but that now "the diffusion of light and progress of improvement" showed that all to be barbaric. Modern thinking was that only a few crimes deserved the ultimate punishment. He then went back to the biblical foundations of the death penalty: "Whoso sheddeth man's blood by man shall his blood be shed," and explained in careful detail that that had never been intended as the basis for determining appropriate punishments, but as a warning that "murder in every age shall beget murder. The overarching principal was 'Thou shalt not kill,' and nothing superseded that."[5] Since the prosecution had opened their case with that particular biblical passage, it was certainly appropriate for Bartlett to present it in a different light.

Even if the jurors felt that the government had the right and the power to execute criminals, he urged them to consider that if the consequence of that enforcement was "unmixed evil," then they had a moral obligation to avoid it. He carefully explained all the reasons why he felt that the death penalty wasn't a deterrent to future crime. He offered as an example a recent execution in England of a pickpocket. He said that while the convict "was struggling in death, fifteen others in the crowd were caught in the act of picking pockets."[6] In fact, this very concern over unruliness was one of the reasons that Pennsylvania, in 1834, was fairly quickly followed by each of the New England states in ending the practice of public executions.[7]

Worse yet, the death penalty sometimes generated sympathy for the condemned criminal, having the opposite of the intended effect. He also noticed that the barbarism exhibited by the government was reflected in the populace. To illustrate this, he read from a speech made by a New York congressman, Edward Livingston (1764–1836), who was opposed to the death penalty and who described an intended public execution in Pennsylvania sometime after 1822. (Pennsylvania seems to have been a much more violent place than New Hampshire. Between 1823 and the date of Abraham's trial, fourteen men were executed in Pennsylvania, one for robbery and the rest of them for murder.)[8]

Above: The Cochrans' hand-dug, rock-lined well with its huge stone cover remained long after their house was gone. Sometimes Prescott, rather than Sally Cochran, would fetch the water. The well was finally bulldozed around 2016. (Leslie Rounds)

Right: The dress Sally wore on the day she was killed featured wide, stuffed sleeves, a narrow constrictive bodice, and a full skirt held out with at least a couple of layers of heavy petticoats, much like this one. (Collection of Leslie Rounds)

Above left: Sally's long hair was held in place on the back of her head with a fragile, oversized tortoiseshell comb similar to this one. Hers was found at the murder scene with just one tooth broken out. (Saco Museum collection)

Above right: Over her comb Sally wore a delicate calash. Thin, stiff yet fragile reeds held the calash open; its wide brim shaded her face from the sun. (Saco Museum collection)

Right: In the days before the murder, Abraham Prescott and Chauncey Cochran worked on cutting brush and building a rail fence with materials from the field they were clearing. Prescott used one of the rails, much like those in this fence, to kill Sally Cochran. (Leslie Rounds)

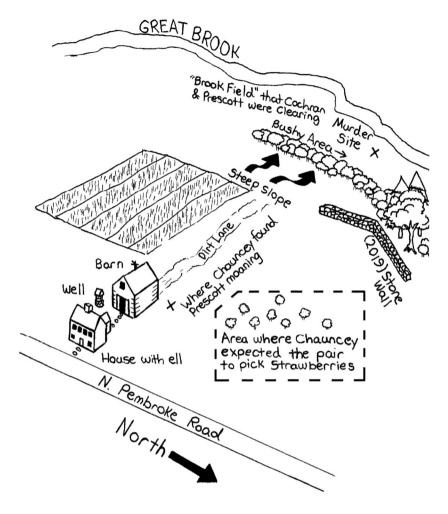

The Cochran farm was located at the top of a hill, close to a dirt lane. The land sloped gradually, then steeply down toward Great Brook. (Emory Rounds)

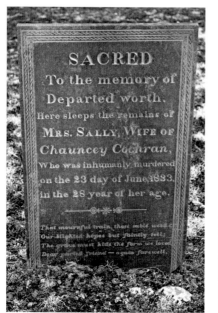

Above left: Sally was buried in the small graveyard located just up the road from her home. (Leslie Rounds) *Above right:* Sometime after Sally's death, a granite marker was erected on the site of her murder. It's now surrounded by dense woods. (Leslie Rounds)

Above: Abraham Prescott was incarcerated in a jail that was attached to the home of his jailer, Andrew Leach. The jail, probably located in a rear wing, is gone, but the home remains in Hopkinton, New Hampshire. (Leslie Rounds)

Above: Abraham Prescott's two murder trails were held in Old North Meetinghouse in Concord. The large meetinghouse burned to the ground in 1873. (Courtesy of the New Hampshire Historical Society)

Left: Charles Hazen Peaslee, one of Prescott's two attorneys, was photographed around the time he began serving in the US House of Representatives (1847–53), twelve years after the second trial. (US House of Representatives collection)

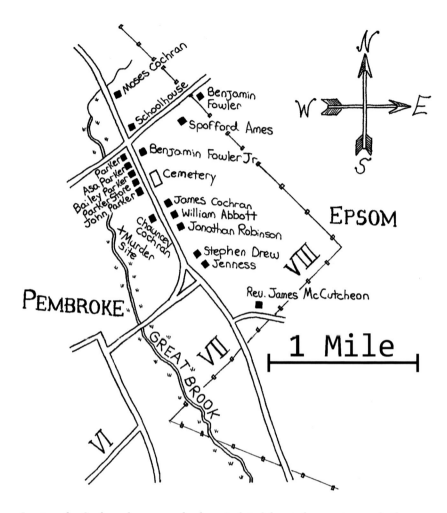

In 1833, the Cochran home was far from isolated, located among several others, all of them now gone. (Emory Rounds)

Left: Supposedly written by an attorney associated with the trial, copies of this admonitory broadside survive in several university collections. (Courtesy of Dartmouth College Library)

Below: By the beginning of the twentieth century, the site of Prescott's execution, once a pasture, had become a country club, its earlier use seemingly already forgotten. (Early twentieth-century postcard)

Above: Perhaps in the early 1880s, aging Chauncey Cochran posed with some of his grown children gathered around his East Corinth, Maine, farmhouse in this stereoscopic view. (Courtesy of Mary Duran Cronkhite)

Left: Sally Cochran's schoolgirl needlework passed down through two more generations of her family before it was donated to the York Institute—now Saco Museum—almost 130 years after her death. (Saco Museum collection)

A poor wretch was condemned to the gallows for murder. The multitude assembled by the tens of thousands. The victim was brought out—all eyes in the living mass that surrounded the gibbet were fixed on his countenance, and they waited with strong desire for the signal fixed for launching him into eternity. There was a delay—they grew impatient: it was prolonged, and they were outrageous. Cries like those which precede the tardy rising of the curtain of a theater were heard. Impatient for the delight they expected, in seeing a fellow creature die, they raised a ferocious cry: but when it was at last announced that a reprieve had left them no hope of witnessing his agonies, their fury knew no bounds, and the poor maniac, for it was discovered that he was insane, was with difficulty snatched by the officers of justice from the violence of their rage.[9]

Bartlett reminded the jury that the death penalty took away "the possibility of correcting the errors of human tribunals, produced by mistaken testimony, false appearances or perjured witnesses."[10] He then noted that the death penalty controverted the Christian faith that death led to a "more spiritual and permanent existence" since it instead associated it with "infamy and horror." Bartlett went on to describe some countries where the death penalty had successfully been abolished. He commented that while on the way to the meetinghouse, he had overheard some respectable men saying, "It is time that somebody should be hanged" for Cochran's murder, a thought that probably did partially sum up the attitude of the community.[11] Most, no doubt, were saying that it was past time for Prescott to pay for his heinous crime.

Hangings were a very popular spectator sport, publicly staged and often generating huge enthusiastic crowds. In England, where executions were more common, vast numbers of people typically turned out, with entrepreneurial vendors hawking their wares and offering—for a high price—good viewing spots in homes and on rooftops. Many traveled long distances to attend an execution or to visit the site of a recent murder, and perhaps collect a souvenir like a hacked-off piece of wall or chunk of flooring from the murder site. But, at least in America, the demographics of the hanging attendees were changing. More and more, the better educated stayed away from these brutal displays.[12]

Finally, Bartlett apologized for his lengthy remarks and promised to begin an examination of the evidence. He noted that there were two components the government needed to establish in this crime: that a person was killed with malice aforethought, and that the killer was of sane mind. This was Bartlett's last opportunity to impress onto the minds of the jury that Prescott was insane, at least when he committed the murder, and he made the most of it.[13]

He began by quoting a French psychiatrist, Etienne-Jean Georget: "An atrocious act, if contrary to human nature, committed without motive, without interest, without passion, opposed to the natural character of the individual, is evidently an act of insanity."[14] While Prescott's act was contrary to human nature, it does, given its level of violence, certainly appear to have been committed with passion, and quite possibly with a motive.

Next, he turned to a fairly recent English civil case that concerned a man who had, ever since the birth of his daughter, believed her to be totally depraved, to the extent he was severely physically and emotionally abusive toward her whenever she had the misfortune to be in his presence. (Fortunately, she spent quite a lot of her childhood at various boarding schools.) After he excluded her in his will from nearly all of his very large estate, she filed a lawsuit against his beneficiaries, claiming that, although sane on other issues, his conduct toward her was insane. The judge who decided the case in 1826, Sir John Nichol, published in book form a lengthy judgment in which he found in favor of the young woman. In part, he felt that insanity was dependent on the presence of delusion. He said, "So that a patient under a delusion, so understood, on any subject or subjects, in any degree, is for that reason, essentially mad or insane, on such subject or subjects to that degree."[15] Later in his decision he stated that since parts of the man's will demonstrated his insanity, that it could not be presumed that other, more rational parts represented thoughts that were not insane. Partial insanity anywhere invalidated the entirety of it.

It should be noted that in the same long explanation, Nichol also remarked on the difference between the standard on insanity in criminal cases compared to civil ones. Nichol stated that partial or intermittent insanity, if the cause of a civil act that was under consideration, could "invalidate the act." In criminal cases, especially in "crimes of great atrocity and wickedness," partial insanity "does not excuse from responsibility, unless insanity is proved to be the very cause of the act."[16] Of course, in Prescott's case, that was precisely the point that the defense wanted to make. Bartlett didn't, however, mention this important distinction to the jury when he described the case.

In fact, the standard for insanity in a criminal case was, at the time, largely based on a crime committed on May 1, 1812, in England, when a man named John Bellingham shot and killed Prime Minister Sir Spencer Perceval. Bellingham claimed that all his problems were caused by Perceval. He was arrested at the scene, and although his attorney requested time to gather witnesses to prepare an insanity defense, that request was denied by the chief justice and Bellingham's trial began just days later. With two witnesses to the shooting and no adequate defense, Bellingham was convicted and executed only seventeen days after the crime. In his summing up the case, Lord Chief Justice James Mansfield stated, "There is a species of insanity where people take particular fancies into their heads, who are perfectly sane and of sound mind on all other subjects, but this is not a species of insanity which can excuse any person who has committed a crime, unless it so affects his mind at the particular period when he commits the crime as to disable him from distinguishing between good and evil or to judge the consequences of his actions."[17]

Bartlett next cited the strange case of Frederick Jensen, which had been written about in 1831 by his physician, phrenologist Dr. Otto of Copenhagen. Frederick, a thirty-seven-year-old workman, had been perfectly normal except for a recent tendency toward "fits of giddiness." After the death of his daughter, one day in 1828 he took his ten-year-old son for a walk, whereupon he was seized with an urge to drown both the boy and himself. A passerby rescued the child, but Jensen demanded to be left alone and was not pulled from the water until an hour later, soggy but alive. After brief treatment in a mental hospital, where, naturally, he was bled and purged to good effect, it was determined that his propensity for murder and suicide probably originated from a congestion of his "organ of destructiveness," most likely related to a fall on the head he had had years before. Frederick was restored to full sanity.[18] Dr. Otto concluded by asking, "whether any body in this case would have admitted responsibility of crime, if the patient really had executed his plan to murder his son?"[19] Although Otto's comment certainly confirmed the defense's stand on the topic of temporary insanity, it seems likely that the legal system would have become involved in the child's death.

Bartlett, having hit his stride, apologized for the "Certainty of being tedious," but said that he intended to review all the testimony, both from defense and prosecution.[20] The jury may have inwardly groaned; he had been speaking for a long time now. He proceeded to go back over, in lengthy detail, the statements of each witness. Finally, he briefly stated what he supposed was the prosecution's version of the events: "That the deceased came to her death by the prisoner at the bar; that he is a person of vicious and violent temper; that for wicked purposes, he induced the deceased, by false pretenses, to a place of concealment, where the death was inflicted; that, at that place, insulting language was used and violence offered; and that he took her life to prevent exposure."[21] It's interesting to note that this is the first mention by either defense or prosecution that Prescott threatened Cochran with violence. In all previous descriptions, he was said to have made an inappropriate comment, presumably propositioning her for (perhaps) a sexual favor, which she rebuffed. Bartlett's description seems to heighten the offensiveness of the assault.

Whatever the case, he now argued that of those five elements of the crime he'd just listed, the defense agreed only to the first. He said that Prescott came from a family with several generations of insane people and that even his childhood illness was evidence of insanity, that he was "a lad of peaceable and quiet habits," that he led Cochran to the field solely for the strawberries, "that there is no proof of any other act of violence than the blows that caused the death," and that his lack of motive and deportment before and after the crime were decisive evidence of insanity.[22] He went on to reiterate the symptoms of Prescott's various forebears. He argued that because the family concealed the insanity from public view, naturally those prosecution witnesses who had testified that they hadn't observed some of the Prescotts' afflictions—Mr. Sanborn, Mr. Batchelder, Mr. Burgin, and Dr. Pillsbury—were just some of the many people who wouldn't have seen the family members acting insane.[23]

He apologized for having called Prescott's parents to testify since he acknowledged that the jury might well suspect their statements were designed to protect their youngest child, but he added, "Poor and uneducated they may be, but no witness has been called to impeach their general reputation for truth."[24] He also explained that Prescott's parents had denied to the Cochrans after the January incident that their son was a habitual sleepwalker because they hadn't wanted to admit it before that attack as that might make the Cochrans wary of him. They couldn't admit to it afterward because then it would seem as if they should have previously warned the Cochrans. To contradict that Prescott had a violent temper, Bartlett said that if the life of any boy accused of murder was examined, then "every expression of passion, or of playfulness" would be questioned. (Considering that Prescott's previous acts included throwing an ax at his brother-in-law, beating the Cochrans senseless with a hatchet, and abusing the cattle so badly that the neighbors commented, this seems a bit disingenuous of the attorney.) He attributed Prescott's "improper language" to "the character of [his] education, or rather want of it."[25]

Then he began to again work his way through the testimony of more of the prosecution's witnesses. Mary Critchett had said that the Prescott boys were "not very pacific, but did not come to blows" and that they seemed angrier than other boys she saw. He asked, "How much of this rests in the poor old lady's imagination?" since she never actually observed them fighting other boys.[26] Francis Bickford, Prescott's brother-in-law, had testified about young Abraham throwing an ax at him when he tried to discipline the child. Bartlett commented that that supposed evidence of a murderous disposition was merely an "instance of provoked petulance in childhood."[27] He claimed that others—Mr. Kimball (Prescott's former employer), Hall Burgin, and even Chauncey Cochran—had not known him to have a "single act of bad temper." But Bartlett knew he couldn't ignore the abuse of animals that Cochran and others had described. He now said that this was not evidence of bad temper but of Prescott's affliction and the proof of that was that he had generally been kind to all the family members; if he had merely been bad tempered, this wouldn't have been possible.[28]

He asked the jury what proof there was that Prescott had left the house with the intention of murdering Sally. He had evidence to the contrary: Sally would never have accompanied him if she had had any suspicion of his intentions; Prescott, if he had an evil intent, would never have asked Chauncey if he wanted to join them; and given the lateness of the season, the field they wandered to was chosen (presumably by Prescott) not because it was isolated but because it was cooler and so it would still have had some strawberries even if they had disappeared elsewhere. Besides that, Bartlett said that at that time of year, on a Sunday, Prescott could not have felt assured that this secluded area would remain that way; there might have been other people out picking strawberries who would have seen them.[29]

Bartlett asked, "When did his wicked purpose first suggest itself to him?"[30] He reminded the jury that Prescott had free "charge of the house" and that sometimes Chauncey was even away and that the farmhand had always been deferential until that fateful moment—what more evidence of "actual madness" when he committed the crime could there be than that he hadn't done it previously when a better opportunity presented itself?

Then he argued that there was no evidence that there had been a struggle between the pair. He said that of all the witnesses who arrived early on the scene and described the diameter of trodden grass, only the Robinsons were so clear-sighted and unbiased as to accurately report that it was just a small area, no more than would be expected if Sally, struck from behind, had just dropped to the ground. He pointed out that Sally's calash and comb were there in the trodden grass. He asked, "Do the Government ask you to believe that they were removed before the blows were given—and by whom?"[31] He asked if they were to suppose that Prescott had removed them, left the victim standing there awaiting her fate while he went to fetch the stake, and then returned and struck her down.

He went on to say that "There can be no doubt that the comb placed high upon the head, as such combs are worn, might with the calash be removed, stooping forward as the deceased probably was, by the blows which were inflicted and by her immediate fall upon her face, without its being more broken than it is represented to be, as the blows were below where it would have been placed."[32] Combs of the era featured a large decorative section that stood up from the head, and very long teeth that extended down into the twisted hair to hold the comb and twisted hair in place.[33] They were usually made of brittle tortoiseshell. Sally may even have repositioned her comb lower on the back of her head in order to accommodate her calash. Blows from a fence post could never have done the vast damage to Sally's skull that they did without also smashing both her comb and her calash, which would have covered her head all the way down to the nape of her neck. There are no reports that the calash was bloody or damaged, which it would surely have been if she were wearing it when she was so brutally struck, while the condition of the comb—one tooth broken out—was reported by several witnesses. When so many were so specific regarding the damage to the comb, it's hard to believe they wouldn't also have noticed and commented on a bloody calash. In fact, one witness had specifically reported examining the calash for blood and finding none. With Prescott's life in serious peril, Bartlett appears to have been trying hard to confuse the jury.

He noted that no one reported that Cochran had other injuries or that there was "discomposure of the dress" (genteelly stated). If the struggle had been anything but very brief, she most likely would have exhibited bruising, especially since she lived on for perhaps fifteen minutes to a half hour after the attack—maybe even longer since Prescott may not have come directly back up to the back of the barn afterward. That would have been ample time for bruising to begin to form, a process that would have concluded when her heart stopped beating. Given the voluminous amount of clothing she would have been wearing—chemise, corset, several petticoats, a dress with a richly gathered skirt, full sleeves, and a cape—Prescott would, however, have had every opportunity to grab her by her clothing to restrain her without leaving any bruises on her body. But no one had yet reported on the condition of the rest of Sally's body—whether or not there was bruising on her arms, legs, or torso.

Bartlett's reference to the "discomposure of dress" implied that there was no sign of a sexual assault, but if Prescott had raped her after striking the blows to her head, Cochran would not have been conscious to fight back and, once again, there may have been no bruising to suggest the attack. Since she wore no underpants, there wouldn't have been any evidence of her clothes being in disarray, especially after he dragged her into the shrubs. Chauncey had rolled his wife over before she died; after death her blood would have pooled in the areas that were lowest. That pooling of blood, lividity, can readily conceal bruising, so it's quite possible that Sally may have had other injuries that went unnoticed.[34]

Unfortunately for Bartlett—and especially, perhaps, for Prescott—there was the matter of his various "confessions." In a time when physical evidence was often far from compelling, and investigative techniques were all but nonexistent, confessions played a critical role in the legal drama. Defendants were repeatedly, doggedly, urged to confess; if nothing else, they were often promised that it would help them make peace with God.[35] Bartlett thought that the confessions, given freely by Prescott, were evidence in themselves of a disordered mind.

Bartlett had already spoken at length, describing the prisoner in all his pathos, summing up the negative effects of the death penalty and the riotous events that executions had become, told of many cases of insanity, and attempted to describe Prescott's acts without presenting them in lurid detail. He had much more to say.

⌐ 16 ⌐

CLOSING ARGUMENTS CONCLUDE

"Executing the Demoniac purpose"
—Ichabod Bartlett

Bartlett reminded the jury of the circumstances of Prescott's confession that he'd given just before his indictment. Prescott had said that he had made an improper proposal to Cochran and, offended, she responded that she would tell her husband and Prescott would be jailed. Having threatened Prescott, she then calmly, according to his confession, returned to picking strawberries, which seems highly implausible, and he took up the fence post and struck her down so that he wouldn't be sent to jail for his indecent comment to her. The attorney told the jury that if Prescott had made an improper proposal to Sally, murdered her because of her response, and then confessed it just before his indictment, well, that was all crazy.

Then, as now, inexplicable false confessions were a curious fact of life. He reminded jurors of the strange tale of the Boorns from "a neighboring state." After their brother-in-law, Russel Colvin, disappeared from Manchester, Vermont, brothers Jesse and Stephen Boorn and their sister, Sally, Russel's wife, went on with their lives.[1] The fact Sally had been away at the time of Russel's mysterious disappearance and was given no good explanation for it by her family, and that it was generally acknowledged that Stephen and Jesse had just been in an angry disagreement with Russel initially raised few eyebrows. Then seven years later, elderly Amos Boorn had three vivid dreams in a row in which Colvin came to him, and reported that he'd been murdered and was buried in a cellar hole. That got people's attention. In quick succession, bones (which turned out to belong to an animal but were nonetheless somehow suspicious) were discovered under a tree stump, and Jesse's barn burned down. When the ruins were searched afterward, an unusual button that was said to have been Russel's was discovered, along with a penknife he'd owned. A larger knife was also found, but nobody knew who it belonged to. Perhaps, neighbors speculated, the barn had been burned deliberately to conceal the long-ago crime. The larger knife could be the murder weapon. Jesse was arrested and confessed that his brother Stephen had murdered Colvin by beating him over the head with a club. Jesse said he was neither a witness nor a participant, but had learned of it only afterward, and that Russel's body *had* been buried in a cellar hole.

The brothers were placed in a cell with Silas Merrill, who later testified to a grand jury that Jesse had confessed to him that after Stephen had beaten Colvin unconscious, Jesse and Stephen's father had helped drag the man to an old cellar hole and the brothers then cut his throat.

Although defense counsel argued that Merrill had much to gain from the tale he was telling, the brothers were held for trial. By the time it occurred in November 1819, Stephen had confessed that he'd killed Colvin in self-defense during a quarrel that the victim himself had started. The brothers were found guilty and sentenced to hang on January 28, 1820. Later, Jesse's sentence was commuted to life imprisonment, since no one had said he was the murderer.

At Stephen's request—he was once again claiming his innocence—a complete description of the missing Colvin was published in a local newspaper by one of his defense attorneys. That curious story was picked up by the *New York Evening Post.* A man from New Jersey was identified as possibly being the missing Colvin. He was brought back to Vermont, where he seemed able to recognize faces of people he'd known, and recall local stories about them. He told his bemused wife, Sally, of their marriage, "That is all over with now."[2] He was accepted as the real Russel Colvin and the Boorns were released.

The motive for Stephen's false confession can only be speculated upon. Perhaps in the face of what the community seemed to regard as damning evidence, he believed that he would be found guilty and would have a chance to avoid the death penalty only by admitting to the killing but

claiming self-defense. (It was just as likely that the Boorn brothers actually were guilty, and the man claiming to be Colvin was a clever fraud
paid by the Boorn family to get the brothers out of jail, as Jesse Boorn
would state years later, long after the Prescott trial ended.)[3]

Jurors for the Abraham Prescott trial would have been familiar with
the Boorn case. It was strange enough, and from a relatively nearby
town. But it's rather unlikely that this was going to inspire any doubt that
Prescott, discovered in his bloody clothing, and able to lead Chauncey to
Sally's body, was innocent. Bartlett's point was that if even innocent men
like the Boorns would confess, what could one expect of a person like
Prescott, young, bewildered, and, he believed, insane at the time of his
crime. Bartlett also reminded the jurors that fifty-five innocent people in
Salem had admitted to the crime of witchcraft. He said, "I cannot imagine that any one of those fifty confessions contained more of extravagance
and improbability than that which is here introduced as evidence."[4]

Bartlett went back again to the January attack. He reminded the jury
that the Cochrans had so trusted Prescott that they had kept him on
afterward, and he said that that crime was as lacking in motive as the
murder. Whatever had precipitated the one had done so for the other:
"The transactions of these different dates must be considered as one and
the same." He asked, "Was he previously nurturing in his bosom the dark
design of murder? Was he with fiendlike malignity, on that night, executing the demoniac purpose?—and was his apparent affection and kindness all hypocrisy?—and has his whole appearance before you been mere
acting?"[5] He reminded the jury that after the attack, Sally had defended
him, and so he was not prosecuted. It must have angered some of those
present when he next said, "What now has put his life in jeopardy, but
the fact that the same malady exhibited in the same form has deprived
him of the testimony of her, who, could her voice be heard, would again
declare to you that "he was unconscious of what he did"—in essence, that
the only reason Prescott might now be convicted was because, unfortunately, he'd murdered the one person who was astute and empathetic
enough to defend him.[6]

Bartlett then spoke at great length about the sad case of Harriet Cornier, a young French woman who, after attempting suicide, kidnapped the
nineteen-month-old daughter of a Paris shopkeeper and, having brought
the child back to the house where she worked as a maid, swiftly beheaded

her and tossed the child's head into the street. Later, she was found to be insane, a case of monomania, and sentenced to hard labor for life. But Bartlett said, "Yet humanity exults, that the high and intelligent tribunal before which she was arraigned, has pronounced a judgment of acquittal."[7]

After reminding the jury again of the solemn and awful weight of the penalty of death, and, in a statement that would be ironically echoed in the O. J. Simpson trial of 1995, he said, "If you doubt as to guilt, you are bound to acquit." Finally, Bartlett closed. He warned the jury not to sentence Prescott just to protect others from an assassin:

> If you have relatives, friends, whom you would protect from the violence of the assassin, you too are friends, husbands, fathers, to those upon whom, in the Providence of God, the calamity which now afflicts this young man may fall. While every grade of mind from the humblest reasoning faculty to the loftiest power of human intellect has been subject to the paralyzing influence of this malady; while its unseen and noiseless approach is unknown until marked by the ruins it has left—who can feel assurance that within the hour he may not be its victim? And while the thousand new forms and modes in which its effects are exhibited are now daily baffling 'the wisdom of the wisest'—who is there may not fear that to such a calamitous visitation of heaven, erring mortals may add the infamy of a public execution upon the gallows. Gentlemen, I here leave the prisoner and his fate with you. May you render a verdict upon which you may hereafter reflect with satisfaction—a verdict which shall not disturb, with misgivings and regrets, the remainder of life—which shall not enhance the dread of death, or the awful solemnity of that scene where we all must soon appear before our final Judge.[8]

The defense rested. The jury and the spectators may have breathed a sigh of relief. The *Patriot* summed up Bartlett's heroic effort: "It was such an effort as we presume has rarely, if ever, been equaled—never surpassed—in our courts."[9] The court adjourned for a late dinner. When everyone had reassembled, Attorney General George Sullivan rose to conclude the state's case.

Sullivan first had to address the defense's strong arguments that the death penalty was such a cruel and inappropriate punishment that the State of New Hampshire had no right to inflict it on Abraham Prescott.

Sullivan presented a step-by-step argument that God had created people who desired and were intended to live in a society; that every society,
government, and individual had the inherent right of self-preservation;
that a convicted murderer sentenced to life imprisonment would have
no reason not to commit further murders since he would have "a perfect knowledge that he can receive no further punishment whatever
murders he may commit."[10] Sullivan argued that "The voice of reason
and of justice as well as the feelings of humanity" all combined to forbid
locking a condemned murderer among the prisoners in the state prison
whom the state had a duty to protect since he might murder them too.
And if the murderous prisoner were kept confined alone in his cell so
he couldn't murder other inmates, then wouldn't that just increase the
man's suffering? However, even though he would suffer more if confined
than if quickly executed, one couldn't even count on that as a deterrent,
since the potential murderers would certainly feel less fear for life imprisonment as compared to death.[11]

Defense attorney Bartlett had stated that some thought life imprisonment would give the murderer time to contemplate his crimes and
eventually repent. (In fact, penitentiaries were called as such with the
idea that they should be places for the penitent.) To that Sullivan responded, "Does experience prove that confinement in the State Prison
will lead men to reflect on their crimes and to repent of them? It shows
very clearly that the State Prison is not the place in which the vicious are
reclaimed; that its tenants, instead of repenting become more hardened
in wickedness."[12] Instead, Sullivan thought that the certainty of immi-
nent death at the hands of the executioner would "feel the necessity of
immediate repentance."[13] It might comfort the jurors to know that sentencing Prescott to death would likely help him straighten things out
with his Creator. Since the defense had cited scripture in an effort to
save Prescott's life, the state would as well. Sullivan offered another couple of biblical passages to prove that the "Whoso sheddeth man's blood
by man shall his blood be shed" was meant as a command to execute
murderers, not as a warning against doing so, as the defense had argued.

He said that in countries where the death penalty had been abolished,
it wasn't true that the rate of murders had gone down. For example, in
Russia, the convicted weren't executed but they were killed anyway by
flogging or being sent to Siberia.[14] In France, too, the death penalty was

abolished, but the experiment didn't last long enough to prove anything. Another reason to execute murderers, Sullivan argued, was that if they were just sent to prison, like highway robbers, then crimes of different degrees of severity would be punished identically, and that wouldn't be fair to the robbers.[15] He said, "In China, those who add murder to robbery, are punished with more severity than those who do not; and it is owing to this difference, that although they rob in China, they never murder; that in Russia, on the other hand, where the punishment of murder and robbery is the same, the robbers always murder."[16] He didn't cite any statistics to prove this, however. He also said that in places where rape and rape followed by murder are punished the same, "it is clear that the life of the unfortunate female would always be taken," a somewhat provocative, prejudicial comment.[17] No one had asserted that Cochran had been raped, but the possibility of it was surely on the jurors' minds.

Having dealt with the death penalty, he moved on to state the facts of the case in a few short sentences, describing the events of that Sunday morning. It was very clear, he said, that only Prescott had had the opportunity to murder Cochran, to say nothing of his having confessed it to her husband immediately afterward, and to many others later. But was Prescott insane? Without peering into his brain, no one could conclusively know his thoughts, Sullivan opined. But he hadn't appeared insane just before the crime, and he hadn't appeared insane just afterward.[18] Then, in a couple of sentences that must have rung quite true to the down-to-earth jurors, he dismissed all the testimony of the defenses' expert witnesses. "In determining when a man destroys the life of another whether he is sane or insane, by what shall we be guided? Shall we follow the idle theories, the airy speculations of visionary writers, or the plain principles of reason and common sense?"[19] He went on to say that one aberrant act—however extreme—could not provide proof of insanity. It would take a series of abnormal acts to provide evidence of the state of the perpetrator's mind. (He did not mention here the "January transaction" even though it certainly may have constituted one of a series.)

Next, he dealt with the issue that Prescott might have been insane because he'd inherited his grandfather's insanity. Sullivan felt the defense had failed to prove that the elder Abraham Prescott was insane. Several people who had lived within a mile or two of the man had testified that they, personally, had never seen him insane, even though they'd heard reports of it. Chase, the old man's son, had testified to his father's insanity, but supposedly had denied in the presence of both William Knox and Norris Cochran (on different occasions) that insanity ran in the Prescott family. Sullivan also took issue with the fact that of Abraham's twelve children, only Chase, father of the accused, testified to Abraham's insanity.[20]

Sullivan stated that Mrs. Blake's supposed but equally unproven insanity was immaterial because "No presumption can arise that a nephew is insane because his aunt was."[21] It's interesting that Sullivan was willing to concede that actual (rather than imagined) insanity could pass down through a family, but that if Abraham's own paternal aunt by blood was afflicted with that inherited trait, it was of no significance. Likewise, the suggested insanity of Benjamin, Martin, and Moses Prescott was also of no importance since they were only uncles and cousins. And besides, he added, if Prescott were acquitted of murder because of insanity in the family, then every single descendant of old Abraham Sr. would also have to be acquitted—if any of them should ever happen to murder someone, rather a stretch in logic. "Are the descendants of Abraham Prescott let loose upon society to murder whom they please with impunity?" he asked incredulously and prejudicially.[22]

He said that it really was of no importance that Sally Blake was melancholy, since it was not due to some disease but because she suspected her husband of infidelity. Furthermore, the testimony regarding the possible insanity of Abraham's half sister Sally Prescott Hodgdon, should not be fully credited since it had come from Abraham's parents and "How strong is their temptation to discolor and to misrepresent facts in order to save [their son] from an untimely and disgraceful death!"[23] He also found fault with Polly Prescott's testimony that Dr. Graves had viewed infant Abraham's condition as possibly hopeless, based on the fact that the doctor had records of only four or five visits to the sick child over the course of several months, and that Graves didn't recall saying it at all.[24] (Of course a statement like that would surely have been quite a bit more memorable to the baby's parents than to the doctor, and the number of visits may have been limited by the impoverished Prescotts' meager finances and quite likely all they could afford or would need since Graves did little to treat Abraham.)

To contradict the many amusing anecdotes that the defense had provided, Sullivan offered a couple of his own in an effort to prove that insane people exhibit delusions and by that evidence can thus be judged insane. He mentioned a man who lived in Boston and who believed that people were attacking him with chlorine gas, causing him to have pain in his head. He locked himself in his chamber, fastened down and caulked his windows, and stuck cotton in his nose and ears. No one could convince him that he was not the victim of such an attack. A young woman believed she was dead and tried and tried to get her doctor to bury her. These people, Sullivan argued, truly were insane. But Prescott didn't have any delusions like that: "strong and convincing evidence that this prisoner was of a sound mind."[25]

Neither did Prescott's supposed history of sleepwalking as a child carry any weight since his parents were the ones who testified to it and "These witnesses are not to be credited."[26] The defense's supposition that heavy work had induced Prescott's spate of insanity was disproven since he had been employed building walls for only two days in the whole season; that in the week before the murder, he mostly "worked on the highway" (which apparently Sullivan did not view as heavy work); and that the day before the murder, he just did household chores.[27]

Sullivan then contradicted the defense's arguments regarding the January attack in a long, quite circuitous, and rather confusing discussion. If Prescott deliberately attacked the Cochrans in January, then he lied to protect himself from punishment and lying would prove that he was sane, or maybe he was just asleep, in which case the whole January event was not of consequence to the June attack. If people had thought he was insane in January, they would have said so and not have believed the sleepwalking story, which some, of course, did not believe. But even if he was insane in January, that certainly wasn't any kind of proof that he was also insane in June.[28]

Sullivan next questioned the defense's proposal that Avery's trial in southern New England had somehow excited Prescott's passion and brought on his insanity. Sullivan pointed out that the trial had been on everyone's mind and tongue for weeks on end. Why, he asked, did Prescott, just then in the meadow, become deranged? Why not earlier? And what evidence was there that Prescott had even read of it, since why would Cochran first lend the borrowed newspaper to his hired boy before reading it himself?[29]

He noted that Prescott's sorrow after the crime appeared to be feigned rather than real. He had cried, but there had been no tears. The very act of pretending to feel sorrow was evidence that he wasn't insane but trying to elicit sympathy, and that he didn't try to escape because he knew that he couldn't get away in time.[30] He then reiterated each element of Prescott's plan, as the prosecution saw it, to get Sally alone in a very private place in order to make an improper proposal to her: that it was Sunday when farmers were at home, that the field was isolated, that Chauncey would not come along with them because he had the trial to read about, and that once Sally refused his advances, he could escape a charge of murder because his sleepwalking ploy had worked once before and would work again. It was a compelling argument, and fit far better into the familiar narrative of early nineteenth-century life than the almost mystical explanations of the defense.

Now Sullivan took the murder story a step further, connecting the dots as it were of the trodden grass, the broken comb, and the calash on the ground. "For what purpose could a struggle have taken place between them, before a blow was given, if it was not for the purpose of having criminal intercourse with her?"[31] In this case, he may have used the word *intercourse* to mean *communication,* a much more common meaning in that time than its contemporary usage to refer to a sexual act, although he might have also been aware of suggesting something far darker.[32] A few sentences later he would describe Prescott as "attempting to dishonor the deceased."[33] Although Prescott's possible intent had been hinted at, Sullivan now spelled it out and then repeated it several times. Finally, he cautioned the jury not to be driven by their natural sympathy for the teen in his current position.

Sullivan concluded passionately, his loud voice filling the large room and drowning out the many other noises of the day: "When the murderer is put on trial our pity is strongly excited in his behalf but how little do we think of him whose life has been destroyed! He is removed from our sight; his connection to the world is at an end; he seems to be forgotten or to be remembered only by his nearest relatives and friends. It is a false, an ill-directed humanity that leads us to bestow all our compassion on the criminal, while we entirely forget the victim of his crime."[34]

Sullivan sat down after speaking for two and a quarter hours. Both defense and prosecution had now had the opportunity to summarize, enhance, and subtly twist the testimony of witnesses and the known facts of the case. It would be left only for the justices to attempt to clarify everything the jurors had heard and explain the law, so that they could then apply their own wisdom to the case.

⊰ 17 ⊱

VERDICT AND RETRIAL

Very little ground of apprehension
—Chief Justice William M. Richardson

Chief Justice Richardson addressed the jury. He took up just where Sullivan had left off, reminding the men that although "the unfortunate youth" was in a situation that would arouse their compassion, they should not let their feelings "warp" their judgment. He told them, "A contest between the State and a humble individual is apparently quite unequal. But the humanity and the wisdom of our laws leave a prisoner very little ground of apprehension on this account."[1] Laws were reasonable and Prescott had been well represented. But he would not be safe from the justice's prejudicial charge to the jury:

> When the deceased left the house of her husband, little did she imagine that she was to return no more; that she was separated forever from the dearest object of her affection. Little did she imagine that she had seen for the last time her infant children, on whose innocent features she had so often gazed with delight. Little did she suspect that the hand of the murderer was soon to be raised against her life; that in a few short moments she was to be sent to the judgment seat of God, and to receive her sentence for eternity. Can a man who has perpetuated such a deed of barbarity and horror deserve your compassion? I will not undertake to describe to you the grief of the aged parents of the deceased; the agony of her husband or the distress of her orphaned children.[2]

He had effectively called up the ghost of Sally and brought her into the courtroom so no one would forget the victim of the attack.

Richardson cautioned the jury that murders had recently become more frequent and that it was *because* compassionate juries had either failed to convict previous murderers, or reduced the charge to manslaughter. He told them, "No feelings of compassion should lead you from your duty."[3] But Richardson was too experienced an attorney and judge to leave it at that. He went through all the components of the crime, detail by detail, and then summed up the conundrum of the case: "In settling the question of sanity in this case, you must constantly bear in remembrance that men who have the use of their reason do not commit crimes of great atrocity at the hazard of their lives without motive."[4] Such a crime, committed *without a motive* was evidence of insanity. But he told the jury there was no evidence that Prescott went out that day with the intent to murder Cochran, contradicting Sullivan's statements and, furthermore, there had been no evidence presented that Prescott had displayed passions for her that would cause him to commit the crime, leaving open the possibility that the killing was without motive. Finally, he destroyed the sleepwalking defense in one sentence: "Nothing could, under the circumstances, have been more wild and incredible than the supposition that he could have been asleep when the blows were given."[5]

If he was insane during the January attack, then it was reasonable to believe he had also been insane during the June attack. But, "If he has been all the time sane, his conduct has certainly been most extraordinary. And on the other hand, if he has been otherwise than sane, it is a very extraordinary case of insanity."[6] He had never seen the like of it. He described the other contradictions: that Prescott had tried to conceal Cochran's body, but left the other evidence of the crime in plain sight and then gone and fetched Chauncey; that he abused the cattle but was always kind to the children and a dutiful employee; that insanity might run in his family and he had been diseased in his head as a child; that he didn't look normal; that he wailed after the murder but shed no tears and slept soundly that night; that he had made no attempt to escape after either the January attack or the murder, but had tried to escape from jail later; and that generally he was sane.[7]

But Justice Richardson didn't explain to the jury any specific legal test for insanity, even though at that point there were the rather limited legal definitions that were based on the case of James Hadfield, who shot at George III: that delusion "unaccompanied by frenzy or raving madness [was] the true character of insanity" or the Justice Mansfield ruling: "a species of insanity which can excuse any person who has committed a crime, unless it so affects his mind at the particular period when he commits the crime as to disable him from distinguishing between good and evil or to judge the consequences of his actions."[8] Surprisingly, Richardson left the jurors to rely on their own opinions and common sense to judge Prescott's sanity, not even providing these basic guidelines that were available to him. While he did, at the beginning of his instructions to the jury, note that they should not pronounce Prescott guilty "until every reasonable doubt of his guilt is removed from your minds," Richardson did not explain what constituted a reasonable doubt, and he immediately followed that up with his highly prejudicial description of the impact of Sally's death on her family. Satisfied that he had provided these men with all they would need to know to make the right decision, he then submitted the case to the jury.

It was, by that time, Friday evening. The court was adjourned until 9 P.M. When all returned to the meetinghouse, lit with flickering oil lamps and alive with dense, moving shadows, it was only to learn that the jury hadn't yet decided upon a verdict. They would return at 8 A.M. on Saturday to learn of Prescott's fate.

The jury retired to the Eagle Hotel and ate supper in the public tavern, mulling over the case under the supervision only of a servant assigned to attend to their needs. It was late and the man who had been charged with keeping them sequestered had gone home to bed for the night. All but two of the jurors visited the barber shop in their hotel, some twice, and had a shave while, if not discussing the case with people who shared the common public opinion that Prescott was guilty, at least overhearing that opinion. One visited the bar a couple of times for some gin, which he also admitted to have been drinking freely in the jury box "for his health." A few visited the post office and stopped in at a local public house; eight in all admitted to drinking with others that evening. Another dropped by to visit a friend. With each contact with others, they heard the opinions of people who had not listened to three full days of testimony but who, nonetheless, were sure what the proper verdict ought to be.[9] At 8 A.M. the following day, the jury returned to the meetinghouse to announce their verdict. Abraham Prescott was found guilty of murder. The *Patriot* reported, "Every eye was instantly turned upon the prisoner at the bar, but we perceived not the least alteration in his features or the expression of his countenance."

The only possible sentence—death—was pronounced at the same session. Prescott calmly listened to the verdict and the sentence, seeming not to react at all to the pronouncement that his life was about to end. Then he was taken from the meetinghouse and returned to the jail under the Leaches' supervision to await his hanging. In the normal course of events, Prescott's execution would follow very shortly after sentencing, often executions taking place within a few weeks. His attorneys immediately appealed. According to the published record of the trial, they, "feeling a positive conviction that he was irresponsible for his acts, either through mental impotency or insanity, sought every possible pretext for a new trial." However, there were other issues easier to prove than to attempt to relitigate the insanity question. Affidavits were immediately gathered that attested to the jury's many improprieties. There were plenty of people who had witnessed their inappropriate activities. After some discussion, the attorneys for defense and prosecution agreed to revisit the issues at the next court session. In December 1834, the Superior Court of Judicature granted Prescott a new trial. For all of the defense's diligent efforts to discover flaws in how Prescott's case had been presented to the jury, it was the misbehavior of those twelve jurors that led to the decision to retry the case.

Abraham Prescott and his defense team now had a fresh chance. The second trial began on September 8, 1835, just about a full year after the first trial. A newly minted justice joined the team. Nathaniel Gookin Upham was born in 1801 into the well-established Upham family in Rochester, New Hampshire, the son of a businessman who served three terms in the United States House of Representatives. Nathaniel attended Exeter Academy and then, like prosecutor Whipple and both defense attorneys, he graduated from Dartmouth College in 1820, just four years before Peaslee. He read law in Rochester, was admitted to the bar, and in 1829, moved to Concord, where he established a successful practice. He was just thirty-two when he was appointed associate justice in 1833, the second youngest man to ever hold the position.[10] According to a glowing biography of him, "His accurate knowledge of law, his success in the practice of his profession, the judicial character of his mind, and his reputation for integrity and general attainments in knowledge, led to his selection for one of the most important and responsible offices in the State."[11] He was not a handsome man, his face featuring an overly large nose and a small, tight mouth. He wore a fringe of sparse whiskers, perhaps trying to appear older than he was.[12] During the second trial, Justice Joel Parker would lead the team in place of the ailing Justice Richardson.

Fifty potential jurors were considered before the jury was seated, almost the same number as the last time. John Pressey, a moderately successful fifty-seven-year-old farmer from Sutton, was selected as the foreman of the jury. He seems to have been the oldest juror selected. Nearly all the other members were married farmers with children, and several were in the thirty to thirty-nine-year-old age bracket, making them somewhat younger than the 1834 jury.[13] Once again, however, they were clearly much more the peers of Chauncey Cochran than Abraham Prescott, with whom they had very little in common. This jury, perhaps even more so than the first, would have been exposed to pretrial publicity. A detailed record of the first trial had come out the previous winter and the first trial had also received a good deal of coverage in the local newspaper.

The trial opened on Tuesday, September 8, 1835, and was held again in the meetinghouse to provide enough room for the large crowd that turned up. Interest in the murder and the coming courtroom drama remained very strong. After the slow business of selecting the jury, and the prosecution's half-hour-long opening statement, which differed very little from a year previously, Chauncey Cochran took the stand and testified much as he had before, although he added that even as recently as a week before, he'd been thinking about Prescott's motive and could come to no conclusion. He was fairly sure that the teen had never been rude to his wife. After his testimony, the court adjourned until 3 P.M. All three of the physicians who had visited the crime scene again testified to Sally's wounds and the wintertime attack on the Cochrans. John Fowler, the coroner, repeated his testimony, and the prosecution rested. Peaslee gave most of his opening statement, taking up the last two hours before court adjourned till the next day at 9 A.M.

Wednesday morning, after Peaslee finished his opening, Attorney General Sullivan announced that there had been a "slight mistake" the previous day. In Prescott's first trial, the defense had attributed the event that had precipitated his sudden onset of insanity to his discussing with Sally the trial of Reverend Avery. However, no evidence had been presented that he had ever done so, making the argument rather speculative. Sullivan announced that Chauncey Cochran had just now recollected that on the morning Sally was murdered, he had read aloud to the family several pages of the Avery trial record. He couldn't recall if Prescott was present for this.[14] The defense must have viewed this both as a satisfying vindication, and with some equal sense of frustration. How exactly, they must have wondered, had Cochran "forgotten" this critical event? But they, of course, had never asked him about it either.

The defense began calling witnesses, the first of whom was Cochran's neighbor, Jonathan Robinson. He said that "Mrs. Cochran was a smart, vigorous woman of good appearance and manners, of irreproachable and unsuspected character." But he went on with some other telling remarks that revealed a rift between him and Chauncey. "At the last trial I was summoned on the part of the prosecution—the Saturday morning of its termination, Mr. Cochran called at our house and seemed to blame our family for aiding for the prisoner. I told him I did not believe in the motive then supported as prompting to the deed. He said he did not. I do not recollect of hearing that motive suggested till the afternoon of the day of the occurrence."[15] Robinson described, once again, the state of the trodden grass and how he tried to preserve that evidence by warning the doctors not to step there. Then he added, "I don't know that at the examination of the prisoner before the justices, previous to his commitment to jail, I represented the grass to have appeared as if there had been a struggle or a scuffle between the prisoner and the deceased before he knocked her down. I could not have done so intentionally, as I never believed it. Mr. Cochran found fault with me for telling two stories, as he intimated."[16]

Robinson's testimony at the September 1833 inquest has not been preserved, but at the first trial he mentioned that he had tried to keep people away from the trodden grass, but he made no comment on the question of a struggle. Presumably, if the area of matted grass was extensive, that provided evidence that Prescott had struggled with Sally.

Robinson seemingly believed Prescott's story that he had come up quietly behind the unsuspecting young woman and struck her down. Cochran preferred to believe that story, too. Although rather confusing, it seems from this testimony that Cochran felt that Robinson was pushing Prescott's jailhouse confession story of propositioning Sally, and the teen's (presumed but not admitted) angry response, which, in fact, was the prosecution's chosen narrative for the murder. That tale, however, left open the possibility that Sally might have been sexually assaulted, and it was this version that Chauncey sought to suppress. He had no desire for there to be any opportunity to sully his dead wife's reputation. Others who had been at the scene of the murder had varied in their opinions as to whether or not there had been signs of a struggle, but after Chauncey's angry confrontation with Jonathan, the Robinson clan were now united with him in their stories. The danger to Sally Cochran's reputation was a real one. The *Kennebunk Gazette and Maine Palladium* commented, "It was a retired place and yet a female might have gone as far as she did without shadowing her own character, or been thought wanting in perception not sooner to have suspected the prisoner's motive."[17] By even mentioning this concern, the *Gazette* was giving the appearance of trying to dampen public titillation, but may have actually been simultaneously suggesting impropriety.

Jonathan Robinson was followed on the stand by four of his adult children: Timothy, William, Lucy, and Clarrissa. Timothy thought, "There might have been a struggle—or not, but would sooner think there had not than had been one."[18] Lucy didn't think there was a struggle. Clarrissa reported that she had thought to go down into the field to pick strawberries that morning, and regretted that she hadn't. She also described Sally's younger sister, Mary Jane, fruitlessly picking through the deep grass trying to find Sally's missing earring, perhaps focused on minutiae in the face of such immense tragedy. However, her careful search through the grass no doubt contributed to the matting of it, and altered what later visitors would observe. Henry Robinson reported that he was the first on the scene at 9:45 by his watch and that, at that time, the trodden grass measured approximately two to three feet by four to six feet in an oval shape. He, too, maintained the uniform Robinson party line that it didn't seem like there had been a struggle.

The defense brought in a couple of new witnesses. Mary Goodhue, a neighbor of the Prescotts, had seen Abraham as a child and confirmed that his head was oversized. Dr. Samuel B. Woodward, the recently appointed first superintendent of the Massachusetts Asylum for the Insane, was in his early fifties, beardless, with graying hair in a high wave and tiny gold spectacles that provided an air of the academic.[19] He, like the other alienists, was full of fascinating stories of the odd behavior of the insane. Most of the "homicidal monomaniacs" he described were now incarcerated at his asylum. He said, "The difference between idiots and madmen, that the latter reason correctly from wrong premises, while the former reason not at all."[20] He also opined that "Any great act of atrocity perpetrated by a deranged man would be likely to recall and perhaps completely restore his wandering intellect." He thought it would be completely impossible for a person to feign madness well enough to deceive an experienced observer like himself. After his testimony, and a long day of court, it was adjourned until the next morning.

When the trial resumed on Thursday morning, the first witness was Dr. William Graves who had treated Abraham Prescott's childhood diseases. Although a witness for the prosecution, he now changed his testimony a little, stating that he did now recall that "the prisoner's head was diseased in infancy." Previously, he had expressed significant skepticism that he wouldn't remember such an illness if it had occurred. Just as with Chauncey Cochran, the passage of a year had, surprisingly, improved his memory. As the day wore on, the prosecution had their opportunity to call further rebuttal witnesses. The primary thrust of many neighbors of the Cochrans seemed to reinforce the idea that there *had* been a struggle before Sally was killed.

One of the last who testified was Sally's younger sister, Mary Jane, who had not been called at the first trial. The main focus of her testimony was to describe how Sally wore her hair, what her hair comb had looked like, and how she, Mary Jane, had searched through the deep, bloodsmeared grass for the missing earring, the poignant scene fully bringing the shock of her loss of her sister into the courtroom. The prosecution must have also known that having Sally's sister on the stand—an attractive young woman who most likely looked much like her older sister— would poignantly remind the jury of the other young woman now lost.

The following morning, Friday, at 9 A.M., the court reconvened to hear closing arguments. Defense attorney Ichabod Bartlett began his, "very powerful and eloquent," and continued speaking until 1 P.M., when there was a break for dinner. The newspaper provided no report of what he covered in his argument. When the court session reopened, he took up where he'd left off and went on for another hour, followed by Attorney General Sullivan, who spoke for a further two and a half hours. After Joel Parker summed up the case, it was 7 P.M. and court was adjourned until the following morning. At 9 A.M. on Saturday, the jury presented its verdict of guilty. At the request of the defense, each member was polled and solemnly repeated that same word—"guilty."

According to a very brief description of the second trial that was included in the 1869 reissue of the publication of the first trial record, "on this fifth day, the jury, much to the disappointment of the public, and especially of the counsel for the defense, rendered a verdict of guilty."[21] If, as the record maintains, this verdict was a disappointment to the public, that fails to explain the events that would occur in December in Hopkinton and Epsom, a town almost all the way across the county from Hopkinton and much closer to Pembroke.

It was Justice Joel Parker who intoned Prescott's sentence and he did not do it with brevity. As his speech was winding down, he counseled Abraham, "Scrutinize yourself closely, and strive to seek out in your heart the horrid impulses that broke out in noonday acts of blood; and during the brief space allotted you on earth—so far as this tribunal of the Government influences your destiny—seek, we beseech you, that only source of healing for the chief of sinners that has been provided in infinite mercy, and spend each remaining moment of your existence in the only manner which can be essential to you—in preparation for that eternity to which you are so rapidly hastening—a preparation to meet your final judge. Listen then to the sentence which is to be the limit of your life; but, while you listen, remember that we claim no power over that which we cannot give, and do not, by our fiat, take away the life of a human being. It is the law that speaks, and not the humble individual whose painful duty it has become to declare its sentence to you. Listen, then, to the sentence which this Court now pronounces upon you, at this last time on earth of our beholding you, which is that you, Abraham Prescott, be taken hence to the prison from which you came, and from thence to the place of execution, and there be hanged by the neck until you be dead. And may God, in His infinite compassion, have mercy on your soul."[22]

It is tragic and telling that the record reports, "During the delivery of the sentence, the prisoner seemed entirely indifferent, and manifested, it is said by those who saw him, not the least emotion. He presented the appearance of a person of very low mental organization, and acted as though he had no idea of the horrible fate to which he had just been sentenced."[23] It was certainly true that nearly all of Parker's erudite speech would have been beyond the comprehension of a person of quite limited intelligence, as many believed Prescott was. His date with the executioner was set for December 23, 1835, between the hours of 10 and 12. He was returned to the jail in Hopkinton, and it would be in that town that his execution would be carried out.

⊰ 18 ⊱

REPRIEVE, RIOTS, AND EXECUTION

Let her die!
—Rioters in Hopkinton, New Hampshire, in December 1835

Prescott's attorneys began a frantic scramble to find some other way to save his life. With the avenue of court appeals now closed to them, they turned to the governor of New Hampshire, William Badger. Badger must have seemed like a hopeful resource for Abraham's lawyers since he had run on a platform of ending capital punishment in New Hampshire. The justices from Prescott's two trials too, unified in their belief that the teen was not criminally responsible, signed a letter requesting a reprieve from Badger. They suggested that the reprieve could last until the legislature would meet again the following June, when the members of that body might commute his sentence, which would have the advantage of leaving Badger politically blameless. Their letter to Badger was reprinted in the *Patriot*.

While they shared the confusion of nearly everybody who was concerned with the case that Prescott's behavior was exceedingly strange and hard to explain, the justices, fully aware of being well-educated men themselves, also expressed significant concern with the power of the jury to completely understand the teen's contradictory acts. "We would express no doubts that the jurors who tried him acted with all good faith, impartiality and honesty and returned such verdicts as they were fully convinced were correct, but the circumstances tending our opinion to excite doubts of the prisoner's sanity, do not appear to have operated

with the same force upon their minds as ours."[1] Their public objection
to the outcome of the trials was most unusual.

The changing medical view of insanity was only slowly embraced by
laypeople in the early nineteenth century. With medical education being
systematized as professional schools opened, physicians had the opportunity to learn that mental illness was not some moral failing or an inva-
sion by the devil, but an actual disease process, even if there was not full
agreement on the causes or the best treatment.[2] At the same time that
physicians were embracing insanity as a disease process, common public opinion was far more negative. The overseers of the poor in Danvers,
Massachusetts, reported in 1818 that "the deranged cannot be pitied, for
they bring on their own misery."[3]

Attorneys, too, were becoming more respected as their professional
schools opened. Increasingly, they were well-educated men, and were
coming to occupy the position of cultural leadership that had previously
been the domain of ministers, who also, of course, promulgated the devil-
possession explanation of mental illness.[4] The justices, too, generally
shared physicians' more modern understanding of mental illness.

However, the farmers who sat on Prescott's two juries were generally less well educated and may have been suspicious of new psychiatric
ideas. Horace Greeley, when retrospectively examining his memories of
the Scotch farms of southern New Hampshire like the one he grew up on
in Amherst, New Hampshire, not far from Pembroke, noted that farmers there had little interest in periodicals that promoted natural science,
even though generally they *were* readers.[5] He felt that farms in southern
New Hampshire were poor because of the farmers' failure to learn about
and embrace modern techniques. Further evidence of that ignorance is
that the first institution of higher learning aimed specifically at agricul-
ture didn't open until 1823, in Maine.[6] Just as these less-educated farmers seem not to have embraced agricultural education, they may have
also been suspicious of the new thoughts on insanity. After all, in their
common rural experience, the insane had always been treated rather
pragmatically, left to wander if they were not violent.

Prosecutor Sullivan had asked in his closing arguments of Prescott's
first trial, "In determining when a man destroys the life of another
whether he is sane or insane, by what shall we be guided? Shall we follow
the idle theories, the airy speculations of visionary writers, or the plain

principles of reason and common sense?" To the less well-educated, less worldly farmers of southern New Hampshire who saw in Prescott a boy who was normal enough that he could work as well as others his age, and who might experience all the passions of other young men, but who had not controlled his, all this speculation of mental illness must have seemed much like a fairy tale. The justices were in the frustrating and disturbing position of knowing that a young man's life was in peril because of the jurors' ignorance.

It seems to have been a difficult decision for the governor. On the one hand, he was personally opposed to capital punishment, and many now thought that Prescott, due to either mental incompetence or insanity, was not completely responsible for his actions. On the other hand, Prescott had killed a young mother in cold blood and had admitted to doing so, and she, too, was surely worthy of public sympathy. Just the previous year, in an address to the legislature, Badger had become one of the first elected officials in New Hampshire to speak out against the death penalty. During his impassioned plea to substitute long-term solitary confinement for execution, Badger said, "But it is the certainty and not the severity of the punishment that prevents crime. The humanity of mankind revolts at the idea of taking the life of a fellow human being. And the result at the criminal tribunal is, that none are convicted unless the criminality is established beyond all doubt, adopting probably the maxim that 'it is better ten guilty escape than one innocent suffer.'"[7] Surely, Badger must have been concerned, after hearing from the justices, that Prescott was that one innocent.

In the end, Badger found the political expedience of safe middle ground. After consulting with the justices of the Superior Court, who were fully in favor of it, he granted a brief reprieve, to last until January 6, 1836. During that period of about two and a half weeks, his council would meet and review Prescott's case and make a recommendation as to whether or not he should be granted some type of further reprieve or clemency. By first granting the short reprieve and then neatly shifting the decision-making process to his council, the governor had abrogated nearly all responsibility for the difficult decision. He would surely be blameless, whatever the outcome.

Meanwhile, the decision to postpone the execution was not well publicized. Since the primary method of doing that was the weekly *Patriot,* the information would be slow to reach many, under the best of circumstances. The issue of Monday, December 21, had a small block of text, just one inch in length, which reported that:

Reprieve of Prescott. We understand that
the execution of Abraham Prescott, now under
sentence of death for the murder of Mrs. Sally
Cochran, which was to have been carried into effect
next Wednesday, has been postponed by Gov. Badger at the unanimous
recommendation of the Justices
of the Superior Court. This decision was made
known on Saturday.[8]

On the day of the expected execution, two days later, an enormous crowd began to gather in Hopkinton, just a small village, not located especially close to any center of population. The county seat, Concord, had about 3,700 residents, but, at a walking pace, was over two hours away from Hopkinton. Manchester, New Hampshire, more than twice as far away, had yet to see the population explosion that new textile mills would shortly bring. It had only 870 residents. New Hampshire's major city of Portsmouth had over 8,000 residents, but was a daunting sixty-five miles away, a vast distance before the advent of railroads.

Although it was a Wednesday, a working day for most men, with farmers less busy in the slack time of winter, there were many people who could take the time to travel to Hopkinton for such a memorable event as the expected hanging. After all, public executions were rare, and this one held all the attraction of a major sporting event—a party-like atmosphere for all but the most important participant.[9] In spite of the frigid weather, whole families were in attendance, bringing their picnic lunches. Around the time set for the execution, an announcement that it had been postponed was finally made to the vast eager audience. With nearly all of the gathering having gone to great trouble to attend, there were few who welcomed that news. Although some, especially those with children, went home, a huge, angry mob continued to hang around the village, no doubt consuming plenty of warming hard cider as they milled about. A rumor moved through the crowd that it was all a trick and that Prescott would actually be hanged that day inside the jail (a tiny space), which further incensed those gathered. Then, fired with their own ire and enthusiasm for a public execution, they resolved to go ahead and hang Prescott themselves. A riot began.[10]

The jail was only a short walk out from the center of town. The loudest of the group beat on the Leaches' door and demanded the keys to Prescott's cell, as the stragglers surged into the Leaches' front yard. Time after time, jailor Andrew Leach came out and shouted to the crowd, trying to calm them and send them home. Nothing could stop the mob's frenzy, however. Determined to gain access to the jail—and Prescott—they pushed forward and scrambled onto a woodpile and then into the prison yard behind the Leach house. From here they could see a tiny window into the jail, which had been covered over with a scrap of wood. They pried it off and a crush of people rushed forward to try to reach in to grab the prisoner. It was only when this effort was frustrated—and it was getting late in the day, so they were now quite cold and hungry—that the rioters began to straggle away.[11]

At home with her parents that afternoon was Clarissa Green Chase, the twenty-two-year-old wife of Capt. Robert Follansbee Chase of Newburyport, Massachusetts, and the Leaches' sole surviving child. They'd previously had two young children buried in the Hopkinton Cemetery. Captain Chase was at sea and Clarissa had come home to Hopkinton to give birth to their second child. He'd been born just two days before, and Clarissa hadn't fared well. She was confined to bed, exhausted and sick. Her twenty-two-month-old daughter, Mary Ann, must have been bewildered by both the change of scenery to Hopkinton and by her mother's illness and the arrival of a noisy little interloper in the form of newborn Robert Green Chase.

Even though it was now fully dark outside, the remainder of the crowd regrouped and decided to have one more go at the jail. When the unruly mob again turned up on the Leach doorstep, holding torches whose flickering light added a frightening element to an already macabre situation, it was Clarissa who begged her father not to turn Prescott over to the lawless gathering. Distraught over what this was doing to her daughter, and probably also very angry, Mary Leach came to the door and raised her voice to the crowd, who, confronted not by a man with whom they could freely express their anger, but with a woman, her face lit by the single candle she held, suddenly quieted to hear what she had to say. Making speeches was far outside the accepted female sphere, but Mary was desperate. She told them of Clarissa's perilous condition and begged them to back down and move away, or else accept responsibility for killing her daughter.

Given their previous behavior, it seems surprising but they did then retreat, sheepishly returning to the center of town, although the newspaper reported that several women in the crowd had shouted back at Mary, "Let her die!"[12] They gathered together some old clothing and swiftly constructed an effigy of Prescott, which they then hung from a large elm tree in front of the Perkins Hotel. That done and their point proven, the mob finally broke up and trailed back to their homes. The dark snowy lanes that led out of Hopkinton were clotted with the departing crowd.

On the day after Christmas, Clarissa died. Just three weeks later, her daughter, Mary Ann, also passed away. The two were buried together under one headstone in the Old Hopkinton Cemetery. When Captain Chase returned from sea a few months later, it was to discover a double tragedy.

Still, his infant son thrived. In October 1841, Captain Chase finally remarried. His new wife accompanied him on his next long sea voyage. The following October, they were sailing along the coast of South America when a storm broke. Their ship was sunk and all hands were lost. Robert was not quite seven when he was parted from the only parent he had ever known. He grew up in the home of his father's parents in Newburyport. After studying for the Episcopal ministry, he was ordained, got married, and became the father of a baby girl they named Mary Ann for the sister he had never known. In July 1867, he and his wife conducted a group of young congregation members on what must have seemed like the trip of a lifetime to the thriving and posh vacation destination of Bar Harbor, Maine. It was a lovely summer day and the group was out for a sailing adventure when a sudden squall came up. The boat overturned. Both Robert and his wife were among those who drowned.

Even after the postponed execution, mob rule reigned. The following week in Epsom, a town not far from Pembroke, a large crowd gathered in response to the governor's decision for a reprieve. If he hadn't been aware of public opinion, at least in the part of the state that was closest to the Cochrans' home, he was now. This crowd didn't bother to take their ire out on a Prescott substitute. They constructed effigies of both

Governor Badger and United States Senator Isaac Hill, and burned them instead. While Badger's role—staying Prescott's execution—was obvious, Hill's was less so. He'd had nothing to do with any of the Prescott trial, but he had previously been the owner and editor of the *Patriot,* which had, of course, printed Prescott's attorneys' appeal to the governor.

In the December 28 issue, the newspaper published an indignant editorial protesting Hill's unfair treatment by the mob.[13] This burning-in-effigy contrasts sharply with the comment in the 1869 record of trial that Prescott's second guilty verdict was a disappointment to the public because of the young man's mental state. Public opinion on insanity had changed by 1869. There is little to indicate that much of the public shared this more enlightened point of view in 1835, although the Saco *Maine Democrat,* also providing contemporaneous coverage, described Prescott as "a mere boy, stupid beyond example if not actually idiotic."[14]"In the weeks leading up to Prescott's scheduled date of execution, however, most seemed to feel it was an appropriate and long overdue sentence.

In the last week of December, the governor's council met to discuss the case and whether or not Prescott should be granted a reprieve until June, when the legislature would next meet. The temptation must have been great to shift the responsibility to that much larger group of men. The council agreed that Prescott's mental state was uncertain. Whether because of insanity or mental incompetence, they acknowledged that there was real doubt about whether he could be morally responsible for Cochran's death. On the other hand, he had been represented by topnotch attorneys, and he had been adjudged guilty not just once but twice by men who had, unlike the council, not only heard all the evidence but who had also had the opportunity to observe Prescott over the course of several days. And if they were stymied by these contradictions, surely the legislature would also be, they agreed.

In the end, they decided not to intervene on his behalf. If Prescott was truly incompetent and so should not be executed, it wouldn't be their fault; the juries that had convicted him were responsible for it. The governor's council would, like the governor, have taken into consideration what the public response would be to whatever their decision was. They were fully aware of the two recent riots. Even if they made their decision based solely upon whether or not they believed Prescott was mentally competent, it would have been hard not to allow their thinking to be influenced by such strong public opinion. They agreed to the date already set for the executioner: January 6, 1836.

Now that it had been confirmed that Prescott would be executed, the various ministers of Hopkinton increased their visits to the doomed young man. They could not hope to save his life, but they still had faith that his soul could be redeemed. Prescott did little to encourage their efforts. The *Boston Post* reported an interview that occurred the day before his execution that involved four of the town's minsters, his jailor Andrew Leach, and finally Lovering, a fellow prisoner whom the newspaper described as a "notorious villain," all reprinted in the *Maine Democrat*. To the ministers, Prescott said that he thought he was prepared to die. When asked if he thought his sentence was just, he replied, "I suppose it wouldn't be fair to hang others for such a thing and let me go."[15] He denied that he ever prayed and didn't appear to think much of an afterlife. But then, not surprisingly, the conversation turned to his motive. Leach had heard that Prescott had provided Lovering with a different motive than the one he'd supposedly offered at the state prison two years previously. The newspaper reported the conversation verbatim:

Question: You have said you intended to kill Mr. Cochran and his wife to get their property—have you ever made any other statement?

Prescott: I never told any one different.

Question: Did you ever make any different statement to Lovering?

Prescott: I never told Mr. Lovering any different from that.

Question: Are you sure?

Prescott: Yes sir: I'm quite sure. Lovering is here by me and you can ask him, if you don't believe what I say.

A person who examined his head phrenologically, and considered the posterior disproportionately large, [now] asked him questions as to the state of his thoughts and wishes before he was a prisoner.

Question: Before you made the assault on Mrs. Cochran in January, what did you used to think most about—what did you desire to be, and like to do?

Prescott: I don't know that I ever desired anything only to be rich—I used to think of this often.

Question: Did you ever lay any plans to become rich?

Prescott: None that ever amounted to anything.

Question: Did it give you any delight to kill animals—such as a fox, a rat, or shoot birds?

Prescott: O yes—I liked to kill them.

Question: Better than anything else?

Prescott: Yes, I think I did.

Question: Did you ever wish to kill people if they opposed or vexed you?

Prescott: I don't know that I did—I used to want to kill the cattle when they didn't act to suit me!

Question: When did you first think of killing Mr. Cochran for the sake of his property?

Prescott: Oh, I don't know. I thought of it a thousand times along through the fall before I attempted it in January.

Question: Then that was your motive then?

Prescott: Yes, that's what I thought on.

Question: What have you most thought of since your reprieve, what have you been thinking of this afternoon?

Prescott: I hav'nt [sic] thought of any thing much, only the execution—and how long it will be before it is over.[16]

On January 6, 1836, the crowds began to gather early in order to secure the best viewing spots. In spite of bad weather—it was cold and snowing heavily—people came from all over; the crowd was estimated to be between six thousand and ten thousand.[17] Considering that the entire population of the State of New Hampshire in 1830 was 269,328—most of them living quite far from Hopkinton—this meant that a very large percentage of people from the immediate area probably elected to attend, although the *Patriot* opined that few in the crowd were actually from Hopkinton itself, perhaps locals feeling rather jaded after the December riot. Fortunately for latecomers, the site selected for the execution was in a small cleared valley. The hillsides, although only slightly sloped, formed a sort of amphitheater. There would be numerous good viewing locations. Many people had traveled all through the previous night in order to arrive in time, but remained in their sleighs until the procession from the jail approached. The weather was just that bad.

Still hoping for a confession that would shed a light on Prescott's two attacks, a small group of ministers gathered outside his cell on the morning of the execution. Prescott commented to the men that he had slept better than he had for the past eleven nights. He was questioned again about motive and, according to the newspaper account, stuck to his story from the day before, but provided more detail:

Prescott: The witnesses did not swear truly at the trial about what I said as regards Mrs. Cochran.

Question: Do you mean to say that the witnesses swore falsely designedly, or that they misunderstood what you said?

Prescott: I mean to say that they did not swear to what I told them—I did not say as they said. They said too they did not harass me, they did harass me.

Question: Do you mean to say, without regard to what you have heretofore stated, that you neither said nor did any thing to Mrs. Cochran in the pasture, which made her threaten to tell her husband—I now put this simple question distinctly to you.

Prescott: I did not say any thing to Mrs. Cochran, that made her say she would tell Mr. Cochran.

Question: Did she threaten to tell Mr. Cochran at all, for any reason whatever, or without any reason?

Prescott: She did not tell me she would tell Mr. Cochran at all, nor nothing like it—she did not say anything.

Question: Did you not know that the property must descend to Mr. Cochran's children?

Prescott: I did not think of property's descending to the children. I knew that it did descend but I did not think of it at that moment. I thought a thousand times of doing it—I thought of getting the property on the 6th of January.[18]

This account of Prescott's two conversations offered an altered and perhaps less unsettling version of his attack on Sally Cochran. The new narrative of events relieved Prescott from the burden of having attempted to sexually assault his gentle surrogate mother; instead, he'd made a highly misguided effort to take the Cochrans' money, having failed, in his diminished mental capacity, to recognize the complete foolishness of such an effort. Besides driving this point home by including the actual (presumably) dialogue twice, the writer also structured his story to reinforce the idea that Prescott was now a victim, too, a poor, mentally incompetent lad bravely facing a desperate situation.

Around 10:45 A.M., High Sheriff Carroll and several other men placed themselves in front of Prescott's jail cell. Carroll read the indictment and "a record of the proceedings thereon through the course of the two trials, the reprieve of the governor, and the warrant for the execution."[19] The record doesn't say how long this took, but presumably it was just summaries of the trials that were read. Rev. Andrew T. Foss, assistant pastor of the Hopkinton Baptist Church, intoned a prayer. Finally, the cell was opened and Prescott's arms were pinioned to his sides. He was led out to a sleigh, accompanied by two officers. His coffin was in the next sleigh in line. Since the condemned man was often conveyed to his execution seated on his own coffin—a sight that was highly favored—it may have been a slight mercy shown Prescott that he was not forced to share space with his, maybe just because of the bad weather. Various officials climbed into a third sleigh. Prescott was said to be trembling, but "more with cold than from fear."[20]

The narrow lanes to the execution site were crowded with people here to catch a glimpse of Prescott, barely parting to make way for the line of vehicles, some shouting rude calls at the young man. Once the procession had passed, these gawkers rushed forward to secure viewing spots for the execution. When they arrived at the gallows, maybe Prescott's fear began to get the best of him. He needed some assistance from Reverend Chase in order to mount the steps of the scaffold, which had been specially built for the day, erected between two enormous boulders in a field that belonged to George Currier. This was to be the first and last execution ever carried out in Hopkinton.

The *Maine Democrat* provided a sad last description of Prescott: "He was handed to a chair, where he sat while the High Sheriff again read his death warrant.—This affected him & he appeared to realize, for the first time, the dreadful fate that awaited him. There was a quivering about his mouth and he drew up his right foot as if suffering intense bodily pain, for a second. At this moment, the expression of his countenance was awfully blanched and vacant. His large dull eyes assumed the glassy appearance of death, his lower lip fell down, and every feature indicated the working of a human being's mind."[21]

After further prayers, a cap was drawn down over his face. If the crowd expected a gallows confession—so popular in the literature of the day—they were disappointed. Prescott's last words were "Lord have mercy! Lord have mercy!"[22] There was one agonizing final indignity. Prescott had an arrangement with the executioner. He would drop a handkerchief when he was ready for the trapdoor beneath his feet to be opened. The men arranged Prescott over the door and tightened the noose around his neck, but they weren't quite prepared to launch him into eternity. Prescott, braced for what would follow, bravely dropped the handkerchief. Nothing happened. One of the men had to pick up the handkerchief and press it into Prescott's trembling fingers for another try. Once again, he released the small white cloth. The trapdoor sprang open at 11:25 A.M. and he dropped to his death. After "scarce a struggle" and hanging for a half hour, he was cut down.

The crowd was not yet fully satiated. The event, after all, had lasted but minutes. Many hundreds returned to the center of town for a warming drink before the long frigid ride home. They managed to break most of the windows in the tavern before they left. By nightfall, the only reminders of this enormous event were the abandoned scaffold and the snow-rutted lanes that led out of Hopkinton.

What became of Prescott's body is not certain. He was convinced that it would be used for dissection—a thought that horrified him. Judge Samuel Burns, a justice of the Court of Common Pleas, later certified that Abraham's body was transported to Rumney, New Hampshire, and buried there, presumably in an unmarked grave since there was almost certainly no one who cared enough about Prescott or had the means to buy a gravestone for him. The January 25 *Patriot* confirmed again that Burns said Prescott was properly buried in Rumney and not dissected. The *Maine Democrat* reported that a friend of Burns took the coffin back to Pembroke for burial, a site that seems to make more sense, given that Prescott's family lived there. However, in order to protect his grave, it wouldn't be surprising for those who knew of his ultimate destination to provide some misinformation.

The record of Prescott's trial ends with these words: "There was some attempt to make political capital out of the execution, but it had no effect, and soon the whole story of the crime, the trial and the execution was permitted to rest."[23] In fact, that was not at all true. Even the *Patriot,* in reporting Prescott's execution, described him as "this miserable boy."[24] Newspaper coverage would report that he was so lacking in intellect that he didn't appear to even be fully aware that he was about to die until the noose was placed around his neck. Although many would soon forget about Prescott himself, they would recall that his death sentence and execution were unsettling. Peaslee would never forget him and his ordeal.

PART III

SOMNAMBULISM, INSANITY, AND PRESCOTT'S LEGACY

The secret operations and sudden derangements of the mind

—JUSTICE JOEL PARKER

⚜ 19 ⚜

NEW HAMPSHIRE'S NEED
FOR AN ASYLUM

"A case of judicial murder"
—Ichabod Bartlett

The records of the time make no secret of the fact that Charles Hazen Peaslee and Ichabod Bartlett were deeply disappointed in the juries' guilty verdicts. In fact, Bartlett later described the outcome as "a case of judicial murder."[1] But it seems to have had the most lasting impact on Peaslee, who was still young at the time of Prescott's execution, with much of his career ahead of him. He became convinced that had there been an institution for the insane in New Hampshire at the time of the trial, then perhaps Prescott might have been sent there rather than being executed. There is no evidence that this alternative was considered at the time of Prescott's trials, but Peaslee didn't forget what he judged to be a most tragic and unfair outcome. A friend of his would later say of him, "When he caught at an idea that was to eventuate in an act, he elaborated the idea clear on to its conclusion, until the terminating act was fully accomplished, never letting it go until the end was fully reached."[2] Prior to his representation of Prescott, Peaslee is not known to have expressed any particular concern for New Hampshire's insane. It seems very likely that his work on Prescott's case focused his attention on the plight—and problem—of the mentally ill.

By the 1830s, treatment for the mentally ill in America varied according to the availability of asylums. In states such as New Hampshire, which lacked an asylum, those who were perceived as mentally ill and who were peaceable enough were generally kept at home if there was family willing to provide the challenging care that might be needed. But remaining at home could present a disastrous outcome, like that of Mary Sewall of Augusta, Maine. Mary was the youngest of the eight children that Henry Sewall had by his first wife, Tabitha. In the late summer of 1824, Mary, who had been educated at the best-known female academy in Portland, Maine, was an unmarried twenty-five-year-old. In August, her older sister Susan set out to convey Mary to a nearby Shaker colony, a religious order that was then thriving, but whose ranks were only ever increased by those who decided to join. The sexes were kept strictly separate, so no new Shakers were ever born.

Whatever Mary's mental state when she arrived at the New Gloucester order, Susan decided that her younger sister should immediately return home, where she took to her chamber. For about three weeks, Mary was highly distressed, whether because she'd been thwarted in her determination to join the Shakers, or because she was lapsing into mental illness. At the end of that time, she fled on foot, headed back to the religious order. Her father sent a man after her and two days later they returned. Now Sewall ordered a chair to confine his daughter. This may have been a variation of the one invented by Benjamin Rush, which kept all of an afflicted person's limbs restrained and included a wooden hood to keep the head immobile, reducing sensory stimuli and theoretically limiting an excess of blood from reaching the overstimulated brain.

When, after about five weeks, this restraint proved ineffective in controlling Mary, he ordered a bunk with a lid that could be shut down to more fully confine her. At some point over the winter, Mary's physician placed a seton in her neck: this was the insertion of a foreign material (sometimes horsehair) under the skin, with the purpose of inducing a localized infection. By placing it in her neck, the doctor probably intended to divert blood from her overworked brain. Mary was also being treated with drugs, and probably with frequent bleeding, and with a sharp restriction in her diet (as sleepwalker Jane C. Rider had been at the Massachusetts asylum). If her body could be reduced through bleeding, physics, reduction in food intake, or even fasting, it was believed that her mind might then also achieve a concurrent diminishing of the problems plaguing it.[3] In early December, she must have been calmer, since her father began to allow her time out of her restraints. By mid-January, she was doing badly, in a weakening condition caused by the destructive, cumulative effects of her various "treatments," and in early March she was so unwell that she no longer had to be restrained at all. Ironically, when she died on March 13, her father reported in his diary that it was "without a struggle."[4]

Others, who were viewed as presenting some kind of danger to themselves or to the public, like Benjamin Rowell of Hopkinton, were confined in local jails, sometimes for years at a stretch. Although Rowell was often allowed to roam under supervision, the more violent might be chained up. Poorhouses provided yet another alternative. They were the final home for many of the elderly who developed dementia but had the misfortune of lacking family resources.[5] Even in states that already had asylums, many of the mentally ill still remained in communities, with their "treatment" very economically assigned to the lowest bidder.[6] In 1841, eight years after the opening of the state asylum, Dorothea Dix reported to the Massachusetts state legislature on the conditions of the impoverished insane in that state: "I procced, Gentlemen, briefly to call your attention to the present state of Insane Persons confined within this Commonwealth, in cages, stalls, pens! Chained, naked, beaten with rods, and lashed into obedience."[7] It was also becoming increasingly difficult, as towns grew, to allow the insane to wander somewhat inoffensively, as the elder Abraham Prescott had done when he was afflicted. Increasing urbanization, a rapidly rising population, and growing family mobility all contributed to the need for better ways to manage the insane.[8]

Although asylums theoretically offered some kind of treatment for the mentally ill that might have been superior to what Mary Sewall suffered through, it was only the rare asylum that didn't resort to restraining troublesome patients. Just as in the community setting, these restraints would include being tied or shackled to chairs and beds, or chained to walls. However, with the large number of patients and limited number of staff, the hospitalized insane were at least far less likely to receive the kind of intensive and harmful medical care that Mary Sewall suffered.

Facilities that featured moral treatment like the McLean Hospital rarely restrained their patients, preferring to seclude problematic individuals until they could calm themselves. But few of the large state-run asylums in the United States had either the necessary room or staff to provide this kind of care. On the other hand, from an outsider's point of view, an asylum could theoretically give care that was up-to-date and thus presumably effective, and would surely offer a far more humane method of management than that available in the community.[9] Although many, if not most, of the large asylums quickly became horrific prisons for most of their inmates, the uninformed public initially viewed them as a safe, necessary, and even benevolent resource.[10]

It was with that understanding of state asylums that some politicians in New Hampshire began to push for the establishment of a facility to care for the insane. Although Prescott's case added impetus to the movement, it had begun before he ever caused trouble. In June 1832, Gov. Samuel Dinsmore, in his address to the legislature said, "I feel no apology need be made, in an age so distinguished for its public and private charities, for calling your attention to a subject which has so much reason and humanity on its side as a measure for the security and recovery of the lunatic or insane. The Legislature of the state has never yet recognized these unfortunate beings as entitled to any special favor from the government."[11] In response, the legislature directed him to gather more information, a way to handle the problem that the politicians of New Hampshire showed themselves to be especially gifted at.

At the opening of the winter session he reported his findings: "In 141 towns, being all from which returns have been received, the whole number of insane is 189—90 males and 99 females—one-third of whom are paupers. The whole of those now in confinement is 76, of whom 25 are in private houses, 34 in poorhouses, seven in cells and cages, six in chains and irons, and four in jail. Of those not now in confinement many were stated to have been at times secured in private houses; some have been handcuffed; others have been confined in cells, and some in chains and jails."[12] The legislature was unmoved. A bill was introduced to establish an asylum, and promptly tabled.

In 1833, Governor Dinsmore tried again without any notable success. Resolutions were introduced to investigate what other states' asylums were like, and to appropriate $10,000 to construct an asylum, but both motions were tabled indefinitely.[13] In 1834, the new governor, William Badger, took up the cause. A new appropriation to build an asylum was tabled. Another year passed. In 1835, a motion was introduced to appropriate twenty-five bank shares to fund the construction of an asylum, but it was also defeated.

In 1836, a little progress was made. Another study was suggested. When a motion to use bank shares to fund an asylum was put forward, it was voted down, but the governor was instructed to find out what voters thought about the scheme. About half the registered voters turned out to weigh in on the question "Is it expedient for the state to grant an appropriation to build an insane asylum?" A majority was not in favor, in spite of the dismal results of a new study, authored, in part, by Peaslee.[14] There were now 312 insane people in the state—a dramatic increase in just four years—and about half of them were fully dependent on public support. Many of the New Hampshire insane were found to be living in horrific conditions. But the report also described in glowing terms the progress being made in other, more modern-thinking states that had already opened asylums. "The patient is to be treated with the greatest kindness and so far from arriving at a madhouse, where he is to be confined, he is come to a pleasant and peaceful residence, where all kindness and attention will be shown him, and where every means will be employed for the recovery of his health."[15] The report to the legislature included detailed descriptions of twelve inmates of the Massachusetts Asylum—"a glorious monument of the liberality and philanthropy of that Commonwealth"— who had all been chained up for periods of years after committing horrific murders, and that who were now clean, calm, reasonable members of the hospital community, thought provoking for Peaslee.[16] The year 1837 saw no action at all.

In 1838, Peaslee was finally in a place to use his powers of oratory and persuasion to bring an asylum to fruition. He was elected to the state legislature. It's not a coincidence that that was the year the bill for the establishment of an asylum was passed and signed into law; Peaslee campaigned enthusiastically and persistently for it. The bill established a corporation, the New Hampshire Asylum for the Insane, which could hold real and personal property necessary for its support, provided that this didn't exceed $30,000. The institution would be managed by a board of twelve trustees, three of whom had to vacate their offices yearly. Eight of the trustees were to be elected by the corporation, and four by a board of visitors. The corporation had to raise $15,000 in donations before the state would provide any money. If they succeeded in raising this very substantial sum, then the state would provide shares of bank stock worth about $18,000. When a power struggle almost immediately arose, the legislature acted again. The governor and his council would appoint all the trustees who would run the corporation, and some of the donations from private individuals would be returned, making the funding somewhat sketchy.[17]

Competition was fierce between towns eager to be the site of the new asylum. In 1840, many towns could see the potential economic value of being the home for a major new institution. The struggle was particularly heated between Portsmouth and Concord. Portsmouth even argued that they had a ready supply of fish, which they presumed to be the very best food for the insane.[18] In the end, Concord judiciously contributed 120 acres for the asylum campus. Since that donation made it possible to shift all the ready money toward the construction of the building, it was quickly a done deal. The asylum would be located between Fruit, Pleasant, and Clinton Streets in Concord, only about a ten-minute walk from where Prescott was tried and convicted.

The architect chosen to design the New Hampshire State Insane Asylum was something of a surprise: Elias Carter of Worcester, Massachusetts. Prior to his involvement in the asylum, his previous work had consisted of several churches in central Massachusetts, and a few homes, but never any large public buildings.[19] Charles Hazen Peaslee was selected as one of the original trustees of the new institution. He served in that role for the rest of his life. The Main Building, as it was called, was completed in 1842 and the first patient admitted in October. A second building quickly followed. This one was named the Peaslee Building in honor of the man who, more than any other, was responsible for New Hampshire finally having a place to house and treat its insane. And he, in turn, had first developed his interest in the need for a state asylum through his unsuccessful defense of a young man who had exhibited clear signs, he thought, of insanity.

⚡ 20 ⚡

THE SLEEPWALKING
DEFENSE EVOLVES

Suicide is almost the natural death of persons of her character
—Annis Merrill

Like Peaslee's impact on the movement to found an insane asylum in New Hampshire, the influence of Prescott's defense would also affect subsequent court cases. Not very many years would go by before the sleepwalking defense would be attempted again, in spite of its notable failure in Prescott's case. Surprisingly, given the facts that were established regarding this murder, the sleepwalking claim would result in an acquittal in a case that would appear to be much less sympathetic to the accused than Prescott's.

Mary Ann "Maria" Dunn Bickford was from Maine, possibly born in Bath to impoverished parents in June 1824.[1] Her father was said to have died when she was very young, leaving her mother to do her best to raise the child alone. Mother and child relocated to Bangor, Maine, by the time Maria reached her teens and she was later placed in service, left in a home to work as a maid.[2]

Unlike Sally Cochran, from the public's point of view in 1845, Maria Bickford was not an entirely sympathetic victim, in spite of the violence of her death and the fact that she was both very young and pretty.[3] An etching that was supposed to be from a daguerreotype taken shortly before her death shows an attractive, slender, and well-dressed young woman who conveys a calm self-assurance. That she was a prostitute, or at least the mistress of more than one man, also seems certain.[4]

In October 1842, about three years after her marriage at the age of sixteen to James Bickford, and only a few months after the death of their year-old daughter, Maria came south from her home in the village of Newburgh, Maine, a town southeast of Bangor, where the couple was registered in the 1840 census. She came without her husband. She met Albert Jackson Tirrell, who was just her age, born in February 1824.[5] Son of a shoe manufacturer, Tirrell had grown up in wealth. Not long before he met Bickford, he married his eight-months-pregnant fiancé. By the time he began to escort Bickford around, he was the father of two very young daughters.

The pair had a tempestuous relationship. He also seems to have had a violent temper. They stayed in hotels around New England, representing themselves as husband and wife. At some point he even brought her to his family home as a houseguest, a situation that his father-in-law put an end to, and that must have been humiliating for his long-suffering wife, Orient. Eventually, Tirrell's very open adultery caught up with him. In May 1845, he was indicted by the grand jury.

On September 29, 1845, Tirrell was arrested, charged with adultery, and jailed. After the judge received a heartfelt plea from a group that included Tirrell's wife, his mother, his father-in-law, and the town councillors of his hometown, Weymouth, who must have been thinking about how badly Tirrell's scandal might reflect on their town and his family, it was agreed that the charge would be suspended for six months. In any case, his brother-in law bailed him out within the week for a substantial $500.

Immediately upon being released from jail, lovesick Tirrell began a desperate search around Boston for his paramour. Maria avoided him for several days, but by late October they had reunited. At that point, Bickford was living at the home and sometime brothel of Joel Lawrence and his wife.[6] Tirrell spent the night in her upstairs back bedroom on October 23, 1845, and then returned again the next night.

In the early hours of the morning of October 25, several people reported hearing raised voices, a shriek, and then a loud thud from Bickford's room, shortly followed by the sound of someone clattering rapidly down the stairs to the front door. The second floor had two other bedchambers, the middle one unoccupied and the front one, where Priscilla Blood and William Patterson, her lover, slept. When their room began to fill with smoke minutes later, they forced open the door to find piles of burning bed linens scattered throughout the upstairs.

The Lawrences and some early morning passersby helped douse the many fires. Only as the last one was put out did they realize that there was a body on the floor of Bickford's bedchamber when they tripped over it in the dark. Clad only in her chemise, a garment that doubled as a daytime slip and nightgown, Bickford lay lifeless between the fireplace and the bed, her face partially burned by the fire that had been lit next to her. The burns failed to conceal that her throat had been brutally cut, her head nearly severed from her body.[7] Beside the pillow on her bed was a large pool of blood; on the floor under her body there was little to no blood. One of her earrings had been torn from her ear and was found on the floor. The washbowl in her room was filled with bloody water. In the middle bedroom there were bloody smears on the bed where someone had pulled off bedcovers that had then been lit on fire in the hallway.

It wasn't long before Tirrell, acting agitated, turned up at a nearby livery stable. He gave a false name and requested a ride to his father-in-law's home. On the way to Weymouth, he told the driver he had gotten into some trouble about a girl—quite an understatement.

Perhaps the prosecution didn't do a good enough job of describing the crime scene, although they called many witnesses who reported the condition of Bickford's body, the presence of Tirrell's clothing left behind in her room, previous arguments the couple had had, and Tirrell's subsequent flight from Boston, then from the country.[8]

The primary counsel for his defense was Rufus Choate, valedictorian of the class of 1819 of Dartmouth College, who graduated just a year before Nathaniel Upham, justice at Prescott's second trial.[9] Given the number of men involved in Prescott's trial who were Dartmouth graduates, that connection led Tirrell's counsel to being both aware of Prescott's claims of sleepwalking, and Choate's subsequent decision to focus on a sleepwalking defense for his client. But sleepwalking was not his only line of defense. First, there would be the suicide claim.

Annis Merrill, cocounsel for the defense, argued that "Suicide is almost the natural death of persons of her character" in describing Bickford.[10] He claimed that she had become distraught in the night that her relationship with the ever-kind Tirrell was ending. Merrill argued that she then must have gotten up in the dark, dragged the blankets from both the bed in which they had been sleeping as well as the bed in the middle room, lit them on fire (for no particular reason), dug her razor out of her trunk, slashed her throat from ear to ear, nearly bled out on the bed, then leapt up and threw herself on the floor, where she somehow caught herself on fire. As for her earring being torn out of her ear, Merrill claimed that the man who owned the house had done that, although when he'd done it wasn't clear. Tirrell must have then arisen, assessed the discouraging situation, realized this would do him no good with his adultery charge, and fled the scene. This circuitous, even bizarre, explanation failed to account for the bloodstains found in the middle bedroom, or the washbasin of bloody water, since it seems very unlikely that Bickford, while bleeding to death, stopped to wash her hands.

Another possibility was that Tirrell was sleepwalking when he committed the offense. To prove that, Choate later took charge and called quite a few witnesses. A half dozen testified that they had seen Tirrell sleepwalking at one time or another. His mother stated that she had seen him sleepwalk at least ten times since he was about four or five years old.

One of these witnesses also helpfully testified to Bickford's bad character. She was, he said, greedy and had said that if she couldn't get herself a blue-black silk dress, she would take a razor to her throat, and that he should not doubt her ability and willingness to do so. More than one confirmed that she was in the habit of keeping a razor in her trunk, in order to shave back her hair on her forehead to ensure that it would be "high," a fashion standard of the day. Many witnesses were called who testified, in contrast, to Tirrell's excellent character, notwithstanding the very public awareness of his propensity for adultery. It would have been common knowledge that his character, being a gentleman of wealth and from a prominent family, must be quite good, and that the character of Bickford, a fallen woman who had abandoned her loving husband in order to live in sin, was equally bad.

As at Prescott's trial, there was a parade of medical witnesses. One of them, Dr. Woodward from the Massachusetts Asylum, who had testified at Prescott's second trial, described many of the same instances of sleepwalking as had Prescott's other physician experts. Miss Ryder of Springfield, the sleepwalking housemaid who became a celebrity, was much in evidence. The ability to sleepwalk and "see" with eyes closed or covered by a blindfold was marveled upon yet again. The same passages in the same professional books were quoted from at length. Prescott's trials served as a playbook for Choate. Usefully, he could consult both his fellow Dartmouth alumni who had been involved in Prescott's case, and also the published trial record.

After Choate's closing argument, which was regarded by some who heard it as one of the most spellbinding speeches of the era, the jury withdrew to consider their verdict. It took them just two hours to find that Tirrell was not guilty. The verdict was followed by resounding applause and cheers from the audience, who clearly viewed Bickford as a depraved enchantress who had led a nice young gentleman astray, rather than as the young, weak victim of violent domestic abuse that she was. There was no effort afterward to find some other perpetrator who might thus have been responsible for Bickford's death. There was too much evidence that the guilty party had just been acquitted.

Not long afterward, Tirrell was tried again. This time the charge was arson for the many fires set at the scene of Bickford's death. As recently as 1836, two men had been executed in Massachusetts for the crime of arson.[11]

Even though Tirrell had managed to be acquitted for murder, he could still face the gallows, since arson remained a capital offense in Massachusetts until 1852.[12] The trial was nearly a repeat performance of the murder trial with Choate in charge and all the same somnambulism testimony, and once again, Tirrell was found not guilty.

Finally, Tirrell was tried for adultery. This time, he was not quite so fortunate. It would be hard to argue that he had conducted his entire relationship with Bickford while asleep. He was found guilty and sent to jail, where he served only about a year. A legend claims that after his release from jail, he wrote to Choate and argued that the attorney should return some of the fees he charged for his successful defense since it had been so easy to get him acquitted that Choate hadn't fully earned his money. There is no record that Choate returned any.

Either Tirrell's long-suffering wife loved him deeply and was a highly forgiving woman, or life presented her with few other options. After his stint in jail, he returned to the family fold. Over the years, he was listed variously as a huckster (salesman), a speculator, a trader, or as unemployed. The value of his home never exceeded a very modest one hundred dollars, so it seems that even if Orient forgave him, the Tirrells did not. He was cut off from the family fortune. Tirrell died in 1880, outliving Bickford by thirty-five years.[13]

The sleepwalking defense was not frequently used afterward, but did appear from time to time. Simon Fraser, a young man in Scotland in 1878, who was described as having a lifelong history of night terrors—extremely vivid negative dreams often accompanied by physical movement and calling out—killed his toddler son by smashing him against a wall, believing the child to be a wild animal that was attacking his family. He was acquitted.[14]

Just the following year in Kentucky, a man named Fain, who had lately lost a good deal of sleep while caring for his sick children and who had been a lifelong sufferer from nightmares and sleepwalking, dozed off in the Veranda Hotel lobby.[15] His friend, George Welch, arranged for them to have a room for the night, but was then unable to awaken Fain. He enlisted the aid of a nearby porter, Henry Smith, who lifted Fain up to awaken him. Fain pulled a handgun and began shooting. After three shots, the unfortunate Smith was dead and Fain then woke up. He was tried and found guilty of manslaughter, but the conviction was overturned on appeal since the jury hadn't been permitted to learn that Fain had had sleepwalking issues and had recently lost so much sleep.[16]

On August 17, 1943, fifteen-year-old Joan Kiger, who was said to suffer from night terrors, got up in the night, found one of her father's many guns, and used it to shoot and kill both her six-year-old brother and her father. She also shot her mother in the hip. When she was tried the following year, her attorney employed a sleepwalking defense and she was found not guilty by reason of insanity. She was sent to a state mental hospital and released the following year as cured.[17]

A study by Rosalind Cartwright, PhD, published in the *American Journal of Psychiatry* in 2004, indicated that 2.1 percent of adults surveyed reported that they had exhibited some form of sleep violence.[18] Typically, violent sleep episodes in adults occur during the transition from non-REM (deep sleep) to REM sleep (highly activated sleep), usually during the first two or three hours of the night. For the purposes of a young man who dozed off while sitting on a tree stump in the warm June sun, this seems to be an unlikely situation. Prescott's sleep in the brook field, if it occurred, would almost certainly have been light and brief. Cartwright also found that the sleep problems of children are characterized by a general placidity and less organized behavior than that of affected adults, who are most often male and aged twenty-seven to forty-eight years.

Considering that Prescott's attorneys had employed the two-pronged attack of both insanity and sleepwalking, and linked the two together as aspects of the same issue, in two cases, in 1910 in Kentucky and then in 1925 in Texas, juries were advised that sleepwalking defendants were necessarily insane when they committed their offenses. In Kentucky, the defendant became drunk in a brothel. After he fell asleep, a friend tried to awaken him. While presumably asleep, he punched his friend, then immediately apologized and shook his hand. Next, he stabbed and killed his friend. He claimed to have been asleep through the whole event. He was found guilty.[19] In Texas, a sleeping man pulled a handgun from beneath his pillow and shot his girlfriend. He, too, was found guilty, but was later acquitted because his attorney hadn't equated sleepwalking with insanity as the Court of Appeals ruled he should have.[20]

Two relatively recent homicidal somnambulism cases demonstrate the continuing conundrum that the sleepwalking defense creates. Early in the morning of May 24, 1987, twenty-four-year-old Kenneth Parks arose from bed and drove fifteen miles to his in-laws' home in Scarborough, Ontario, driving through at least one complex intersection that would have required some attention to navigate safely. Parks was already in serious trouble, having just been fired by his employer after it was discovered that he had embezzled money to pay off gambling debts. In addition, he had borrowed heavily.[21] Now the whole sordid story was emerging.

Parks's wife knew of his legal problems and he had promised her that he would tell her parents and his grandmother the following day. When he arrived at his in-laws' home, he attacked them in their bed with a knife he'd found in their kitchen, killing his mother-in-law and severely wounding his father-in-law. At some point he walked upstairs and stood outside the bedroom of two others in the home, seemingly listening to see if he had awakened them. After the attack, he drove himself to a nearby police station (still supposedly asleep) and confessed in somewhat garbled language to killing the couple. At the time, he had serious knife injuries of his own, but seemed unaware of them.

Parks had exhibited several incidences of sleepwalking since childhood. In one case three years before, he violently attacked his sister when she tried to keep him from leaving the house while asleep. He was under considerable stress. Finally, and perhaps most significantly, his electroencephalograph was found to be abnormal during sleep, creating some objective evidence for a physical disorder. However, the prosecution argued, the abnormality could also have been a result of severe stress.[22] He was acquitted of murder.

In contrast is the case of Scott Falater.[23] On the night of January 16, 1997, Scott attacked his wife of twenty years with a knife, stabbing her forty-four times, but not quite killing her. A little while later, wearing gloves, he then dragged her as she was dying to their Phoenix, Arizona, swimming pool, pulled on gloves, rolled her into the water, and held her head underwater until she drowned. He later said that he couldn't recall any of this and that he must have attacked her while sleepwalking. In fact, it was the police who allegedly awakened him from bed when they came to his house in response to a report from the Falaters' neighbor, who observed Scott ordering his dog to lie down just before he drowned his wife.[24]

Falater was an electrical engineer, deeply involved in an important project at his workplace. Although he had a major role in the project, Scott was convinced that it wouldn't succeed and was extremely conflicted about whether or not to share that information with his employers, or, as his wife advised that evening, to just tell them what they wanted to hear. His wife also told him that the filter in their swimming pool was acting up.[25]

After working on several projects, including the pool filter, he went to bed at around 9:30 P.M., but didn't remove his contact lenses, as was his usual habit. At around 10 P.M., the neighbor was awakened by the sound of a woman screaming. He looked over a wall and saw that a body lay next to the Falaters' pool, but he assumed that the woman was drunk. He could see Scott moving around in his house. Around 10:50, Scott, now wearing gloves, returned to the pool area to roll his wife into the water, prompting the neighbor to call 911. The police discovered that Scott had received some minor injuries during the attack on his wife; he had applied bandages to these. Falater had also put his bloody gloves and clothing, along with the knife he'd used, into a plastic container and placed that in the spare tire well of his car.[26]

In the face of what seemed to be some rather damning evidence, the defense contended that an overtired Falater got up in his sleep and tried to repair the pool filter while sleepwalking. They said that his wife had attempted to bring him back to bed and that that was when he attacked her with the knife he was using on the filter. The prosecution stated that the Falaters' marriage was not as idyllic as Falater claimed, and that his wife was found to no longer be wearing her wedding ring. In addition, a prosecution witness said that Falater had discussed the Kenneth Parks case at work a few weeks before his wife's murder, proving that he was aware that a sleepwalking defense could bring an acquittal. The prosecution pointed out that the entire event was quite lengthy, unusual for sleepwalking violence, and that Falater appeared to exhibit significant planning—putting on gloves, calming his dog, and hiding the murder evidence—which contradicted the typical more random behavior of a sleepwalker.[27]

However, by drowning his badly wounded wife in the pool, he ended up staining the water with her blood. If this was a deliberate act, it was poorly conceived. Hiding that evidence from their two teenaged children, sleeping inside, and the neighbors would be all but impossible. There was the very strong contradiction of Falater seeming to try to conceal the crime and of leaving ample evidence (like a bloody body in the pool) on display, although if he planned to later claim that she had been murdered by someone else, hiding his bloody clothing, the weapon, and the gloves would make sense. Falater also had a history of sleepwalking problems, but several nights in a sleep lab revealed nothing to either support or contradict his defense. He claimed to have been sleeping poorly before the attack, so he was somewhat sleep deprived. A jury found Falater guilty of first-degree murder and he was sentenced to life imprisonment. His appeal was denied.[28]

In general, witnessed attacks that are brief and more obviously random in nature—like Fain's abrupt shooting of the hotel porter when the man attempted to pick him up, and Simon Fraser's quick but lethal attack on his toddler son—are easier to defend with a claim of sleepwalking than Scott's complex, nearly hour-long attack. While Kenneth Parks was acquitted of his long and complex murderous attack, there remain many who find that result questionable.

⊰ 21 ⊱

THE INSANITY PLEA

Violent conduct at various times
—State v. Jones

Surely without any intention to do so, Abraham Prescott and his attorneys' novel defense would leave a lasting impact on New Hampshire law, inspiring a thoughtful evolution of the definition of legal insanity that would continue through most of the twentieth century. The troubling uncertainty of Prescott's mental status and his attorneys' impassioned defense put a human face on the issue of criminal responsibility, but it was probably his gradual postmortem change from murderer to a rather pathetic second victim that did more to encourage this exploration of the role of mental disability in crime in New Hampshire.[1] Even by the time of Prescott's execution, there may have been a growing number of people in the state who no longer believed he had full possession of his senses, or at least enough possession to understand the wrongness of his act, a key test of criminal responsibility at the time.

Legal definitions of insanity had been slowly evolving. Whether or not all juries were instructed on the latest definition was less clear. In 1724, in England, Edward Arnold shot but failed to kill Lord Thomas Onslow. Arnold had such a reputation for insanity that he had been commonly called "mad Ned." He believed that Onslow had caused "chamber devils and imps" to disturb his sleep.[2] He generally went about talking to himself and suffered from delusions. However, the prosecution was able to prove that Arnold could read and write, work sums, conduct business, and go into shops to purchase things in spite of his affliction.[3] It seemed at the time highly contradictory that a man who was capable of all these very normal behaviors could also fail to understand that shooting Lord Onslow was wrong. The trial judge instructed the jury that they had to decide if Arnold's understanding was "no more than a wild beast, or a brute, or an infant."[4] If his understanding exceeded that very low threshold, then he must be responsible for his crime. The jury agreed that it did and convicted him. He was sentenced to death, but spared only because Lord Onslow pleaded for the man. This now created the first notable insanity test for English courts: the perpetrator might be spared if he recognized what he had done but lacked the mental capacity to know his act was wrong, what is called *mens rea* or guilty mind.

The next development that preceded Prescott's trial was the case of James Hadfield, who attempted to shoot King George III in 1800. He was found not guilty by reason of insanity, but was held in an asylum for the rest of his life rather than released back to his family to resume his place—whatever it was—in the community, previously the typical outcome for those who were found to lack criminal responsibility because of insanity. Hadfield had been a member of the Light Dragoons and received a severe saber wound to his head in 1794. He was left for dead by fellow soldiers, but was eventually found and treated. His delusion was immediately obvious afterward.[5] He'd become convinced that God had determined he should die, but he had to die at the hands of someone other than himself. Surely killing the king would result in just the outcome he was after.[6]

He wasn't insane by the then current "wild beast" test, and he knew that his attempt to kill the king was wrong, but he was unable to resist the power of his delusion.[7] His defense counsel argued that an irresistible delusion was, in effect, a form of insanity. Lord Kenyon, the justice at Hadfield's trial, ruled that such a delusion provided an exception to the knowing-right-from-wrong rule.[8] (It was just such a delusion test that, more than two decades later, would guide the decision of Sir John Nichol to rule in favor of the young woman who had been cut out of her father's will, as mentioned previously.)

The next significant case was that of John Bellingham in 1812. Justice James Mansfield stated, "There is a species of insanity where people take particular fancies into their heads, who are perfectly sane and of sound mind on all other subjects, but this is not a species of insanity which can excuse any person who has committed a crime, unless it so affects his mind at the particular period when he commits the crime as to disable him from distinguishing between good and evil or to judge the consequences of his actions."[9] This created the concept that an accused murderer might be insane if his delusion was so severe that he was unable to distinguish good from evil, but might not exhibit any other evidence of mental illness.

The next trial of note in the evolution of the insanity defense would be that of Daniel McNaughton (or sometimes M'Naghten or McNaughten). Daniel McNaughton was the illegitimate son of a wood turner, born in Glasgow, Scotland, in 1813.[10] He grew up under the care of his mother until her death, and then moved into his father's home and became an apprentice in his shop. After a brief stint as an actor, Daniel set up his own wood-turning shop in 1835.[11] By 1840, signs of mental illness may have been appearing. He sold his business and traveled around for the next few years. In 1841, he complained to his father, the chief of police, and others that he was being followed and persecuted by Tories.[12] In January 1843, he began loitering around the center of government in London. On January 20, he fell in behind the prime minister's private secretary, Edward Drummond, pulled out a pistol, and shot the man point-blank in the back. Only the quick work of a nearby policeman prevented McNaughton from firing a second pistol. Although never proven, McNaughton is said to have believed that Drummond was the prime minister, his actual target. Five days later, after aggressive, highly debilitating medical "treatment," Drummond died and McNaughton was charged with murder. At trial prosecutors argued that although McNaughton suffered from a delusion of persecution, he was able to distinguish right from wrong and knew he was committing a crime. The defense argued that McNaughton suffered from an irresistible delusion such that he had lost "all restraint over his actions."[13] He was found to be innocent by virtue of his insanity, but, like Hadfield, was sent to an asylum, where he lived out the rest of his life, dying in 1865.

After the verdict, there was a public outcry, reinforced by Queen Victoria, who had previously been attacked by similarly deluded people. As a consequence, following an early custom, the House of Lords put questions to the twelve justices of the Court of Common Pleas in order to clarify what constituted legal insanity. The most important outcome of those questions was this statement, which became known as the M'Naghten Rule: "To establish a defence on the ground of insanity it must be clearly proved, that, at the time of committing the act, the party accused was labouring under such a defect of reason from disease of the mind, as not to know the nature and quality of the act he was doing, or if he did know it, that he did not know that what he was doing was wrong."[14]

While this rule didn't especially differ from the "irresistible delusion" concept that had been evolving since Hadfield's trial, it was more clearly stated and more specific. This rule of law would remain the standard for determining legal insanity in both Great Britain and most American states—except in New Hampshire—for years to come.[15] New Hampshire was a small state with a small population, and perhaps influences from the past had a greater impact there than in other places. In 1869, New Hampshire rejected the M'Naghten Rule in favor of a much different view of how courts should handle a claim of insanity. While it might appear to begin with the case of Josiah Little Pike, it was inspired by Justice Richardson's very limited instructions to the jury regarding insanity in the Prescott case, calling upon the jurors to use their own judgment as to the teen's mental status.

Josiah Pike was born in 1837 in Newburyport, Massachusetts, one of eight sons and two daughters of nearly impoverished parents.[16] He, like his father and most of his brothers, became a shoemaker. In 1859, he married, and was the father of one child. Sometime in the 1860s, he began to drink heavily, a condition that was referred to at his trial as "dipsomania," which then meant an uncontrolled craving for alcohol.[17]

In the 1860s, Pike worked for a time as a farmhand for Thomas Brown, a well-to-do farmer in Hampton Falls, New Hampshire, and his wife, Elizabeth. They lived in a large farmhouse on the road to Amesbury, Massachusetts. On May 7, Pike, after consuming a liberal amount of alcohol, decided to pay a call on the elderly couple, knowing that Brown often seemed to have a good amount of cash on hand.[18] When he arrived at the farm in the evening, drunk and with a plan to rob them, he noticed an ax in the dooryard. He seized the ax and politely knocked on the door. Elizabeth, seventy-three years old, didn't immediately recognize Pike in the dim light, but then recognition dawned and she said his name in surprise—just before he struck her with the ax. Next, he assaulted Thomas, seventy-five, who didn't even have time to rise from his chair. Pike ransacked the house and eventually fled with about $500 and some of the Browns' personal possessions. Neither of the couple was dead. Elizabeth passed away the following day, but Thomas lived for five days, long enough to regain consciousness and name his killer. Pike was found, drunk, back in Newburyport with the damning evidence of the Browns' belongings on him.[19] There was little doubt that he had killed the Browns, but did his chronic alcoholism and inebriation at the time of the crime render him insane?

The judge, stepping away from the M'Naghten Rule, which might have provided a defense for Pike, instructed the jury: "whether there is such a thing as dipsomania, and whether the defendant had that disease, and whether the killing of Brown was the product of such disease, were questions of fact for the jury."[20] The jury, given the opportunity to consider each of these points as a question of fact, found Pike guilty. On November 9, 1869, he was hanged at the prison in Concord, but only after delivering an apologetic speech from the gallows that had been written by the prison pastor.[21] He had the dubious honor of being the first person to be executed within the walls of the prison, finally ending the era of public executions in New Hampshire. Less than a year after his death, Hiram Jones's case would become the next important step in framing the New Hampshire definition of insanity.

On June 4, 1870, Jones, a sixty-four-year-old man who had spent nearly his entire life farming in central Maine, murdered his wife, Ann.[22] Hiram was well known for his rabid temperament. Shortly before the crime, Hiram and his family relocated to Newmarket, New Hampshire, not far from Portsmouth. Jones initially found work as a deckhand on the packet boat *Factory Girl,* but then was fired from his job.[23] During the spring of 1870, he began to believe that his wife, the mother of his three young-adult children, was having an affair with a man named French.[24] (There were several young to middle-aged men named French in town who might have been the potential paramour. However, at that time, Hiram's son was living with Nathaniel and Adeline French, both aged fifty-eight, and their twenty-one-year-old son, Frank, not far away in Newburyport, Massachusetts, perhaps a coincidence, or maybe a clue to the identity of "Mr. French.")[25] Ann was a bit younger than her tall, blue-eyed, gray-haired husband, aged forty-nine at the time of her death.[26] Almost nothing else is known of her except that she became the victim of her husband's brutality or, as he claimed, his delusion.

On May 22, the police had been called to the Joneses' home. Hiram, angry and perhaps ranting, was threatening to kill himself and maybe Ann as well in "violent demonstrations" that had ended by the time the policeman arrived. The officer seems to have questioned Ann apart from Hiram, maybe to see if she felt safe staying with him.[27] She remained, whatever her feelings, probably seeing few other options.

On June 4, Jones took up a razor and slashed his wife's throat deeply, with at least one of their offspring, perhaps their youngest son, present in the small house. Ann died immediately. Jones then attempted to cut his own throat, but didn't manage to inflict a lethal wound on himself.[28] After recovering from his injury, he was tried the following October. His attorneys argued that he had been suffering from such a severe delusion of his wife's infidelity that he was unable to control the urge to kill her. Jones was found guilty and sentenced to be executed on November 9, 1871.[29]

According to his appeal, "the State was allowed to prove, to a large extent, the history of the defendant, including his temperament, excitable nature, quarrels, wrangling, making preparations and threats to shoot a neighbor, and violent conduct at various times during a period of many years before the death of his wife."[30] They had also introduced evidence that there was a rumor in town that Ann was having an affair, so perhaps Jones wasn't suffering from a delusion.

The justices, at his appeal, ruled that "all symptoms and all tests of mental disease are purely matters of fact, to be determined by the jury." If he had an irresistible impulse to kill his wife, that, too, was a matter of fact the jury must decide, as they apparently had.[31] This ruling broadened the "question of fact" ruling of the Pike case. Jones's death penalty was allowed to stand. However, his death sentence was later commuted to life in prison, an outcome he was said to have been dissatisfied with, preferring a quick end. Since he died on December 21, 1871, only a few weeks after his scheduled date with the executioner, he seems to have gotten his wish.[32]

As the law stood in New Hampshire after the Jones case, a defendant claiming insanity would not be judged upon whether he could distinguish right from wrong at the time of the crime (a judgment on the quality of his thinking), but upon whether or not the jury believed beyond a reasonable doubt that he was suffering from insanity at that moment. The law did not define what constituted insanity as the M'Naghten Rule did; that decision was instead left up to the jury. The rest of the states continued to use the M'Naghten Rule right up until a 1954 US Court of Appeals case in the District of Columbia called *Durham vs. US.*

Monte Durham was a young man with a long history of mental illness, beginning with his discharge from the navy in 1945 at the age of seventeen, when he was found to be suffering from "a profound personality disorder." Over the next several years, Durham was repeatedly arrested for various crimes, and jailed or held involuntarily in a mental hospital. He was discharged from a hospital just two months before being arrested for breaking and entering a residence, and found guilty by a lower court.[33] The Court of Appeals agreed that the knowing-right-from-wrong test was entirely outmoded and that it failed to take into consideration a new understanding of the characteristics of mental illness.[34] The Durham Test, as it came to be known, was that a person would not be responsible for criminal behavior if "his unlawful act was the product of mental disease or mental defect."[35] Although Durham would later be superseded nationally by a new test of mental illness in *United States vs. Brawner* in 1972, in New Hampshire it was fully embraced and incorporated into Statute 628.2.1: "A person who is insane at the time he acts is not criminally responsible for his conduct. Any distinction between a statutory and a common law defense of insanity is hereby abolished and invocation of such defense waives no right an accused person would otherwise have."[36] Thus, the Durham Test, which was considered in New Hampshire to be largely a reaffirmation of the Jones and Pike rulings of the nineteenth century, became the law for that state and remained so in 2019.[37] The insanity defense in New Hampshire doesn't require a medical diagnosis of insanity from a physician. Juries decide what constitutes insanity.

Many of the other states continue to rely on the M'Naghten Rule or a modified version of it to determine the claim of insanity in criminal cases. A few use the Model Penal Code definition, which requires both a medical diagnosis of a mental defect and either a determination that the defendant didn't realize that his conduct was criminal, or that he was unable to conform to the law, which harkens back to the "irresistible delusion" that affected Hadfield when he tried to kill King George.[38] New Hampshire is not the only outlier; Kansas has entirely abolished the insanity defense. In Idaho, Utah, and Montana, the insanity defense has been abolished, but courts may rule that a defendant was "guilty but insane."[39]

New Hampshire's long and sometimes uneasy relationship with the death penalty came to an end after the hanging of Howard Long on July 13, 1939. Found guilty of the assaults on two young children in Massachusetts, Long eventually relocated to Alton, New Hampshire, where he sexually assaulted and murdered two ten-year-old boys. Although others were sentenced to death after Long, who was unsuccessful in his insanity defense, none was executed. In the spring of 2019, both houses of the New Hampshire legislature voted to repeal the death penalty, with significantly more votes available than needed to override a veto by the governor, who signed the repeal into law.

Although the chain of cases from Prescott to Pike to Jones, and then to Durham was each based one upon another, it might appear to be specious to conclude that the verdict in Prescott's trial was so important and lasting that it led inexorably to New Hampshire's somewhat out-of-sync definition of legal insanity. However, the outcome of the Prescott case began New Hampshire's discomfort with the uncertain qualities that define diminished responsibility, and that skepticism or mistrust has continued to filter down through courtroom decisions until the present time, even though its roots have been obscured. Ultimately, that young man, "this miserable boy," with his downward gaze and questionable level of intelligence, became a far more sympathetic character than either drunken Josiah Pike or angry and abusive Hiram Jones.

⊰ 22 ⊱

THE QUESTION OF
RESPONSIBILITY

'Twas this for which I did the deed
—Abr'm Prescott's Confession, of the Murder of
Mrs. Sally Cochran, of Pembroke, N.H.
—June 23, 1833. By a private individual at the Bar. Period broadside

Ultimately, it's important to try to make sense of Abraham Prescott's behavior in the light of new understanding of somnambulism, mental illness and disability, and criminal behavior. Which, if any, of his several contradictory stories should be believed?

As understanding of sleep behaviors has grown and the somnambulism defense has become slightly more common, it provides the opportunity to revisit the sleepwalking version of the Prescott case. Recent science indicates that those who are sleepwalking during non-REM sleep have "no mental interaction with the outside world."[1] They don't form memories of the event, they don't have any ability to perceive, and they do not respond to their environment. If awakened during one of these sleepwalking events, they will be groggy. Additionally, sleepwalking has been found to have a very strong familial incidence, often recur in the same person, and to typically be associated with exacerbating factors like stress, sleep deprivation, or alcohol or drug use. None of these are known to apply to Prescott's situation.

However, his January attack on the Cochrans seems far more typical of a sleepwalking event than does his murder of Sally. During the winter event, unlike in June, he would have had time to fall deeply asleep, the period when sleepwalking behavior occurs. However, he does seem to have shown some awareness of his environment and been responsive to it since he fetched and lit a candle, then brought it with him into the Cochrans' bedchamber before he attacked them. It's not clear whether he added wood to the fire and got the buffalo-skin robe while sleepwalking or if he had briefly awoken and completed those tasks. If he did those things while asleep, that would certainly indicate that he was aware of being cold, and exhibiting clear "mental interaction with the outside world." But if he had awoken and then gotten the robe and tended the fire, then it's extremely unlikely that he would have reached the state of deep sleep again so soon. All of these contradictions make it improbable that he was sleepwalking in January. The situation in June—that he dozed off while sitting on a tree stump and then immediately got up to murder Cochran—fails to align at all with a modern understanding of sleepwalking and indicates that he almost certainly was not asleep when he attacked her.

Even though Prescott does not appear to have been a young man of much intelligence, he may well have recently heard of a sleepwalking case. Chauncey Cochran had, of course, recalled at the second trial that he had read to the family about Reverend Avery. Sharing interesting and unusual stories may have been commonplace in their family, and talk could certainly have turned to some unique sleepwalking case. However, what is far more significant than whether or not Prescott was sleepwalking or lying about it in January is that afterward he both knew that a claim of sleepwalking could protect him from prosecution, and that his employers were vulnerable, if taken by surprise.

Whatever way Prescott first fixed upon the idea of explaining his actions by claiming to be asleep, his was a novel defense. Even though his claim did not secure his exoneration, his case brought a great deal of attention to the concept of a sleepwalking defense. The work that his counselors did certainly helped Choate and Merrill win an acquittal for Tirrell in Boston just a few years later, and that notable success would go on to inspire others to use the somnambulism defense.

In June, Prescott had even more control over the situation than he had had in the winter as he was alone with Sally in the field. He either initiated the idea of strawberry picking, or willingly acquiesced to it. Although they initially visited a field that was easily visible from many houses, later he deliberately led Sally to a place that was extremely isolated. It was far down a hill that was so steep, it was hard to scramble down. It certainly was possible that they could have encountered others out picking strawberries—but they didn't. If they had, his limited plan would have changed. His crime was opportunistic.

Now he was alone in a lonely place with a pretty young woman. He may recently often have thought of what it would be like to enjoy her sexual favors, but the opportunity hadn't been quite right until Sunday morning. That, however, was likely the full extent of his plan; he lacked the necessary intellect for anything much more complicated. Having gotten her into a position where he held all the power, he propositioned her. If his initial approach was violent, like grabbing her and attempting to kiss her—which would have made her angry and very scared—then it is impossible that she would have merely threatened him with Chauncey's angry response, and then just have calmly gone back to picking berries. She didn't.

When she rejected his attention, whatever that consisted of, either verbal or physical, he was both humiliated and angry. He responded with all the spontaneous, uncontrolled rage he'd previously inflicted on the equally defenseless farm animals. He had learned in January that if his blows were hard enough and properly placed, he could kill. He did. In attacking Cochran, he exhibited all the tendencies of a "disorganized killer," not planning the murder, using a readily available weapon, demonstrating "overkill" or extreme, unnecessary force, not making any real effort to conceal the crime or even to protect himself from being discovered as the killer.[2]

After he struck her, and then began to calm down, he made a rudimentary attempt to conceal her body, maybe initially thinking to flee the area, although the complications of fully developing a plan like that defeated him entirely. Then a seemingly more rational and certainly easier idea emerged. He fell back on the greatest lesson that January had provided to him: people would believe a claim of sleepwalking. Everything would be okay, he hoped.

He didn't fully anticipate the response her killing generated; he just accepted that his sleepwalking claim would suffice to protect him, but he was not a person who understood people well. When the sleepwalking claim seemed not to work, he fell back on a toned-down version of the truth, trying as much to deflect the disdain of his jailors as to prove his innocence.

Much later, if the newspaper account can be believed, he came up with an even less credible explanation for the murder—that he had killed Sally and intended to then murder Chauncey in order to gain possession of their farm. In spite of that conversation in the jail, which was attributed to him by the newspaper (but no one else), this plan seems like a bizarre combination of a complicated scheme that he was ill-suited to develop, and also demonstrated a remarkable level of ignorance. It's very hard to imagine that even a young man of limited intellect would think that he would become the owner of the Cochran farm if Sally and Chauncey were to die at his hands. Almost certainly, in the course of his very long incarceration, Prescott invented a new narrative that at least exonerated him from the heinous idea that he would proposition and then murder the young woman who had been his surrogate mother. Being driven by money and not by lust might have seemed to him a more acceptable excuse once his sleepwalking claim was rejected. He wasn't intelligent enough to recognize that his new explanation was unbelievable.

Although his attorneys would make a valiant effort to attribute the murder to insanity, there is no indication, based on a modern understanding of mental illness, that Prescott was suffering from the disease. However, his mental status should still be considered. So many people described his flat affect, downcast eyes, and appearance of low intelligence. Likely having a genetic mutation that had left him with an enlarged head and some clear signs of being on the autism spectrum, Prescott was not of normal intellect even though, in 1834 and 1835 when he was tried, there was no test for mental capabilities that would have proven this.

Many who saw or knew Prescott did recognize that he was in some way mentally deficient and it seems like it was this aspect of him that most disturbed his attorneys and the justices at his trials, although it was a quality that was hard to quantify, especially to the pragmatic jurors. Prescott was fully capable of caring for himself, following directions from his employers, completing a hard day's work, and functioning within a family setting. Almost everyone present surely knew people who couldn't manage any of those tasks because they were so intellectually deficient. Prescott seems to have fallen into some gray area where he wasn't quite normal but wasn't so impaired as to be fully abnormal either.

In 1986, the US Supreme Court stated, "For today, no less than before, we may seriously question the retributive value of executing a person who has no comprehension of why he has been singled out and stripped of his fundamental right to life. Similarly, the natural abhorrence civilized societies feel at killing one who has no capacity to come to grips with his own conscience or deity is still vivid today. And the intuition that such an execution simply offends humanity is evidently shared across this nation. . . . Whether its aim be to protect the condemned from fear and pain without comfort of understanding, or to protect the dignity of society itself from the barbarity of exacting mindless vengeance, the restriction finds enforcement in the Eighth Amendment."[3] These comments call to mind the image of Prescott sitting impassively as the jury in both trials pronounced him guilty. He did not appear to comprehend the significance of their decision.

A study conducted in 2003 in Texas found that 23 percent of the people entering the prison system in 2002 scored below 80 on IQ tests, and a subsequent study found that the average IQ nationally for repeat adult offenders was 85, indicating that the culpability of the mentally disabled remains a significant issue.[4] Returning, as many states have, to the test of "knowing right from wrong," the justice system is confronted with complex issues. Does a person who is an adult but has the mental age of a child have the capability to know right from wrong and act on that knowledge? For the most part, the justice system appears (judging by the number of incarcerated people with mental disabilities) to have decided that knowing right from wrong does not represent a significant intellectual challenge for the mentally disabled. There is some evidence that Prescott did meet that low standard in that he made efforts to first conceal Cochran's body, and later to explain away his attack on her. If he had not recognized her murder as wrong, it seems unlikely he would have bothered to conceal it. It's possible that in a more modern criminal justice system he would not have been executed, but even that is highly uncertain. It is disappointing and tragic that, after the passage of nearly two hundred years and notable advances in the study of the human mind, the issues raised in Prescott's trial have not been resolved.

It's easy to understand why the murder of Sally Cochran has never been completely forgotten, as have most other capital crimes of the nineteenth century. Here was a young, well-to-do wife and mother, the very picture of innocence and mildness. It was a rural community, surely a place where things like this just couldn't happen. The murder occurred on a bright June Sunday, not a dark and portentous night. Prescott, too, seemed so very innocent: young, perhaps a bit dim-witted, but kindly with the children, mostly obedient, and all but a member of the family. It wasn't seemingly a crime that could be expected. It presented enormous shock value.

But aside from the provocative aspects of the murder, it was the uncertainties that kept the case alive for so long afterward. Writers have discussed it many years after the events. Ultimately, in judging whether the guilty verdicts were appropriate for this youth and this crime, one must either choose to trust the juries who decided his fate, or his attorneys and the justices who also sat through all the testimony and had plenty of time to observe Prescott, and who made it perfectly clear afterward that they believed the juries had erred.

EPILOGUE

It seems likely that Chauncey Cochran must have been haunted by guilt. Twice, he failed in his duty as a husband to protect his wife, who, in the sensibility of the time, was fully dependent upon him for that protection. Even if Prescott was kept on at their farm after the January attack because his wife pleaded with Cochran to trust the teen, it was a mistake— *his* mistake as the paternalistic responsible party. Further adding to his burden of guilt, he refused to accompany her strawberry picking for the most indolent of reasons—he did not want to interrupt his reading of a murder trial that happened far away and was none of his concern. Surely, some of that guilt must have motivated him to first confront his neighbor, Jonathan Robinson, and then not long afterward, to pack up and leave behind his family farm and heritage, his mother and brother, his dead wife's parents, and nearly all else that he had loved.

By the time of Abraham's first trial, Chauncey Cochran had sold his Pembroke farm, gathered up his children and his possessions, and made the long journey to East Corinth, Maine. It's possible that he sent a friend, Thomas Edes, ahead to scout out the prospects. That twenty-seven-year-old man died in Corinth in June 1834. He was the first to be buried in the Chauncey Cochran plot in Corinthian Cemetery, although his body must have been moved there later since he died long before the cemetery opened. His headstone was purchased from Exeter, New Hampshire, a town near Pembroke, and was carved by stonecutter Timothy Eastman, who also carved Sally Cochran's stone, which is the only one of its type in Corinthian Cemetery. It seems likely that Chauncey was the one who brought it up there.

Initially, Chauncey worked as a "trader" or merchant in Maine. In 1838, he traveled back to New Hampshire to marry Maria Gay of New

London, on the far northwestern edge of Merrimack County. Maria, who was twenty-eight at the time of their marriage in February 1838, was the daughter of Abigail Carpenter and William Gay. This William Gay was the same man who was the last of the jurors to be chosen in Abraham Prescott's first trial, which would account for how Chauncey had met her. Sally's two children did not fare well. Sarah died at the age of twenty-one on October 11, 1849, and was buried in the plot in Corinthian Cemetery. On the 1860 census, their son, Giles Newton, was listed on the census as "Invalid." He died on July 7, 1869, never having married. Engraved on the granite stone that marks the graves of the Cochrans in Corinth is Sally's name and her birth and death dates, even though she remained buried in faraway Pembroke.

Chauncey and Maria had nine children together, including two sets of twins. Two of the children may have died at birth as their names are not recorded on any headstones in the family plot. Of the remaining seven, John would die four days before his first birthday and Chauncey only one day before his ninth birthday. Only one of Chauncey's surviving offspring ever married.

On the main road in East Corinth, Chauncey moved into a Cape Cod–style home with a barn behind it. Perhaps sensing that nearly all of his now adult children would never leave home, in the 1880s Chauncey raised the roof, creating a second full story and walk-up attic, and added fashionable bow windows to the front. The house still stands on Main Street, largely unaltered, although the barn is gone. He became very active in the Corinth Methodist Church, where he was a trustee, and served many roles in local government, including one stint as a state representative in 1851. Although a local history reports that he switched careers, from trader to farmer, in around 1850 due to ill health, he lived on until April 6, 1884. In the years after his career change, he farmed 150 acres, with 125 in active use. Maria died of angina on December 14, 1901.

Chauncey's son Jasper left the state to pursue his education, studying first at Wesleyan University in Middletown, Connecticut, and then attended medical school in New York City. He returned to Maine and opened a medical practice on Main Street in Saco. In 1899, when he was forty-eight, he married Ida May Hutchins of Fryeburg, Maine, who was a decade younger. They had two children. When Chauncey was born in 1901, Jasper named him either for his father or perhaps for his only dimly remembered older brother. In 1902, Sarah (who was called Sally during her childhood) was born. After Ida died in 1915, Jasper married his English live-in housekeeper, Annie Whitworth, who was thirty years younger. He died on July 5, 1924.

After that time, Annie ran a rooming house, assisted off and on by Sally, who never married but who worked in an office for the rest of her life. Jasper's son, Chauncey, became an auto mechanic in Saco. When he died in 1941, he was interred in the Cochran plot in Laurel Hill Cemetery. Jasper's descendants still live in the Saco area.

Sally's sampler, stitched so long ago in 1818, traveled to Corinth with Chauncey as a treasured memento of his lost wife. Sometime before Jasper died in 1924, it came into his possession. Since he was the only one of Chauncey's children to have any descendants, passing it on to him would have made sense. It may have hung in the 92 Elm Street home that Annie inherited and Sally shared. In 1961, they donated the sampler to the York Institute, which was later renamed the Saco Museum. If they were familiar with Sally's very sad story, they didn't share that information when they donated the sampler, and the remaining members of the Cochran family also had never heard the story.

The place where Prescott was executed—the only execution ever held in Hopkinton—was a farmer's pasture, deep in snow at the time of the execution, chosen both because it was close to town and because it was shaped like a natural amphitheater, providing excellent views for the thousands expected to turn out for such an event. It remained a field for many decades, passing from the well-to-do Currier family to even wealthier Horace G. Chase in the 1880s. The son of a successful Hopkinton tanner, Horace built a summer "cottage" (more like a rambling Victorian mansion) on part of the property. With its one-time use probably long forgotten, the land was turned into the Beech Hill Golf Club around 1900, providing recreation for the many guests of the huge Perkins Inn, located just a block away. After the hotel was lost to arson in 1907, the golf club fell on hard times. Later, part of the site was excavated to form a small pond and cabins were built around it, creating a modest new vacation destination. Now the cabins are gone and it is a town-owned recreational facility. The two enormous rocks that Abraham's scaffold was perched between were moved long ago; only the bowl shape of the land (largely hidden by woods and water) gives a hint as to where it may have stood.

Prescott's parents disappeared into obscurity after his two trials. A family tree on Ancestry.com reports that Abraham's father, Chase, died in Epsom, New Hampshire, on February 24, 1835, which would have meant that he did not, mercifully, live to see his youngest son executed. Perhaps Polly was also spared that fate, but there is no certain record of her death. None of the Prescott offspring ever rose to the level of financial success that would permit buying a home, but all of them stayed with their wives and children, getting by and leaving no record of having any trouble with the law.

Sally's parents remained in Pembroke after Chauncey left with their two young grandchildren. Jenny died at the age of fifty-eight on September 21, 1837, surviving long enough to see her daughter's killer executed. Moses lived until August 27, 1841. They are both buried beside Sally in Pembroke. Chauncey's mother, Lettice, who had witnessed so much but was never called to testify, didn't accompany Chauncey to Corinth, moving in with her next-youngest son and Sally's sister instead, since Chauncey sold the family home—her home—before he left. She died in Pembroke on October 31, 1838.

Mary Jane, Sally's younger sister, who gave birth to her first child only six months after her marriage to Chauncey's younger brother, James, was pregnant with her second child at the time of Sally's murder. She would have ten children altogether, the last one born when she was forty-five. Of those, four would die as children, including three who passed away within a month of each other in the early fall of 1853. James, who began to use "Cofran" as his last name, worked as a farmer and a shoemaker, but never did well financially. He died on April 19, 1864. Mary Jane would live another twenty-three years, also never well off. She passed away on December 11, 1887, in Springfield, New Hampshire, but she, James, and many of their children are buried in the Old Pembroke Cemetery, where Sally lies. Their descendants have spread across the country.

Charles Hazen Peaslee, one of Abraham's defense team, would serve three terms in the US House of Representatives, then was appointed by President Pierce—a New Hampshire native who had attended Dartmouth with Peaslee and also was for a time his partner in a law practice—as the collector of the Port of Boston, a highly lucrative position gained through the spoils system, which would last until presidents James Garfield and Chester Arthur replaced it in the 1880s with a merit system for civil servants. After serving in that position until 1857, Peaslee relocated to Portsmouth, New Hampshire. He died of apoplexy (usually either a heart attack or a stroke) on September 18, 1866, while on a visit to St. Paul, Minnesota.

Ichabod Bartlett, Abraham's other attorney, lived out the rest of his life in New Hampshire. He never married. He served two more terms in the New Hampshire legislature and was selected as a delegate to the New Hampshire Constitutional Convention of 1850. He spent the last years of his life in a Portsmouth boardinghouse, even though he owned $6,000 of real estate, a farm of 150 acres in Portsmouth. He died October 21, 1853, in Portsmouth and was buried there. Upon his death, the *New England Historical and Genealogical Register* noted that he was among the most talented attorneys of his era, and that while serving in the US Congress, "he attracted great attention in that body, and from him the arrogance of Henry Clay received a rebuke which was never forgotten."

George Sullivan was the elder of the men prosecuting Abraham, and was attorney general at the time of the trial. He stepped down from that post in 1835. He was the husband of Clarissa Lamson and father of at least ten children, six of whom lived short lives. He died on June 14, 1838, in Exeter, New Hampshire, and is buried there with his wife and three of his children.

John Whipple, Merrimack County solicitor, married Hannah Ralston Chase. They were parents to at least five children. After serving as solicitor for another couple of years, Whipple turned his attention to the private sector and became the treasurer of the N. E. Mutual Fire Insurance Company. He may have done well in that role. At the time of the 1850 census he was living in a large and expensive home in Concord located in a neighborhood of similar houses. He died there on August 28, 1857.

Chief Justice William Merchant Richardson remained on the court, although not always active, until his death on March 15, 1838. He had been severely afflicted by a fever around the time he first joined the court and had suffered from uneven health ever since. But he was not a man to coddle himself; he apparently didn't believe in any heat sources except fireplaces and his chambers were known for their frigidity. He married and was the father of seven children, six of whom survived to marry. In his later years Richardson was recognized as a talented gardener and orchardist as well as having a brilliant legal mind. Richardson's death

EPILOGUE   217

resulted in the publication of both an admiring biography and a lengthy funeral discourse on the quality of the man.

Associate Justice Joel Parker moved up to become chief justice to replace Richardson. In 1840, he served on a committee that revised New Hampshire statutes. In 1847, he was appointed Royall professor of law at Harvard. Two months later, he married a widow with two children, and in June 1848 he resigned from the court and moved to Cambridge, Massachusetts. He taught at Harvard until 1868. On the 1870 census, he was living in a large and valuable home in Cambridge. He died there of a "disease of the bowels" on August 17, 1875, becoming the last of the many attorneys involved in the Abraham Prescott case to die. Some years after the murder, a granite monument was erected on the site—as people recalled it—of Sally's death. It remains there, deep in thick woods, long after the Cochran home disappeared and then was replaced with a more ramshackle structure, also now gone.

Now, there is almost nothing left to remind us of a tragic and sordid tale except Sally's poignant sampler. On fine, tightly woven linen, with sleek silk threads she stitched each complex motif: delicate deep-pink roses, checkerboard pot, and striped cornucopia. In tiny black cross-stitches, she carefully recorded the names of everyone in her family and their birth dates. In the interest of thoroughness, she left spaces for her parents' and siblings' death dates, filling those in for her two deceased older siblings and, four years later, adding the death date for Betsy, her tiny baby sister. She added a deeply sad epitaph below, and then, finally, she worked a neat vine-wrapped double oval and stitched: "Wrought by Sally Cochran aged 13," having no idea that she had only fifteen more years to live and that this triumph of stitchery would outlast every other memory of her life.

NOTES

1. THE KILLING

1. The weather in southern New Hampshire on June 23, 1833, and for the spring of 1833 is based on diary notations by Benjamin Simpson in his Saco, ME, diary 1781–1849 (owned by the Dyer Library, Saco, ME) and the diary of Sally Brown, Plymouth Notch, VT, quoted by Tom Kelleher, curator, Old Sturbridge Village.

2. John D. Lawson, LLD, "Trial of Abraham Prescott for the Murder of Mrs. Sally Cochran Concord, New Hampshire 1834," *American State Trials; A Collection of the Important and Interesting Criminal Trials Which Have Taken Place in the United States, from the Beginning to the Present Day* (St. Louis, MO: F. H. Thomas Law Book Co., 1916), 5:746, https://books.google.com/books?id=hvMUAAAAYAAJ&pg=PA925&lpg=PA925&dq=trial+of+abraham+prescott+american+state+trials+volume+V&source=bl&ots=6bWseE5uVG&sig=ACfU3U2tca6-ZA7-RnxSjqoJKZJCq9J_hw&hl=en&sa=X&ved=2ahUKEwi-4-3nhbrkAhVQnlkKHb_qAHUQ6AEwA3oECAcQAQ#v=onepage&q&f=false. Two other similar versions of the trial narrative exist. Unfortunately, the more commonly used 1869 version, published by a local newspaper, deletes most of the arguments of the attorneys. All of the references to the trial are based on this version, but the records were all consulted to help eliminate errors.

3. David Richard Kasserman, *Fall River Outrage, Life, Murder, and Justice in Early Industrial New England* (Philadelphia: Univ. of Pennsylvania Press, 1986), 6–12, 120–26.

4. Tara Vose Raiselis, *From the Elegant to the Everyday: 200 Years of Fashion in Northern New England* (College Station, TX: Virtualbookworm Publishing, Inc., 2014), 3, 26. Throughout the nineteenth century, women carefully followed fashion as documented in publications like *Godey's Lady's Book*, even remaking their gowns to match the styles emerging from Paris and London.

2. THE COCHRAN FAMILY

1. All of the information on these Scotch-Irish settlers was found at http://www.1718migration.org.uk/s intro.asp, which provides a lengthy and scholarly look at this migration. For several preceding years, the northern part of Ireland had suffered from a series of bad harvests due to persistent drought. Sheep were dying from a disease called *rot* and smallpox was becoming more prevalent. This had all led to a general recession, which also affected the price of linen, the primary agricultural product of the area. Many of the group, in addition to farming, also worked at spinning and weaving linen, so this was a double economic blow. A fourth factor, beyond the bad harvests, rampant disease, and the recession, was that many of the leases on their farmland, most of which ran for periods of thirty-one years, were coming due and landlords, feeling the pinch but also fueled by greed, planned to raise rents substantially by auctioning off the leases to the highest bidder.

2. *Patrick Griffin, The People with No Name: Ireland's Ulster Scots, America's Scots Irish, and the Creation of a British Atlantic World, 1689–1764* (Princeton, NJ: Princeton Univ. Press, 2001), 90.

3. "Nutfield Rambles," http://www.londonderrynh.net/2013/01/potatoes/59797.

4. Londonderry Historical Society, http://www.londonderryhistory.org/townhist.

5. Rev. Edward L. Parker, *History of Londonderry Comprising the Towns of Derry and Londonderry, N.H.* (Boston, MA: Perkins and Whipple, 1851), 30–66.

6. Nathan Franklin Carter, *History of Pembroke, N.H. 1730–1895 in Two Volumes* (Concord, NH: Republican Press Association, 1895), 2:35. This is the source for all Cochran genealogical information.

7. George L. Haskins, "The Beginnings of Partible Inheritance in the American Colonies," *Yale Law Journal* 51, no. 8 (1942): 1280, https://digitalcommons.law.yale.edu/cgi/viewcontent.cgi?article=4259 . . . ylj.

8. Carter, *History of Pembroke, N.H.,* 82.

9. Howard S. Russell, *A Long, Deep Furrow Three Centuries of Farming in New England* (Hanover, NH: Univ. Press of New England, 1976), 103.

10. Russell, *A Long, Deep Furrow,* 107.

11. Jane C. Nylander, *Our Own Snug Fireside* (New York: Alfred A. Knopf, 1993), 21.

12. Their children were James, born Dec. 4, 1798, and who married Lucinda Danforth; Polly, born Nov. 17, 1800, and died May 18, 1801; Sally, born Oct. 28, 1802, and who died Sept. 22, 1804; Sally, with whom Jenny was pregnant when the first Sally died, born Feb. 24, 1805; Robert, born Aug. 19, 1807, and who would later marry Phebe Holt; Mary Jane, born Feb. 24, 1811—on

her sister Sally's sixth birthday—who would later marry James, the younger brother of Sally's husband, Chauncey, and move in right across the lane; John, born Feb. 27, 1813, who married Mary Ann McConnell; George, born Nov. 27, 1816, and who married Sarah Swain; Betsey, born Nov. 19, 1819, and died Mar. 22, 1822; and Charles Lewis, born Jan. 25, 1824, and who married Elsie Jane Cochran, his first cousin.

13. Nylander, *Our Own Snug Fireside,* 26.

14. Nylander, *Our Own Snug Fireside,* 32. Her experience was typical of the era.

15. Robert V. Wells, "Family Size and Fertility Control in Eighteenth Century America: A Study of Quaker Families," *Population Studies* 12 (Mar. 1971): 73.

16. "Achievements in Public Health, 1900–1999 Family Planning," http:/www .cdc.gov/mmwr/preview/mmwrhtml/mm4874a1.htm.

17. While cloth condoms had existed in some form for a millennium, they were not in common use. Abstinence remained the only reliable method of controlling family size and since the period in a women's cycle when she was fertile was unknown, the abstinence had to be relatively complete to be effective. Midwives of the eighteenth and nineteenth centuries were familiar with herbs that could be used to encourage abortion and by 1800, at least one patent medicine, Dr. Rolfe's Aromatic Female Pills, advertised that if taken by a pregnant woman, it would most certainly produce miscarriage—although this was stated as a supposed warning rather than a (thinly veiled) suggested use. Termination of a pregnancy before quickening—when fetal movement was first perceived by the mother—was generally legal in the United States up until the 1840s. Since a woman couldn't be sure she was pregnant until that moment, and taking into consideration that the baby wasn't perceived to be alive until it had begun moving, it was perfectly acceptable to try to restore menstruation with drugs, since "blocked menses" presented a potential peril to health. Laura Thatcher Ulrich*, A Midwife's Tale: The Life of Martha Ballard Based on Her Diary 1785–1812* (New York: Vintage Books, 1990), 170.

18. Michael R. Haines. "The Urban Mortality Transition in the United States, 1800–1940," *Annales de Demographie Historique* no. 1 (2001): 14.

19. Their children were Samuel, born only five months after his parents' marriage in Dec. 1788 and who died unmarried in 1818; Betsey, born in 1790; John, born in 1792 and died unmarried in Natchez, MS, before 1819; Mahala, born in 1797 and who married and moved to Concord, NH; Chauncey, born in 1799 and who died in 1801; Chauncey, born Nov. 24, 1801—shortly after his toddler namesake's death—and who would marry Sally Cochran; and finally, James, born in 1804 and who would marry Sally's younger sister, Mary Jane Cochran.

20. Susan McKinnon, "Cousin Marriage, Hierarchy, and Heredity: Contestations over Domestic and National Body Politics in 19th-Century America," *Journal of the British Academy* 7, no. 20 (May 2019): 64.

3. SALLY AND CHAUNCEY COCHRAN

1. George Waldo Browne, *The Amoskeag Manufacturing Company of Manchester, New Hampshire, A History* (Manchester, NH: Mills of Amoskeag Manufacturing Company, 1915), 47. For example, although a cotton mill had been constructed in nearby Manchester in 1804, it wasn't until about 1830, with the construction of new buildings, that the enterprise began to turn the type of profit that would lead to explosive growth.

2. Leslie Rounds, *I My Needle Ply with Skill* (College Station, TX: Virtualbookworm Publishing, Inc., 2013), 3.

3. Mark J. Sammons, "The District Schools of Early New England," Families and Children, in *Dublin Seminar for New England Folklife Annual Proceedings 1985* (Boston, MA: Boston Univ., 1985), 78.

4. Sammons, "The District Schools of Early New England," 79.

5. Claire Perry, *Young America Childhood in the 19th-Century Art and Culture* (New Haven, CT: Yale Univ. Press, 2006), 53.

6. Patsy Parker, PhD, "The Historical Role of Women in Higher Education," *Administrative Issues Journal: Connecting Education, Practice, and Research* 5, no. 1 (Spring 2015): 6. Mount Holyoke (https://www.mtholyoke.edu/about/history) was founded by Mary Lyon, who spent a stint at Adams Female Academy, which was established when Pinkerton Academy—Sally Cochran's school—decided to stop educating girls in 1821. Lyon was forced out of Adams because she disdained the teaching of the female arts, preferring to dedicate instruction time to academic subjects, a very controversial idea at the time.

7. Betty Ring, *Girlhood Embroidery* (New York: Alfred A. Knopf, Inc., 1993), 8.

8. Ring, *Girlhood Embroidery*, 9.

9. Glee Krueger, *A Gallery of American Samplers* (New York: E. P. Dutton, 1978), 18.

10. Krueger, *A Gallery of American Samplers*, 15.

11. Ring, *Girlhood Embroidery*, 22.

12. Previously owned and sold by Stephen and Carol Huber at www.antiquesamplers.com.

13. Tara Raiselis and Leslie Lambert Rounds, *Industry and Virtue Joined* (College Station, TX: Virtualbookworm Publishing, Inc., 2015), 109–10.

14. Raiselis and Rounds, *Industry and Virtue*, 113.

15. Courtesy of Stephen and Carol Huber.

16. Ethel Stanwood Bolton and Eva Johnston Coe, *American Samplers* (Boston, MA: Thomas Todd Co., 1921), 255–354. In 1921, these two members of the Massachusetts Society of Colonial Dames made an extended effort to document all known samplers and record their verses. Sally's verse is not included in their very extensive and comprehensive list.

17. Clive Oppenheimer, "Climatic, Environmental and Human Consequences of the Largest Known Historic Eruption: Tambora Volcano (Indonesia) 1815," *Progress in Physical Geography* 27, no. 2 (2003): 230.

18. "1816: The Year without a Summer," http://www.newenglandhistorical society.com/1816-year-without-a-summer/.

19. Nylander, *Our Own Snug Fireside*, 63.

20. Nylander, *Our Own Snug Fireside*, 258.

21. Ulrich, *A Midwife's Tale*, 141. A young woman often "went to housekeeping" sometime after the wedding, once all the arrangements were secure.

22. Carter, *History of Pembroke*, 1:412. Long before 2010, there was a ramshackle mid-twentieth-century home on the property, seemingly constructed approximately over the site of the Cochran home. By 2016, this home, the dug well, and the still-visible granite foundation of the barn were also gone.

23. Carter, *History of Pembroke*, 1:412.

24. By this time, some of the more progressive farmers were switching over to purebred livestock from the mongrel animals of earlier days. This movement began with wealthier, better-educated farmers who subscribed to new innovative farm journals, but market pressures created a trickle-down effect so that by the 1830s, many farms showed significant improvements in livestock.

25. Nylander, *Our Own Snug Fireside*, 85.

26. Water would have to be fetched for household needs. A comment in the trial testimony shows that Cochran generally went for the water herself. She was quite grateful when one morning, hired farmhand Prescott did it for her, an apparently notable act of kindness. On a laundry day, a large kettle would be filled with as much as fifty gallons of water, involving numerous trips to the well with a heavy, two-gallon pail. Rinsing would involve just as many more pails of water. Nylander, *Our Own Snug Fireside*, 169.

27. Nylander, *Our Own Snug Fireside*, 48.

28. Nylander, *Our Own Snug Fireside*, 44.

4. NIGHTTIME ATTACK

1. Nylander, *Our Own Snug Fireside*, 130.

2. "Sleighing," *Patriot*, Jan. 4, 1833.

3. William Waterston, *A Cyclopedia of Commerce, Mercantile Law, Finance, Commercial Geography and Navigation* (London: Henry G. Bohn, 1863), 143.

4. "Somnambulism." *Patriot*, Jan. 14, 1833.

5. John D. Lawson, ed., "The Trial of Abraham Prescott for the Murder of Mrs. Sally Cochran Concord, New Hampshire 1834," in *American State Trials; A Collection of the Important and Interesting Criminal Trials Which Have Taken Place in the United States, from the Beginning to the Present Day* (St.

Louis: F. H. Thomas Law Book, 1916), 5:751. Since somnambulism constituted a truly unusual and really rather amusing tale, Dr. Sargent's story was picked up by other newspapers as well.

6. "An Extraordinary Example of Somnambulism," *Maine Democrat,* Jan. 23, 1833.

7. Hyman Kuritz, "The Popularization of Science in Nineteenth-Century America," *History of Education Quarterly* 21, no. 3 (Autumn 1981): 259.

8. Lawson, "The Trial of Abraham Prescott," 748.

9. Lawson, "The Trial of Abraham Prescott," 749.

10. Lawson, "The Trial of Abraham Prescott," 749.

11. "Pigs," https://www.nps.gov/grsm/learn/historyculture/pigs.htm.

12. Lawson, "The Trial of Abraham Prescott," 800.

5. THE PRESCOTT FAMILY

1. Although the population of Pembroke in 1830 was 1,312, there were only about 280 men of approximately the appropriate age to be heads of households.

2. A figure obtained by averaging the size of all the numerous farms listed.

3. Irvine Loudon, "Deaths in Childbed from the Eighteenth Century to 1935," *Medical History* 30 (1986): 3. Loudon cites a British mortality rate of about six deaths per thousand births, which is considerably lower than the statistic that Laurel Thatcher Ulrich reported in *A Midwife's Tale* of anywhere from 7.5 to a horrifying 222.2, but her number was from hospital deliveries in Dublin and London; these births were considerably more perilous than home births of the era (173). By comparison, the maternal mortality rate for the United States in 2018 was .207 (https://www.americashealth rankings.org/explore/health-of-women-and-children/measure/maternal_mortality). It must also be taken into consideration that women in the late eighteenth century were experiencing many more pregnancies than women do currently, greatly multiplying the risk of maternal demise. The US National Center for Health Statistics reported (https://www.pewresearch.org /fact-tank/2019/05/22/u-s-fertility-rate-explained/) that in 2018 the average number of births per woman reached a new low of 1.73. So the lifetime risk of dying in childbirth in 2018 is about .358 per 1,000 and was in 1800 about 48 per 1,000. Even taking that very high risk into consideration, infectious disease was, by far, the greatest cause of death for people in 1800. However, this fact is heavily skewed because the largest percentage of those dying from infectious disease were children under the age of five. For those who achieved adulthood, the risk of dying of infection was much lower.

Polly was also probably not the daughter of Nathaniel Lear and Susanna Lincoln, born in New Castle, New Hampshire, on Feb. 8, 1767. Neither could she be the Mary "Polly" Lear, who was the daughter of Tobias Lear and Mary Stilson Lear, baptized on Dec. 30, 1760, in Portsmouth, NH, since that Mary Lear later married Samuel Storer of Wells, ME.

4. See Ancestry.com.

5. Both Eliza and Lucy Salter Lear were daughters of Alexander Lear, who was born after 1761 in Portsmouth, NH. His parents were Samuel Lear and Mary Lucy, married there on Dec. 25, 1761. If Abraham's mother was the Polly who was Alexander's younger sister, born in 1773, then her two sons married their first cousins, and she lied—substantially—about her age at Abraham's trial. If she was Alexander's younger sister, then she would have been around forty-three at the time of her last child's birth, which seems much more probable than that she was around fifty-five, as she would claim.

6. Stanley Lebergott, "Wage Trends, 1800–1900," in *Trends in the American Economy in the Nineteenth Century* (Princeton, NJ: Princeton Univ. Press, 1960), 457, https://pdfs.semanticscholar.org. In 1825 a New England farm laborer could expect to earn $8.50 per month, compared to the monthly wages of a mason ($52.50) or a carpenter ($45).

7. Recorded in the 1810 US Federal Census for Deerfield, NH. The US census did not start reporting information on home ownership until much later in the century, so statistics are unavailable. However, the Prescotts lived in farming communities yet lacked a farm of their own, and with Chase's low wages, most likely completely lacked the capability to acquire one.

8. QuickStats: Infant Mortality Rates for Single Births, by Age Group of Mother—United States, 2006, https://www.cdc.gov/mmwr/preview/mmwr html/mm5946a6.htm. The infant mortality rate in 2006 for babies born to mothers aged forty-five and older was three times higher than the rate for mothers aged twenty-five to thirty-nine.

9. "Genetic Risk Maternal Age," https://embryology.med.unsw.edu.au /embryology/index.php/Genetic_risk_maternal_age.
The risk of a chromosomal abnormality in a child rises with each year of maternal age: 1 in 526 at age 20, 1 in 20 at age 45, and 1 in 8 at age 49.

10. Concealing one's age is not a modern deceit. There are many extant samplers where someone, presumably the maker, has later carefully picked out the stitches that identify her birth year.

11. Lawson, "The Trial of Abraham Prescott," 789.

12. Jason L. Lifshutz, MD, and Walter D. Johnson, MD, "History of Hydrocephalus and Its Treatments," *Neurosurgery Focus* 11 (2001): 2.

13. Lifshutz and Johnson, "History of Hydrocephalus," 2. Taking into consideration the incidence of hydrocephaly, about two to three per thousand live births, Abraham's macrocephaly might well have been the only case Dr. Graves had ever seen.

14. Stephen Klein, Pantea Sharifi-Hannauer, and Julian A. Martinez-Agosto, "Macrocephaly as a Clinical Indicator in Genetic Subtypes of Autism," *Au-*

tism Research (Feb. 6 2013): 51–56, https://www.ncbi.nlm.nih.gov/pmc/articles
/PMC3581311/.

15. Lawson, "The Trial of Abraham Prescott," 789.

16. C. B. Cosby, "James Currie and Hydrotherapy," *Journal of the History of Medicine and Allied Sciences* 5 (Summer 1950): 286.

17. Russell, *A Long, Deep Furrow,* 109.

18. Lawson, "The Trial of Abraham Prescott," 803.

19. Russell, *A Long, Deep Furrow,* 110.

20. "Wage Trends 1800–1900," https://pdfs.semanticscholar.org.

6. INDICTMENT AND INCARCERATION

1. Nylander, *Our Own Snug Fireside,* 9–10.

2. Nylander, *Our Own Snug Fireside,* 9.

3. "Murder," *Patriot,* July 1, 1833.

4. *Report of the Trial of Abraham Prescott on an Indictment for the Murder of Mrs. Sally Cochran, before the Court of Common Pleas, Holden at Concord, in the County of Merrimack. on the First Tuesday of Sept., 1834* (Concord, NH: M. G. Atwood and Currier & Hall, 1834), https://books.google. com/books?id=4LJjAAAAcAAJ&pg=PA3&lpg=PA3&dq=trial+of+abra ham+prescott+1833&source=bl&ots=hen6FOS103&sig=ACfU3U29aAm avdKx32TAZPpCR7jycoffng&hl=en&sa=X&ved=2ahUKEwjo5vXKnLrk AhXLhOAKHcZJC7c4ChDoATACegQICBAB#v=onepage&q=trial%20 of%20abraham%20prescott%201833&f=false. This is yet another version of the trial record, and the only one including information about Prescott's first court appearance.

5. Thomas Coffin, *Diary of a Farmer in Boscawen, New Hampshire,* New Hampshire Historical Society collection, M 1967–044.

6. C. C. Lord, *Life and Times in Hopkinton, N.H.* (Concord, NH: Republican Press Association, 1890), 131.

7. Lord, *Life and Times in Hopkinton,* 90.

8. Lawson, "The Trial of Abraham Prescott," 805.

9. Lawson, "The Trial of Abraham Prescott," 805.

10. Ancestry.com.

11. Albert Deutsch, *The Mentally Ill in America: A History of Their Care and Treatment from Colonial Times* (New York: Columbia Univ. Press, 1949), 137.

12. Lord, *Life and Times in Hopkinton,* 284.

13. Louis P. Masur, *Rites of Execution Capital Punishment and the Transformation of American Culture, 1776–1865* (New York: Oxford Univ. Press, 1989), 61. "Early History of the Death Penalty," https://death, penaltyinfo.org/ facts-and-research/history-of-the-death-penalty/early-history-of-the-death -penalty.

14. "Early History of the Death Penalty."
15. "Early History of the Death Penalty."
16. Masur, *Rites of Execution*, 78.
17. "Chronological History," https://www.nh.gov/nhdoc/chronological.html.
18. Masur, *Rites of Execution*, 82–83.
19. Martin J. Hershock, *A New England Prison Diary* (Ann Arbor: Univ. of Michigan Press, 2012), 136.
20. Hershock, *A New England Prison Diary*, 143.
21. Dartmouth College, Shattuck Observatory Meteorological Records, 1827–present [1853–1966], DA-9, Dartmouth College Library Special Collections, Dec. 1995. The handwritten weather records of Ebenezer Adams Sr. reveal that the first twelve days of January 1835 were bitterly cold.
22. Daniel Drayton, *Personal Memoirs of Daniel Drayton: Four Years and Four Months a Prisoner (For Charity's Sake) in Washington Jail* (Boston: Bela Marsh, 1853), 41.
23. Robert Mackenzie, *The Nineteenth Century: A History* (New York: Thomas Nelson & Sons, 1909), 80.
24. Mackenzie, *The Nineteenth Century*, 103.
25. Mackenzie, *The Nineteenth Century*, 105.
26. "Trial of Prescott for Murder," *Patriot*, Sept. 8, 1834.
27. "Robbery Trial," *Patriot*, Sept. 14, 1833.
28. Coffin, *Diary of a Farmer*.
29. Records of New Hampshire State Prison.
30. Lawson, "The Trial of Abraham Prescott," 749–50. All of the meeting at the prison is described on these pages.
31. Lawson, "The Trial of Abraham Prescott," 749.
32. Lawson, "The Trial of Abraham Prescott," 806.
33. "Fifth Amendment Activities *Miranda v. Arizona*," https://www.uscourts.gov/educational-resources/educational-activities/facts-and-case-summary-miranda-v-arizona.
34. "Fifth Amendment Activities *Miranda v. Arizona*."
35. Lawson, "The Trial of Abraham Prescott," 742.
36. Lawson, "The Trial of Abraham Prescott," 742.

7. THE PROSECUTION PRESENTS ITS CASE

1. United States Congress, "George Sullivan (id: S001052)," in *Biographical Directory of the United States Congress*, https://www.loc.gov/item/2003533078.
2. Natt Head, *Report of the Adjutant General of the State of New Hampshire for the Year Ending June 1, 1868* (Manchester, NH: John B. Clarke, Printer, 1868), 227.

3. James O. Lyford, ed., *History of Concord, New Hampshire from the Original Grant in Seventeen Hundred and Twenty-Five to the Opening of the Twentieth Century* (Concord, NH: Rumford Press, 1903), 719.

4. "Executions in the U.S. 1608–1972: The Espy File," https://deathpenalty info.org/executions/executions-overview/executions-in-the-u-s-1608–2002 -the-espy-file. In this list of executions by state, 1608 to 1972, New Hampshire is ranked forty-fourth.

5. Artemus Rogers and Henry B. Chase, *The Trial of Daniel Davis Farmer for the Murder of the Widow Anna Ayer at Goffstown on the 4th of April A. D. 1821* (Concord, NH: Hill and Moore, 1821), 21.

6. *Journal of the American Temperance Union* 10 (Sept. 1, 1846): 133, http://books.google.com/books?id=JspOAAAAYAAJ&pg=RA1-PA133&dq=an drew+howard+murdered+phebe+hanson&hl=en&sa=X&ei=5DKeUr6bGq_ MsQTkqYGIDw&ved=0CC8Q6AEwAA#v=onepage&q=andrew%20how ard%20murdered%20phebe%20hanson&f=false.

7. Duane Hamilton Hurd, *History of Merrimack and Belknap Counties, New Hampshire* (Philadelphia, PA: J. W. Lewis Co., 1885), 1.

8. Coffin, *Diary of a Farmer.*

9. "Sounding the North Church Bell," https://www.concordmonitor.com /vintage-views-north-church-bell-21963271.

10. Lawson, "The Trial of Abraham Prescott," 752. Attorney Peaselee called them "the vast numbers who have assembled."

11. Lawson, "The Trial of Abraham Prescott," 809.

12. "Trial of Prescott for Murder." *Patriot,* Sept. 8, 1834.

13. "Cylinder Cooking Stove," *Patriot,* Oct. 24, 1831.

14. All of this information regarding jurors comes from research on Ances-try.com and Familysearch.org.

15. "Religion and the Founding of the American Republic," https://www.loc .gov/exhibits/religion/re102.html.

16. Lawson, "The Trial of Abraham Prescott," 743.

17. Lawson, "The Trial of Abraham Prescott," 743–44.

18. Lawson, "The Trial of Abraham Prescott," 744.

19. Lawson, "The Trial of Abraham Prescott," 745.

20. Lawson, "The Trial of Abraham Prescott," 746.

21. "Murder," *Patriot,* July 1, 1833.

22. Lawson, "The Trial of Abraham Prescott," 747.

23. Lawson, "The Trial of Abraham Prescott," 747.

24. Lawson, "The Trial of Abraham Prescott," 749.

25. Terrie E. Moffitt, "Male Anti-social Behavior in Adolescence and Be-yond," *Nature Human Behavior* 2 (Feb. 2018): 7, https://www.ncbi.nlm.nih .gov/pmc/articles/PMC6157602/. Some of the behaviors exhibited by teens that psychiatry now associates with a tendency for future violence are: being

somewhat withdrawn and socially isolated; is easily influenced and yet victimized by peers; overindulging in alcohol; is inclined to dwell on past injustices in life; overreacts to criticism with a desire for revenge; is preoccupied with violent behavior; and is fascinated with potential weapons. Recent studies have shown that the type of antisocial behavior that persists into adulthood, resulting in the creation of "career criminals," begins in early childhood. These children exhibit problems with impulsivity, difficulty with verbal communication and understanding, and problems with inattention and executive function (the mental skills involved in managing oneself in order to complete tasks). They also score somewhat lower in intelligence tests than their peers who aren't exhibiting antisocial behavior. These problems are often first noted in infancy; infants who are hard to nurture may have subtle neurological deficits that predispose them to these later behavioral problems.

26. Lawson, "The Trial of Abraham Prescott," 750.

27. Joan Severa, *Dressed for the Photographer* (Kent, OH: Kent State Univ. Press, 1995), see photos on pp. 33, 49, 138, and 174.

28. Severa, *Dressed for the Photographer*, 10.

29. Lawson, "The Trial of Abraham Prescott," 750.

30. Today, Prescott's clothing would be analyzed for the pattern of blood spatter, which would provide a clearer picture of the positions of both assailant and victim during the attack. In 1834, all that could be discerned was that there was blood on his clothing.

31. R. K. Ressler and A. W. Burgess. "Crime Scene and Profile Characteristics of Organized and Disorganized Murders," *FBI Law Enforcement Bulletin* 54, no. 8 (Aug. 1985): 19. The FBI notes that the disorganized criminal "Acts spontaneously, targets people he or she knows, depersonalizes the victim, keeps conversation with victim to a minimum, creates a chaotic crime scene, attacks victim with sudden violence, does not use restraints, may have sex with corpse, leaves weapon and leaves a variety of evidence."

32. Lawson, "The Trial of Abraham Prescott," 750.

33. Lawson, "The Trial of Abraham Prescott," 751.

34. Kasserman, *Fall River Outrage*, 12.

35. Kasserman, *Fall River Outrage*, 144.

36. Kasserman, *Fall River Outrage*, 12.

37. Nylander, *Our Own Snug Fireside*, 39.

38. Severa, *Dressed for the Photographer*, 17, 99.

39. Lawson, "The Trial of Abraham Prescott," 751.

40. Lawson, "The Trial of Abraham Prescott," 751.

41. Lawson, "The Trial of Abraham Prescott," 751.

42. Charles Varle, *Moral Encyclopedia or Varle's Self-Instructor, No. 3* (New York: M'Elrath & Bangs, 1831), 295–98. For example, Varle spelled out a long abecedary list of "Rules of behavior for Young Ladies," which included "Avoid

everything masculine. . . . Be not too often seen in public . . . Boast not of your appetite, strength, &c., nor say anything that conveys an indelicate idea . . . Never deal in scandal . . . Pride yourself in modesty . . . Refrain from talking much." Many other behavioral guides reinforce these concepts of delicacy.

8. THE DEFENSE'S OPENING ARGUMENT

1. "Liberty versus Tyranny under the U.S. Constitution," https://sixth amendment.org/the-right-to-counsel/history-of-the-right-to-counsel/liberty -versus-tyranny/.

2. "Liberty versus Tyranny under the U.S. Constitution."

3. "The Story of the Scottsboro Boys in *Powell v. Alabama*," https://sixth amendment.org/the-right-to-counsel/history-of-the-right-to-counsel/the -story-of-the-scottsboro-boys/. That was just the beginning of a long legal ordeal for the young men. Even though one of the supposed rape victims later recanted her accusation, the teens were tried three more times, with the Supreme Court having to intervene a second time on their behalf. In 1937, the first four were released from prison after all charges were dropped. Five ultimately served long prison terms.

4. Susan Katcher, "Legal Training in the United States: A Brief History," https//hosted.law.wisc.edu>wordpress.wilj>files>20012/02>katcher.

5. "Bartlett, Ichabod," http://bioguide.congress.gov/scripts/biodisplay.pl ?index=B000205.

6. "Peaslee, Charles H. (1804–1866)," https://www.nhhistory.org/object /259855/peaslee-charles-hazen.

7. *Memorial Biographies of the New England Historical Genealogical Society*, vol. 6, *1864–1871* (Boston: New England Historical Genealogical Society, 1905), 188.

8. In 2010, the population of New Hampshire was 1,316,807, and there were 22 murders that year, or one for every 59,854 people. The population of New Hampshire in 1820 was 183,858 and the state was averaging only one murder every several years.

9. David Baker, *Women and Capital Punishment in the United States: An Analytical History* (Jefferson, NC: McFarland and Company, Inc., 2016), 78.

10. Rogers and Chase, *The Trial of Daniel Davis Farmer*, 3.

11. Nancy Hathaway Steenburg, *Children and the Criminal Law in Connecticut: Changing Perceptions of Childhood* (New York: Routledge, 2005), 74.

12. *Trial of Seth Elliot, Esq. for the Murder of His Son, John Wilson Elliot: Before the Supreme Judicial Court at Castine, October Term, 1824* (Belfast, ME: Fellowes and Simpson, 1824), 15, https://iiif.lib.harvard.edu/manifests/view /drs:5811332$60i.

13. *Trial of Seth Elliot,* 12.

14. *Trial of Seth Elliot,* 6.

15. *Trial of Seth Elliot,* 5.

16. *Trial of Seth Elliot,* 4.

17. *Trial of Seth Elliot,* 27. That led to a long discussion of whether or not bleeding was still considered an effective treatment for insanity. The defense argued that the book they cited, which advised bleeding as a treatment, was included in the library at nearby Bowdoin College and that that was prima facie evidence that it was a current and effective treatment.

18. *Trial of Seth Elliot,* 41, 42.

19. George A. Wheeler, *History of Castine, Penobscot and Brooksville, Maine* (Bangor, ME: Burr & Robinson, 1875), 174.

20. "Trial of Prescott for Murder," *Patriot,* Sept. 8, 1834.

21. Lawson, "The Trial of Abraham Prescott," 752.

22. Lawson, "The Trial of Abraham Prescott," 753.

23. Lawson, "The Trial of Abraham Prescott," 756.

24. Lawson, "The Trial of Abraham Prescott," 757.

25. Lawson, "The Trial of Abraham Prescott," 757–58.

26. Lawson, "The Trial of Abraham Prescott," 759.

27. An eminent barrister of the inner temple, *The Trial of James Hadfield for High Treason* (London: C. Barber, 1800), 4.

28. Joel Peter Eigen, *Witnessing Insanity: Madness and Mad-doctors in the English Court* (New Haven, CT: Yale Univ. Press, 1995), 49.

29. Sir William Oldnall Russell, *A Treatise on Crimes and Misdemeanors* (Boston: Wells and Lilly, 1824), 1:17.

30. "Trial of James Hadfield," https://books.google.com/books?id=NrVaAA AAcAAJ&printsec=frontcover&source=gbs_ge_summary_r&cad=0#v=onepage &q&f=false.

31. Edward Rowe Snow, *Women of the Sea* (Carlisle, MA: Commonwealth Editions, 2004), 60.

32. *American Railroad Journal and Advocate of Internal Improvements* 2, no. 19, New York (May 11, 1833): 13.

33. Lawson, "The Trial of Abraham Prescott," 760.

34. Lawson, "The Trial of Abraham Prescott, 766.

35. Lawson, "The Trial of Abraham Prescott," 766.

36. Lawson, "The Trial of Abraham Prescott," 769.

37. Lawson, "The Trial of Abraham Prescott," 768.

38. Lawson, "The Trial of Abraham Prescott," 769.

39. Lawson, "The Trial of Abraham Prescott," 771.

40. Lawson, "The Trial of Abraham Prescott," 772.

9. THE DEFENSE DISCUSSES SLEEPWALKING

1. "Sketch of the Life and Character of William M. Richardson, Extracted from a Charge Delivered to the Grand Jury of Cheshire County (N.H.) at the Last April Term of the Superior Court," *American Jurist and Law Magazine* 20, no. 39 (Oct. 1838): 120, https://search.proquest.com/openview/fe55ebofd 9096c212caa85a7a5c7395b/1?pq-origsite=gscholar&cbi=24511.

2. Joel Parker, *Report of the Trial of Daniel H. Corey on an Indictment for the Murder of Mrs. Matilda Nash at the Term of the Superior Court of Judicature Holden at Keene in the County of Cheshire on the First Tuesday of October 1830* (Newport, NH: French & Brown, 1830), 7.

3. *Proceedings of the American Academy of Arts and Sciences* 11 (May 1875–May 1876): 336–38.

4. Corey was then confined in the county jail for several years, but he escaped around 1836, quite possibly with the assistance of officials who were tired of paying to support the troublesome man. Accompanied by his remarkably loyal family, he relocated to upstate New York, where his mental illness quickly worsened to the degree that he was said to have been kept caged in the family home for nearly the rest of his life, dying in 1853.

5. Lawson, "The Trial of Abraham Prescott," 772.

6. Lawson, "The Trial of Abraham Prescott," 772.

7. Lawson, "The Trial of Abraham Prescott," 773.

8. Patrice Pinnel, "The Genesis of the Medical Field: France, 1795–1870," Dans *Revue française de sociologie* 52 (May 2011): 117.

9. Lawson, "The Trial of Abraham Prescott," 773.

10. Lawson, "The Trial of Abraham Prescott," 773.

11. John Abercrombie, MD, FRS, *Inquiries Concerning the Intellectual Powers, and the Investigation of Truth* (Boston: Otis, Broaders, and Company, 1841), 237, as quoted by Peaslee.

12. Dr. Benjamin Rush, *Medical Inquiries and Observations upon the Diseases of the Mind* (Philadelphia: Grigg and Elliot, 1835), 302.

13. Lawson, "The Trial of Abraham Prescott," 775.

14. Lawson, "The Trial of Abraham Prescott," 776.

15. Lawson, "The Trial of Abraham Prescott," 776. Sudhansu Chokroverty and Michael Billiard, eds., *Sleep Medicine: A Comprehensive Guide to Its Development, Clinical Milestones and Advances in Treatment* (New York: Springer Science and Business Media, 2015), 378.

16. Robert MacNish, *The Philosophy of Sleep,* (Glasgow: W. R. McPhun, 1834), 167.

17. Jeremiah Chaplin, *Life of Benjamin Franklin* (Boston: D. Lothrop & Co., 1876), 27.

18. Lawson, "The Trial of Abraham Prescott," 776.

19. Lawson, "The Trial of Abraham Prescott," 777.

20. Lawson, "The Trial of Abraham Prescott," 778.

21. Lawson, "The Trial of Abraham Prescott," 779.

22. "Case of Somnambulism," *Thomsonian Botanic Watchman*, Feb. 1, 1834.

23. "Case of Somnambulism." However, Peaslee was only slightly paraphrasing a tale that can be found in Walter Cooper Dendy, *A Philosophy of Mystery* (London: Longman, Orme, Brown, Green and Longman's, 1841), 315. Dendy cited *The Gazette of Augsburg* of the twentieth of an unnamed month or year, but clearly well before 1841, since Peaslee was quoting it in 1834. Dendy had a few previous publications in which the tale might have appeared. It was also quoted in other later nineteenth-century publications.

24. Lawson, "The Trial of Abraham Prescott," 780.

25. Dr. L. W. Belden, *An Account of Jane C. Rider* (Springfield, MA: G. & C. Merriam, 1834), 9.

26. Probably William, the only Rider on the 1830 census in Brattleboro, and his wife, who—tellingly—had died of "a disease of the brain."

27. Belden, *An Account of Jane C. Rider,* 30.

28. Three years previously she had suffered from chorea, involuntary movements that in the time before antibiotics were often a consequence of rheumatic fever, resulting from an untreated streptococcal infection. Or it's possible the movements may have been a symptom of a psychiatric disorder.

29. The Stebbins family and Dr. Belden became convinced that Rider could see clearly with her eyes closed, apparently part of the marvelousness of her condition, and conducted a series of experiments with coins, cards, and books that she was supposed to read. She cooperated nicely (in her sleeping state) and was able to read even the faintest things without opening her eyes. Dr. Belden participated in later experiments when he oversaw the covering of her eyes himself. He noticed that she would raise the cards with the writing up to a normal reading position, but that she couldn't read cards that were held before her with the print turned away from her. He didn't attach any great relevance to that observation, accepting the seemingly magical accomplishment at face value. Since her condition was receiving coverage in the New England press, crowds of people came to watch her perform. For Rider, formerly just a domestic servant, the fame must have been exhilarating. Even if she was—improbably—accomplishing all of her clever tricks while asleep, she still got to reap the benefits in her waking state.

Belden, ever credible, described on page after page the parlor tricks that she could successfully complete, all in the name of science. After her transfer to the Worcester institution, life became much less pleasant for Rider. She was treated with many popular therapies. Her feet were soaked in nitromuriatic acid almost every day, which she apparently found soothing as they had been habitually cold. She was also given tincture of guaiacum and tincture of sanguinaria, both herbal remedies, and the cure-all drug of the age, calomel, which was mercury and likely to cause long-term, devastating side effects at even low doses. These were all given "with the intention of affecting a secretion," but in case that wasn't sufficient, her head was shaved and she was periodically administered blisters: first to that "organ of marvelousness" on her head, but later to her arms and legs as well. Her diet was restricted to gruel, weak coffee, and porridge. With all of that "treatment" and near-constant retesting of her remarkable blind-reading skills, Rider stopped performing altogether and thus was considered to be well again.

30. Belden, *An Account of Jane C. Rider*, 65.

31. In Dec. 1837 in Springfield, George O. Kingsley of Peoria, IL, married Rider. She may have died shortly afterward. George, who was also born in Brattleboro, VT, returned to Peoria, where he married an Ohio girl, Fanny Eams, in Jan. 1841. There is no record of Rider's burial in the Kingsley plot.

32. Lawson, "The Trial of Abraham Prescott," 752.

10. THE AVERY CONNECTION

1. "Gregor Mendel, Botanist," https://www.britannica.com/biography/Gregor-Mendel.

2. Nancy Fix Anderson, "Cousin Marriage in Victorian England," *Journal of Family History* 11, no. 3 (Sept. 1, 1986): 285.

3. George Man Burrows, *Commentaries on the Causes, Forms, Symptoms and Treatment, Moral and Medical, of Insanity* (London: Thomas and George Underwood, 1828), 101.

4. Margaret, E. Derry, *Art and Science in Breeding: Creating Better Chickens* (Toronto: Univ. of Toronto Press, 2012), 21.

5. Lawson, "The Trial of Abraham Prescott," 783.

6. Lawson, "The Trial of Abraham Prescott," 784.

7. Kasserman, *Fall River Outrage*, 5.

8. David H. Ela, *A Vindication of the Result of the Trial of Rev. Ephraim K. Avery* (Boston: Russell, Odiorne and Co., 1834), 33.

9. Ulrich, *A Midwife's Tale*, 155.

10. Kasserman, *Fall River Outrage*, 213.

11. Among the fictional works are Mary Cable's *Avery's Knot* (New York: G. P. Putnam's Sons, 1981) and Raymond Paul's *The Tragedy at Tiverton* (New York: Ballantine Books, 1984). The nonfiction began in 1833 with Avery's own tome on the subject, but also include David Richard Kasserman's *Fall River Outrage: Life, Murder, and Justice in Early Industrial New England* (Philadelphia: Univ. of Pennsylvania Press, 1986) and Rory Raven's *Wicked Conduct: The Minister, the Mill Girl, and the Murder That Captivated Old Rhode Island* (Charleston, SC: History Press, 2009).

12. Lawson, "The Trial of Abraham Prescott," 784.

13. Lawson, "The Trial of Abraham Prescott," 785.

14. Lawson, "The Trial of Abraham Prescott," 785.

15. Lawson, "The Trial of Abraham Prescott," 785–86.

16. Lawson, "The Trial of Abraham Prescott," 786.

17. Lawson, "The Trial of Abraham Prescott," 786.

18. M. Cox et al., "Eighteenth and Nineteenth Century Dental Restoration and Treatment and Consequences in a British Nobleman," *British Dental Journal* 189 (Dec. 9, 2000), https://www.nature.com/articles/4800839.

19. Burrows, *Commentaries,* 345.

20. Rush, *Medical Inquiries,* 16, 13, 33.

21. Lawson, "The Trial of Abraham Prescott," 786.

22. "Trial of Prescott for Murder," *Patriot,* Sept. 15, 1834.

11. MENTAL ILLNESS IN THE PRESCOTT FAMILY

1. This was partially attributed, by the minister, to Caleb's terrible upbringing and partly to the fact that in the same town eight years previously, a twelve-year-old African American slave named Anne had murdered her owner's five-year-old daughter, Martha Clark, when the child annoyed her, and that Adams certainly knew of this crime. It didn't help, no doubt, that Anne was lashed, branded, and imprisoned for the rest of her life—but not executed, which might have offered a better warning to Adams.

2. "Appendix," http://www.calebadams.org/appendix.htm.

3. Elijah Waterman, "A Sermon, Preached at Windham, November 29th, 1803, Being the Day of the Execution of Caleb Adams for the Murder of Oliver Woodworth," http://www.calebadams.org/sermon.htm.

4. Ancestry.com.

5. Lawson, "The Trial of Abraham Prescott," 786.

6. Abraham Sr. was the father of three daughters: Abigail, born 1742; Ann, born 1744; and Sally, his last child, born 1766. Which of his daughters Mary is referring to is unknown.

7. Lawson, "The Trial of Abraham Prescott," 787.

8. Abraham Prescott had a son, Abraham Jr., born Aug. 3, 1748. That Abraham (who had a brother, Benjamin) married Hannah Crum and they were the parents, it is believed, of four children: Sally, Benjamin, Polly, and Abraham, born July 5, 1789. Abraham Jr. is thought to have died Mar. 15, 1815, so, if true, he was not the Abraham testifying.

9. Lawson, "The Trial of Abraham Prescott," 787.

10. Hannah's identity is also questionable. John Huntoon Jr. and Elizabeth Beede are credited by some genealogists with having two sons with similar names, Elijah, born in 1768, and Elisha, born in 1771. Elijah is said to have mar-

ried Hannah French, born Aug. 30, 1788, in 1805, and Elisha to have married Hannah Worthen, born Mar. 17, 1772, in 1788. Since Hannah Huntoon testified in 1834 that she had worked for Sally Prescott about forty years previously, if the Elijah/Elisha information is correct, it seems likely that the "right" Hannah would be Hannah Worthen Huntoon, who would have been aged about twenty-two rather than Hannah French Huntoon, who would have been only about six years old around 1794. Hannah French Huntoon was the mother of eight children in 1834 and lived until 1850. Hannah Worthen Huntoon was the mother of five children and died in 1854.

11. Lawson, "The Trial of Abraham Prescott," 788.
12. Lawson, "The Trial of Abraham Prescott," 788.
13. Lawson, "The Trial of Abraham Prescott," 789.
14. Lawson, "The Trial of Abraham Prescott," 789.
15. Moffitt, "Male Antisocial Behavior," 9.
16. Lawson, "The Trial of Abraham Prescott," 789.
17. Lawson, "The Trial of Abraham Prescott," 790.
18. C. B. Cosby, "James Currie and Hydrotherapy, 286.
19. Nylander, *Our Own Snug Fireside*, 144.
20. Even at the end of the nineteenth century, it was possible to buy from the major retail catalogs a "flesh brush" intended for dry cleaning the skin. The *electric* flesh brush took this one stage further; it promised to clean and also cure a variety of diseases, aches, and pains.
21. Lawson, "The Trial of Abraham Prescott," 790.

12. THE PHYSICIANS BEGIN THEIR TESTIMONY

1. "University of Pennsylvania School of Medicine: A Brief History," www .archives.upenn.edu>histy>features>schools>med.
2. J. Bailey Moore, *History of the Town of Candia, Rockingham County, New Hampshire from Its First Settlement to the Present Time* (Manchester, NH: G. W. Browne, 1893), 107.
3. *Records of the New Hampshire Medical Society from Its Organization in 1791 to the Year 1854* (Concord, NH: Rumford Printing Co., 1911), 178. This alienation from his contemporaries may have been one motivating factor in the move he made in 1826 from Deerfield, New Hampshire, to the city of Lowell, Massachusetts, where he opened a medical practice that he later shared with his son. Here there would be more than enough patients to go around. It would also be far easier and less risky to obtain fresh corpses in a metropolitan area.
4. Linda Gordon, *The Moral Property of Women: A History of Birth Control in America* (Urbana: Univ. of Illinois Press, 1974), 27–28.

5. Charles Cowley, *A History of Lowell, Massachusetts* (Boston: Lee & Shepard, 1868), 75.

6. "Descendants of William Graves," http://sites.rootsweb.com/~nhcsandw/Bios/w_graves.html.

7. "Sanford Mason American 1798–1862," http://www.artnet.com/artists/sanford-mason/portrait-of-dr-william-graves-of-lowell-Lmh5B1rtvy31SX7uRyAomw2.

8. Lawson, "The Trial of Abraham Prescott," 790.

9. Lawson, "The Trial of Abraham Prescott," 791.

10. Lawson, "The Trial of Abraham Prescott," 791.

11. "William Graves," https://www.ancestrylibrary.com.

12. Diary of Thomas Coffin.

13. Eric T. Carlson and Lay F. Chale, "Dr. Rufus Wyman and the McLean Asylum," *American Journal of Psychiatry* 116, no. 1 (May 1960): 1034.

14. S. Olson and D. R. Gerstein, "Alcohol in America: *Taking Action to Prevent Abuse*" (Washington, DC: National Academies Press, 1985), 1. In the 1830s, the average adult consumption was about 7 gallons of pure alcohol per year; today it is estimated to be about 2.4 gallons per year. W. J. Rorabaugh reports that the consumption of distilled spirits in 1830 reached about 5 gallons per person, but that drinkers also consumed about 15 gallons of hard cider. He caps pure alcohol consumption at a more modest 4 gallons per year. W. J. Rorabaugh, *The Alcoholic Republic: An American Tradition* (Oxford: Oxford Univ. Press, 1979), 8–10.

15. Carlson and Chale, "Dr. Rufus Wyman," 1037.

16. Morrill Wyman, *A Brief Record of the Lives and Writings of Dr. Rufus Wyman and His Son Dr. Morrill Wyman* (Cambridge, MA: Riverside Press, 1908), 10.

17. Lawson, "The Trial of Abraham Prescott," 792.

18. Lawson, "The Trial of Abraham Prescott," 793.

19. Lawson, "The Trial of Abraham Prescott," 793.

20. Lawson, "The Trial of Abraham Prescott," 794.

21. Lawson, "The Trial of Abraham Prescott," 794.

22. Lawson, "The Trial of Abraham Prescott," 794.

23. Lawson, "The Trial of Abraham Prescott," 795.

13. MORE PHYSICIANS FOR THE DEFENSE

1. "Murder at Harvard: Dr. George Parkman (c. 1790–1849)," https://www.pbs.org/wgbh/americanexperience/features/murder-dr-george-parkman/.

2. Paul Collins, *Blood & Ivy: The 1849 Murder That Scandalized Harvard* (New York: W. W. Norton & Co., 2018), 44. It was that strong focus on money

that would lead to his murder by a Harvard chemistry professor, John White Webster, who, having lived above his financial station for years, was deeply in debt to him. Parkman may have been pressuring Webster to repay. After luring Parkman to his laboratory at Harvard on Nov. 23, 1849, White murdered him. A reward was offered for help in finding the missing Parkman. Later, White was observed by a curious janitor carrying a mysterious bundle, and since Parkman was known to have planned to visit the laboratory, police searched it. The janitor, who lived in the building and had plenty of opportunity to investigate, thought that the chemist tried to keep police away from his privy. From another cellar room, the determined and apparently quite suspicious janitor later drilled into the walls of the privy and found body parts there. Webster was eventually convicted—after the judge instructed the jury that they "must" find him guilty—and executed. The highly sensational case was intensively covered by the press. One of the reasons that this murder commanded so much attention is that both the victim and the murderer were gentlemen, among Boston's poshest residents. That made Webster's crime all the more unseemly and entertaining.

3. Lawson, "The Trial of Abraham Prescott," 795.

4. Lawson, "The Trial of Abraham Presccott," 795.

5. "Trial of Prescott for Murder," *Patriot,* Sept. 15, 1834.

6. Lawson, "The Trial of Abraham Prescott," 796.

7. Ancestry.com.

8. Lawson, "The Trial of Abraham Prescott," 796–97.

9. George Chandler, *The Chandler Family: The Descendants of William and Annis Chandler Who Settled in Roxbury, Mass.* (Worcester, MA: Press of Charles Hamilton, 1883), 588.

10. A native of Jaffrey, NH, born in 1787, Cutter was educated at Yale and opened a medical practice in 1818 and then a mental hospital in Pepperell in about 1819.

11. Lawson, "The Trial of Abraham Prescott," 797.

12. Lawson, "The Trial of Abraham Prescott," 797.

13. Lawson, "The Trial of Abraham Prescott," 798.

14. Lawson, "The Trial of Abraham Prescott," 799.

15. Lawson, "The Trial of Abraham Prescott," 799.

16. Rudolf Pintner, "Feeblemindedness," in *A Handbook of Child Psychology* (Worcester, MA: Clark Univ. Press, 1930), 587.

17. For example, the Constitution of the State of Mississippi, in spelling out voting rights, begins, "Every inhabitant of this state, except idiots and insane persons, who is a citizen of the United States of America," http://www.sos .state.ms.us/ed_pubs/constitution/constitution.asp.

18. Lawson, "The Trial of Abraham Prescott," 799.

19. Lawson, "The Trial of Abraham Prescott," 800.

20. Ancestry.com.

21. Lawson, "The Trial of Abraham Prescott," 800.

22. Lawson, "The Trial of Abraham Prescott," 800.

14. THE PROSECUTION REBUTS

1. Lawson, "The Trial of Abraham Prescott," 800.

2. Lawson, "The Trial of Abraham Prescott," 800.

3. Lawson, "The Trial of Abraham Prescott," 801.

4. Lawson, "The Trial of Abraham Prescott," 801.

5. Lawson, "The Trial of Abraham Prescott," 802.

6. Lawson, "The Trial of Abraham Prescott," 802.

7. Lawson, "The Trial of Abraham Prescott," 803.

8. Lawson, "The Trial of Abraham Prescott," 803.

9. Lawson, "The Trial of Abraham Prescott," 803.

10. Lawson, "The Trial of Abraham Prescott," 803.

11. Lawson, "The Trial of Abraham Prescott," 803.

12. Lawson, "The Trial of Abraham Prescott," 803.

13. Lawson, "The Trial of Abraham Prescott," 804.

14. Lawson, "The Trial of Abraham Prescott," 804.

15. In a review of literature related to the predictive value of previous behavior, Chaiken, Chaiken, and Rhodes noted, "Children who throw heavy or sharp objects at their parents are likely to hit their siblings or peers and to lie, set fires, and be truant from school." Jan Chaiken, Marcia Chaiken, and William Rhodes, "Predicting Violent Behavior and Classifying Violent Offenders," *Understanding and Preventing Violence*, vol. 4, Commission on Behavioral and Social Sciences and Education (Washington, DC: National Academy Press, 1994).

16. Lawson, "The Trial of Abraham Prescott," 804.

17. Lawson, "The Trial of Abraham Prescott," 804.

18. Since all the people who describe Prescott and mention his eyes use the phrase "a downcast eye," do they mean that only *one* of his eyes was downcast? The 1828 edition of Noah Webster's *American Dictionary of the English Language* defined *downcast:* "a. Cast downward; directed to the ground; as a downcast eye or look, indicating bashfulness, modesty or dejection of mind." It seems that both of Prescott's eyes were typically focused downward.

19. Lawson, "The Trial of Abraham Prescott," 804.

20. Lawson, "The Trial of Abraham Prescott," 804.

21. Lawson, "The Trial of Abraham Prescott," 805.

22. Lawson, "The Trial of Abraham Prescott," 805.

23. Lawson, "The Trial of Abraham Prescott," 806.

24. Lawson, "The Trial of Abraham Prescott," 806.
25. Lawson, "The Trial of Abraham Prescott," 806.
26. Lawson, "The Trial of Abraham Prescott," 806.
27. Lawson, "The Trial of Abraham Prescott," 807.

15. THE DEFENSE BEGINS ITS CLOSING ARGUMENT

1. Kasserman, *Fall River Outrage*, 135, 210.
2. Nathan Kilbourn Abbot, *Diaries 1824–1874*, New Hampshire Historical Society collection, 1986–2012. In this diary, Abbot spells out, year after year, nearly all of his farm tasks, the dates he began them and when he finished. It's a fascinating, pragmatic look at managing a small, mixed New England farm.
3. *State v. Prescott*, 7 N.H. (1834), 289.
4. Lawson, "The Trial of Abraham Prescott," 808.
5. Lawson, "The Trial of Abraham Prescott," 812.
6. Lawson, "The Trial of Abraham Prescott," 817.
7. Masur, *Rites of Execution*, 94.
8. "Index by State—Pennsylvania—1801–1900," https://deathpenaltyusa.org /usa1/state/pennsylvania2.htm.
9. Lawson, "The Trial of Abraham Prescott," 818.
10. Lawson, "The Trial of Abraham Prescott," 819.
11. Lawson, "The Trial of Abraham Prescott," 822.
12. Masur, *Rites of Execution*, 95–96.
13. Lawson, "The Trial of Abraham Prescott," 823.
14. Georget (1795–1828) had made himself rather famous in France for his strong arguments that monomania, a form of insanity that was evidenced only under certain particular circumstances in a patient who otherwise appeared normal, was a probable factor in many serious crimes, and that in these cases it would be necessary to have a psychiatrist available in the courtroom to provide medical information. Many in France, especially in the judiciary, felt that Georget was providing a too-easy excuse for most serious crimes. Georget commissioned a French artist, Theodore Gericault, to paint ten portraits of various men and women who were incarcerated in asylums to demonstrate the apparently readily identifiable faces of mental illness. Of these, five moving portraits remain.
15. Sir John Nicholl, *A Report on the Judgment in Dew v. Clark and Clark*, ed. John Haggart (London: A. Strahan, 1826), 88.
16. Nicholl, *A Report*, 88.
17. Horace W. Fuller, ed., *The Green Bag: An Entertaining Magazine for Lawyers* (Boston: Boston Book Company, 1897), 9:436.
18. Lawson, "The Trial of Abraham Prescott," 826.

19. James Johnson, MD, ed., *The Medico-Chiurical Review and Journal of Practical Medicine* (New York: Richard & George S. Wood, 1831), 14:254.

20. Lawson, "The Trial of Abraham Prescott," 827.

21. Lawson, "The Trial of Abraham Prescott," 828.

22. Lawson, "The Trial of Abraham Prescott," 828.

23. Lawson, "The Trial of Abraham Prescott," 830.

24. Lawson, "The Trial of Abraham Prescott," 831.

25. Lawson, "The Trial of Abraham Prescott," 831.

26. Lawson, "The Trial of Abraham Prescott," 833.

27. Lawson, "The Trial of Abraham Prescott," 833.

28. Lawson, "The Trial of Abraham Prescott," 833.

29. Lawson, "The Trial of Abraham Prescott," 834.

30. Lawson, "The Trial of Abraham Prescott," 835.

31. Lawson, "The Trial of Abraham Prescott," 836.

32. Lawson, "The Trial of Abraham Prescott," 836.

33. Severa, *Dressed for the Photographer,* 10.

34. "Livor Mortis," https://www.sciencedirect.com/topics/medicine-and-dentistry/livor-mortis.

35. Judith Flanders, *The Invention of Murder* (New York: St. Martin's Press, 2013), 237. Flanders says, "to be convicted of murder was one thing; to have relays of the well-meaning pressing endlessly for a confession must have been like being pecked to death by beady-eyed fowl. Confessions were an integral part of the emotional narrative of trial, conviction and execution. For much of the first half of the [nineteenth] century, confession was seen in its religious aspect: the sinner repented, and was therefore, after an earthly punishment, forgiven by a beneficent God."

16. CLOSING ARGUMENTS CONCLUDE

1. Edwin M. Borchard, *Convicting the Innocent, Errors of Criminal Justice* (New Haven, CT: Yale Univ. Press, 1932), 15–22. Primary sources were *Trial of Stephen and Jesse Boorn for the Murder of Russel Colvin* (Rutland, VT: Fay & Burt, 1820), and Honorable Leonard Sargeant, *The Trial, Confessions and Conviction of Jesse and Stephen Boorn for the Murder of Russel Colvin and the Return of the Man Supposed to Have Been Murdered* (Manchester, VT: Journal Book and Job Office, 1873). That author was the Boorn brothers' defense counsel and thus had intimate familiarity with the details of the case.

2. Borchard, *Convicting the Innocent,* 20.

3. Gerald McFarland, *The Counterfeit Man: The True Story of the Boorn-Colvin Murder Case* (New York: Pantheon Books, 1990), 183.

4. Lawson, "The Trial of Abraham Prescott," 839.

5. Lawson, "The Trial of Abraham Prescott," 841.

6. Lawson, "The Trial of Abraham Prescott," 843.

7. Lawson, "The Trial of Abraham Prescott," 845.

8. Lawson, "The Trial of Abraham Prescott," 851.

9. "Trial of Prescott for Murder," *Patriot,* Sept. 15, 1834.

10. Lawson, "The Trial of Abraham Prescott," 856.

11. Lawson, "The Trial of Abraham Prescott," 856.

12. Lawson, "The Trial of Abraham Prescott," 857.

13. Lawson, "The Trial of Abraham Prescott," 857.

14. Lawson, "The Trial of Abraham Prescott," 859

15. Lawson, "The Trial of Abraham Prescott," 859.

16. Lawson, "The Trial of Abraham Prescott," 860.

17. Lawson, "The Trial of Abraham Prescott," 860.

18. Lawson, "The Trial of Abraham Prescott," 863.

19. Lawson, "The Trial of Abraham Prescott," 864.

20. Lawson, "The Trial of Abraham Prescott," 867.

21. Lawson, "The Trial of Abraham Prescott," 868.

22. Lawson, "The Trial of Abraham Prescott," 871.

23. Lawson, "The Trial of Abraham Prescott," 869.

24. Lawson, "The Trial of Abraham Prescott," 870.

25. Lawson, "The Trial of Abraham Prescott," 872–73.

26. Lawson, "The Trial of Abraham Prescott," 873.

27. Lawson, "The Trial of Abraham Prescott," 874.

28. Lawson, "The Trial of Abraham Prescott," 875–76.

29. Lawson, "The Trial of Abraham Prescott," 876.

30. Lawson, "The Trial of Abraham Prescott," 877.

31. Lawson, "The Trial of Abraham Prescott," 882.

32. In fact, the word *intercourse* was first used in reference to coitus in 1798. In 1804, the same Dr. Abernathy whom Peaslee had so often quoted used it again in that way in *Surgical Obstetrics.* It's probable that Sullivan's use of the word may have had a broader definition than either coitus or the more common usage of *communication*—almost any sexual touching as well as a sexual proposition would have fit into the category of *criminal intercourse. Oxford English Dictionary* (Oxford: Clarendon Press, 1933), 5:390.

33. Lawson, "The Trial of Abraham Prescott," 882.

34. Lawson, "The Trial of Abraham Prescott," 884.

17. VERDICT AND RETRIAL

1. Lawson, "The Trial of Abraham Prescott," 889.

2. Lawson, "The Trial of Abraham Prescott," 886.

3. Lawson, "The Trial of Abraham Prescott," 887.

4. Lawson, "The Trial of Abraham Prescott," 890.

5. Lawson, "The Trial of Abraham Prescott," 891.

6. D. Hack True, MD, LLD, *A Dictionary of Psychological Medicine* (London: J. & A. Churchill, 1892), 302.

7. Lawson, "The Trial of Abraham Prescott," 893–94.

8. Lawson, "The Trial of Abraham Prescott," 833; "The Defence of Insanity in Criminal Cases," *The Law Journal* (Nov. 22, 1884): 702, https://books.google.com/books?id=pltNAQAAMAAJ&pg=PA702&lpg=PA702&dq=a+spe cies+of+insanity+which+can+excuse+any+person&source=bl&ots=GUPDXS wRbP&sig=ACfU3U18dnmH4ojjQiGDwHoO4PVnaVWOTw&hl=en&sa=X &ved=2ahUKEwj8xvvdoqnoAhWDj3IEHR-kCjcQ6AEwCnoECAoQA Q#v=onepage&q=a%20species%20of%20insanity%20which%20can%20ex cuse%20any%20person&f=false.

9. *State v. Prescott, 7 N. H.* (1834), 287–89. All of the jurors' movements that violated their sequestration were described in the trial record of Prescott's appeal.

10. Conrad Reno, "Nathaniel Gookin Upham," *Memoirs of the Judiciary and the Bar of New England for the Nineteenth Century* (Boston: Century Memorial Publishing Co., 1901), 1:64–65.

11. Daniel J. Noyes, DD, *Memoir of Nathaniel Gookin Upham Read at the Annual Meeting of the New Hampshire Historical Society, June 14, 1871* (1871), 8, https://archive.org/stream/memoirofnathanieoonoye/memoirofnathanie oonoye_djvu.txt.

12. His photograph appears as the frontispiece in the Noyes memoir.

13. Ancestry.com.

14. "Capital Trial," *Patriot*, Sept. 14, 1835, is the sole source for coverage of the second trial. Although lacking the depth of the published trial record of 1834, it was still extensive, filing an entire page of the newspaper.

15. "Capital Trial," *Patriot*, Sept. 14, 1835.

16. "Capital Trial."

17. "Conviction of Prescott," *Kennebunk Gazette and Maine Palladium*, Sept. 26, 1835.

18. "Capital Trial."

19. "Dr. Samuel B. Woodward: A 19th Century Pioneer in Psychiatric Care," https://escholarship.umassmed.edu/lib_postpres/5/.

20. "Capital Trial."

21. *Report of the Trial of Abraham Prescott for the Murder of Mrs. Sally Cochran, of Pembroke, June 23, 1833. Executed at Hopkinton, January 6, 1836* (Manchester, NH: Daily Mirror Office, 1869), 31.

22. *Report of the Trial of Abraham Prescott*, 41.

23. *Report of the Trial of Abraham Prescott*, 43.

18. REPRIEVE, RIOTS, AND EXECUTION

1. "Prescott," *Patriot,* Dec. 28, 1835.

2. Mary Ann Jimenez, *Changing Faces of Madness: Early American Attitudes and Treatment of the Insane* (Hanover, NH: Univ. Press of New England, 1987), 79.

3. Jimenez, *Changing Faces of Madness,* 81.

4. Daniel A. Cohen, *Pillars of Salt, Monuments of Grace: New England Crime Literature and the Origins of Popular Culture, 1674–1860* (New York: Oxford Univ. Press, 1993), 29.

5. Lapping, *Long, Deep Furrow,* 197.

6. Lapping, *Long, Deep Furrow,* 197.

7. Jonathan Simon and Richard Sparks, eds., *The SAGE Handbook of Punishment and Society* (Thousand Oaks, CA: Sage Publications, Inc., 2013), 313.

8. "Reprieve of Prescott," *Patriot,* Dec. 21, 1835.

9. Masur, *Rites of Execution,* 19–20. Although it occurred during a rainstorm in 1849 within the prison yard, a huge, rowdy crowd gathered in hopes of getting a glimpse of the death of Washington Goode in Boston.

10. David Grimsted, *American Mobbing 1828–1861* (New York: Oxford Univ. Press, 1998), 3–4. It came in a season of riots, if there is such a thing. Under the influence of Jacksonian democracy, 1834 and 1835 saw a sharp rise in mob violence all across the country.

11. Lord, *Life and Times,* 131.

12. "The Execution of Abraham Prescott," *Maine Democrat,* Jan. 27, 1836.

13. "Prescott," *Patriot,* Dec. 28, 1835.

14. "Execution of Abraham Prescott," *Maine Democrat,* Jan. 27, 1836.

15. "Execution of Abraham Prescott," *Maine Democrat.*

16. "Execution of Abraham Prescott," *Maine Democrat.*

17. "Execution of Abraham Prescott," *Maine Democrat.*

18. "Execution of Abraham Prescott," *Maine Democrat.*

19. "Execution of Abraham Prescott," *Patriot,* Jan. 11, 1836.

20. Lawson, "The Trial of Abraham Prescott," 901.

21. "Execution of Abraham Prescott," *Maine Democrat.*

22. Lawson, "The Trial of Abraham Prescott," 901.

23. Lawson, "The Trial of Abraham Prescott," 902.

24. "Execution of Abraham Prescott," *Patriot,* Jan. 14, 1836.

19. NEW HAMPSHIRE'S NEED FOR AN ASYLUM

1. *Report of the Trial of Abraham Prescott for the Murder of Mrs. Sally Cochran, of Pembroke June 23, 1833. Executed at Hopkinton, January 6, 1836,* 43.

2. *Memorial Biographies of the New England Historical Genealogical Society,* vol. 6, 1864–1871 (Boston: New England Historical Genealogical Society, 1905), 191.

3. Laurel Thatcher Ulrich, "Derangement in the Family: The Story of Mary Sewall, 1824–1825," in *Medicine and Healing* (Boston, MA: The Dublin Seminar for New England Folklife Annual Proceedings, 1990), 173. This is the source for all of Mary's story.

4. Ulrich, "Derangement in the Family," 170.

5. Gerald N. Grob, *The Mad Among Us: A History of the Care of America's Mentally Ill* (New York: The Free Press, 1994), 17.

6. Peter Sturmey, *Reducing Restraint and Restrictive Management Practices* (Basel, Switzerland: Springer International Publishing, 2015), 74.

7. Sturmey, *Reducing Restraint,* 75.

8. Grob, *Mad Among Us,* 25.

9. Grob, *Mad Among Us,* 25.

10. Grob, *Mad Among Us,* 36.

11. *Sixth Annual Report of the Board of Managers of the Prison Discipline Society* (Boston, MA: Perkins & Marvin, 1832), 9.

12. Henry Mills Hurd et al., *Institutional Care of the Insane in the United States and Canada* (Baltimore, MD: The Johns Hopkins Press, 1916), 30.

13. Paul Shagoury, "History of Psychiatric Hospitals," https://www.dhhs .nh.gov/dcbcs/nhh/history1.htm.

14. "Concord State Hospital," http://www.asylumprojects.org/index.php /Concord_State_Hospital.

15. *Report Made to the Legislature of New Hampshire on the Subject of the Insane, June Session 1836* (Concord, NH: Cyrus Barton, Printer, 1836), 10.

16. *Journal of the House of Representatives of the State of New Hampshire at Their Session Holden at the Capitol in Concord Commencing June 1, 1836* (Concord, NH: William White, 1836), 221.

17. "Concord State Hospital."

18. Shagoury, *History.*

19. Seemingly, his design was viewed as a success since not long afterward he was engaged to design the main building of the State Manual Labor School in Westborough, Massachusetts, a reform school for boys that would later become an insane asylum as well.

20. THE SLEEPWALKING DEFENSE EVOLVES

1. Daniel A. Cohen, "The Murder of Maria Bickford: Fashion, Passion, and the Birth of a Consumer Culture," *American Studies* 31 (1990): 20.

2. Shortly after her murder, a "friend of her youth," who claimed to be a minister from Brunswick, Maine, and who was coyly identified only by his

initials, published a collection of letters she supposedly sent to a variety of people. These included both a young man, Theodore Maxwell, who was from Georgia, with whom she engaged in a passionate and highly literary exchange of letters, and also an attorney from Eastport, Maine. Oddly, the collection includes all of her letters to Theodore, but none that he sent to her, so it seems strange that she would have in her possession the letters she had sent, and be able to pass them onto the Eastport attorney, as the editor of the collection claimed. *The Early Love Letters and Later Literary Remains of Maria Bickford: Murdered in Boston, October 25th, 1845. Edited by a Friend of Her Youth* (Boston, MA: Silas Estabrook, 1846), http://reader.library.cornell.edu/docviewer/digital?id=sat:1907#page/1/mode/1up. Except her future husband, none of the people named in the letters, nor the minister/editor of the collection, could be found on census records, making it possible that many letters, or perhaps the entire volume, was a fabrication, reflective of the evolution of the earlier gallows confession pamphlet into a biographical (if mostly imagined) narrative. The flowery, highly literate letters seem unlikely to have been penned by a young woman who grew up poor and was probably only marginally educated. A second set of literary letters, supposedly exchanged between Maria and her husband, James Bickford, were published by him (the pamphlet claimed) in 1846. These letters vividly depicted her wicked fall from grace and his earnest, kindly, and unending attempts to bring her home and restore her good name. That pamphlet had the added merit of providing a moralistic tale.

3. *The Early Love Letters*, 10.

4. *The Early Love Letters*, 6.

5. Daniel A. Cohen, *Pillars of Salt, Monuments of Grace: New England Crime Literature and the Origins of Popular Culture, 1674–1860* (New York: Oxford Univ. Press, 1993), and his shorter work, "The Murder of Maria Bickford: Fashion, Passion, and the Birth of Consumer Culture," *American Studies* 31 (1990): 5–30, are the sources for nearly all the information regarding the murder of Maria Bickford.

6. "The Murder of Maria Bickford," 10.

7. Cohen, "The Murder of Maria Bickford," 10.

8. He had traveled to Montreal, planning to board a ship for England, which later turned back to New York due to stormy weather. There, he boarded a steamboat, the *Sultana,* for New Orleans, where he was finally arrested and charged with Bickford's murder. This was not the same *Sultana* that would famously explode on the Mississippi River in 1865 and kill about seventeen hundred Civil War soldiers returning home at the war's end.

9. Cohen, "The Murder of Maria Bickford," 15.

10. Cohen, *Pillars of Salt*, 219.

11. Simeon L. Crockett, *A Voice from Leverett Street Prison, or, The Life, Trial and Confession of Simeon L. Crockett, Who Was Executed for Arson, March 16, 1836,* 3rd ed. (Boston, MA: Printed for the Proprietors, [1836?]),

http://nrs.harvard.edu/urn-3:FHCL:3899540. Simeon Crockett, aged twenty-six, and Stephen Russell, twenty-seven, were both out of work. Crockett seems to have abandoned months earlier both his wife and old style of life in Bangor, Maine, and Russell, a drifter, never had done much anyway. Discovering an advertisement for carpenters needed to repair a tenement, they began work on the near-derelict building that nonetheless still housed between twenty-five and thirty mostly Irish immigrant families in desperate squalor. After working on the building for about six weeks, the pair was supposedly heartily disgusted with the immigrants' living conditions. On October 22, 1835, after a night of heavy drinking, they resolved to do something about the situation. Unfortunately, in their inebriated state, they lit the all-wooden, ramshackle structure on fire in what they thought was a humanitarian gesture. Although it was the dead of night and the building burned remarkably fast, somehow the nearly 130 individuals who lived there managed to escape, but lost what few worldly possessions they owned.

Since they had been spotted at the building, police had no difficulty identifying them as the arsonists. They were quickly arrested and tried. Although Russell didn't have much to say about his reason for the crime, Crockett fully attributed his behavior to alcohol. A jailhouse confession in his own hand read:

> I now under a deep sense of my situation, wright a few lines to leave on earth, after I leave the world in memore of me, while my spiret is gone into the world of spirots ... No wonder so many Crimes are Comited with the drunkard when his brains is boiled in gin, rum and brandy, when the natural man has fled and rum and brandy has changed a man in to a beast, and destroys the finest works of nature ... The RETAILERS are no more Guiltles than the men that drinks it. I feel to render the most tender and piteful feelings towards sutch people.

12. Kathleen J. Burns, "A Chronicle of the Death Penalty in Massachusetts: Part One," *Lawyers Journal* (Jan. 1999), www.nodp.org/ma/stacks/Chronicle.doc. It was not until 1852 that Massachusetts abolished the death penalty as the punishment for arson, treason, and rape.

13. Around 1850, Bickford's body was exhumed, according to Massachusetts death records, and returned to Maine. Her final resting place is unknown. Her long-suffering husband, who remained a seemingly loyal presence in her short life and who testified against Tirrell, remained in Newburgh through 1860, living very modestly and unmarried. After that, he disappeared from public records.

14. Matthew J. Wolf-Meyer, "Sleepwalking Killers and What They Tell Us About Sleep," *Psychology Today* (Dec. 13, 2012), https://www.psychologytoday.com/us/blog/day-in-day-out/201212/sleepwalking-killers-and-what-they-tell-us-about-sleep.

15. This man may have been Wilson Fain, a young farmer in District Four of Jessamine County, Kentucky.

16. "Fain v. Commonwealth," www.kentlaw.edu/faculty/rwarner/classes/ carter/ . . . kentucky_com.

17. William Seabrook, "Jury Acquits Girl Who Slew in Her Sleep," *World's News,* May 6, 1944.

18. Rosalind Cartwright, "Sleepwalking Violence: A Sleep Disorder, a Legal Dilemma, and a Psychological Challenge," *American Journal of Psychiatry* 161, no. 7 (July 2004): 1149–58.

19. Mike Horn, "A Rude Awakening: What to Do with the Sleepwalking Defense?" *Boston College Law Review* 46 (Dec. 1, 2004): 165.

20. Horn, "A Rude Awakening."

21. Shreeya Popat and William Winslade, "While You Were Sleeping: Science and Neurobiology of Sleep Disorders and the Enigma of Legal Responsibility of Violence During Parasomnia," *Neuroethics* 8, no. 2 (2015): 203.

22. Popat and Winslade, "While You Were Sleeping," 208.

23. Most information regarding the Falater murder comes from "Sleepwalking Killer Gets a Wake-up Call," https://forensicfilesnow.com/index.php /tag/scott-falater/.

24. "Sleepwalking Killer Gets a Wake-up Call."

25. "Sleepwalking Killer Gets a Wake-up Call."

26. "Sleepwalking Killer Gets a Wake-up Call."

27. "Sleepwalking Killer Gets a Wake-up Call."

28. "Sleepwalking Killer Gets a Wake-up Call."

21. THE INSANITY PLEA

1. Even by 1869, when the trial record was reissued, Prescott was depicted with pathos.

2. P. Holmes Reed, "Insanity as a Defence in Criminal Law," Historical Theses and Dissertations Collection, Cornell Law Library, Scholarship@ Cornell Law: A Digital Repository, 1895, 3, https://scholarship.law.cornell. edu/historical_theses/index.3.html.

3. Reed, "Insanity as a Defence," 3.

4. Reed, "Insanity as a Defence," 4.

5. Donald K. Freedheim, ed., *Handbook of Psychology* (Hoboken, NJ: John Wiley & Sons, Inc., 2003), 392.

6. Freedheim, *Handbook of Psychology.*

7. "The Defence of Insanity in Criminal Cases," *The Law Journal* (London: F. E. Streeten, Nov. 22, 1884), 673.

8. Freedheim, *Handbook of Psychology,* 393.

9. "The Defence of Insanity," 702.

10. Freedheim, *Handbook of Psychology,* 38.

11. "The Defence of Insanity," 702.

12. "The Defence of Insanity," 702.

13. "The Defence of Insanity," 393.

14. "Insanity Defense," https://www.law.cornell.edu/wex/insanity_defense.

15. Freedheim, *Handbook of Psychology,* 393.

16. Ancestry.com.

17. "Supreme Judicial Court of New Hampshire State v. Pike," *American Law Register* 20, no. 4, New Series vol. 11 (Apr. 1872): 234, https://www.jstor.org/stable/3303702?seq=26#metadata_info_tab_contents.

18. "Supreme Judicial Court of New Hampshire State v. Pike," 233.

19. "Execution of the Murderer Pike in Concord, New Hampshire," *Sacramento* (CA) *Daily Union,* Nov. 18, 1869.

20. "Supreme Judicial Court of New Hampshire State v. Pike," 235.

21. "The Death Penalty: Execution of the Murderer Pike in Concord, New Hampshire His Last Words from the Scaffold—His Crime," *New York Times,* Nov. 10, 1869.

22. "State v. Jones," *American Law Times Reports* (Aug. 1872): 270.

23. "State v. Jones," 271.

24. "State v. Jones," 271.

25. Ancestry.com.

26. Records of the Concord State Prison.

27. "State v. Jones," 271.

28. "State v. Jones," 270.

29. "State v. Jones," 270.

30. "State v. Jones," 271.

31. Augustin Derby, *Cases on Criminal Law* (Indianapolis, IN: Bobbs-Merrill, Co., 1923), 309.

32. Ancestry.com.

33. *Durham v. United States* 214 F. 2d 862 Court of Appeals Dist. of Columbia Circuit 1954, 864, https://scholar.google.com/scholar_case?case=1244686235948852364.

34. *Durham v. United States,* 870.

35. *Durham v. United States,* 875.

36. "United States v. Brawner," https://h2o.law.harvard.edu/collages/1432.

37. *Durham v. United States,* 875.

38. "Insanity—Prior Law," https://www.justice.gov/jm/criminal-resource-manual-636-insanity-prior-law.

39. "The Insanity Defense among the States," https://criminal.findlaw.com/criminal-procedure/the-insanity-defense-among-the-states.html.

22. THE QUESTION OF RESPONSIBILITY

1. Popat and Winslade, "While You Were Sleeping."

2. R. K. Ressler and A. W. Burgess, "Crime Scene and Profile Characteristics of Organized and Disorganized Murders," *FBI Law Enforcement Bulletin* 54, no. 8 (Aug. 1985): 18–25.

3. *Ford v. Wainwright,* 477 U.S. 390, 410 (1986), https://www.hrw.org/reports /2001/ustat/ustat0301–04.htm#P592_111736.

4. "Intelligence and Crime," https://criminal-justice.iresearchnet.com/ crime/intelligence-and-crime/3/.

SELECTED BIBLIOGRAPHY

This selected bibliography lists sources that provided most of the information for this work. Additional resources can be found in the further readings section that follows.

Abbot, Nathan Kilbourn. *Diaries 1824–1874.* New Hampshire Historical Society collection 1986–2012.

Abercrombie, John. *Inquiries Concerning the Intellectual Powers, and the Investigation of Truth.* Boston, MA: Otis, Broaders, and Company, 1841.

American Railroad Journal and Advocate of Internal Improvements 2, no. 19, New York (May 11, 1833). https://books.google.com/books?id=xYFDAQA AMAAJ&pg=PA301&lpg=PA301&dq=Captain+Paddock+american+rail road+journal&source=bl&ots=K2sfHvvzRQ&sig=oqp9dm_dczz7g9Kp WHMM-Wmlbco&hl=en&sa=X&ved=oahUKEwiYh5m8q8bZAhVD xYMKHZNDCX8Q6AEINDAB#v=onepage&q=Captain%20Paddock %20american%20railroad%20journal&f=false.

Belden, Dr. L. W. *An Account of Jane C. Rider,* Springfield, MA: G. & C. Merriam, 1834.

Bickford, James, ed. *The Authentic Life of Mrs. Mary Ann Bickford Who Was Murdered in the City of Boston on the 27th of October, 1845.* Published by the Compiler, 1846. https://iiif.lib.harvard.edu/manifests/view/drs:5807102$9i.

Bolton, Ethel Stanwood, and Eva Johnston Coe. *American Samplers.* Boston, MA: Thomas Todd Co., 1921.

Borchard, Edwin M. *Convicting the Innocent, Errors of Criminal Justice.* New Haven:YaleUniv.Press,1932.http://library.albany.edu/preservation/brittle _bks/Borchard_Convicting/chpt3.pdf.

Browne, George Waldo. *The Amoskeag Manufacturing Company of Manchester, New Hampshire, A History.* Manchester, NH: Mills of Amoskeag Manufacturing Company, 1915.

Burns, Kathleen J. "A Chronicle of the Death Penalty in Massachusetts: Part One." *Lawyers Journal* (Jan. 1999). www.nodp.org/ma/stacks/Chronicle.doc.

Burrows, George Man. *Commentaries on the Causes, Forms, Symptoms and Treatment, Moral and Medical, of Insanity.* London: Thomas and George Underwood, 1828.

Carter, Nathan Franklin. *History of Pembroke, N.H. 1730–1895 in Two Volumes.* Vol. 2. Concord, NH: Republican Press Association, 1895.

Cartwright, Rosalind. "Sleepwalking Violence: A Sleep Disorder, a Legal Dilemma, and a Psychological Challenge." *American Journal of Psychiatry* 161, no. 7 (July 2004): 1149–58.

Chaiken, Jan, Marcia Chaiken, and William Rhodes. "Predicting Violent Behavior and Classifying Violent Offenders." In *Understanding and Preventing Violence*, vol. 4. Commission on Behavioral and Social Sciences and Education, Washington, DC: National Academy Press, 1994.

Chandler, George. *The Chandler Family: The Descendants of William and Annis Chandler Who Settled in Roxbury, Mass.* Worcester, MA: Press of Charles Hamilton, 1883.

Chase, Robert Greene. *Sermons preached in the Chapel of the Church of Saint Matthias, Philadelphia.* Philadelphia, PA: Samuel D. Burlock, 1868.

Chokroverty, Sudhansu, and Michael Billiard, eds. *Sleep Medicine: A Comprehensive Guide to Its Development, Clinical Milestones and Advances in Treatment.* New York: Springer Science and Business Media, 2015.

Coffin, Thomas. *Diary of a Farmer in Boscawen, New Hampshire.* New Hampshire Historical Society collection, M 1967–044.

Cohen, Daniel A. "The Murder of Maria Bickford: Fashion, Passion, and the Birth of Consumer Culture." *American Studies* 31 (1990): 5–30.

———. *Pillars of Salt, Monuments of Grace: New England Crime Literature and the Origins of Popular Culture, 1674–1860.* New York: Oxford Univ. Press, 1993.

Collins, Paul. *Blood & Ivy: The 1849 Murder That Scandalized Harvard.* New York: W. W. Norton & Co., 2018.

Cox, M., J. Chandler, A. Boyle, P. Kneller, and R. Haslam. "Eighteenth and Nineteenth Century Dental Restoration and Treatment and Consequences in a British Nobleman." *British Dental Journal* 189 (Dec. 9, 2000). https://www.nature.com/articles/4800839.

Cox, Rowland, ed. "State v. Jones." *American Law Times Report.* Aug. 1872. Washington City: Rowland Cox, 1873.

Crockett, Simeon L. *A Voice from Leverett Street Prison, or, The Life, Trial and Confession of Simeon L. Crockett, Who Was Executed for Arson, March 16, 1836.* Boston, MA: Printed for the Proprietors, [1836?]. 3rd ed. http://nrs.harvard.edu/urn-3:FHCL:3899540.

Derry, Margaret E. *Art and Science in Breeding: Creating Better Chickens.* Toronto: Univ. of Toronto Press, 2012.

Deutsch, Albert. *The Mentally Ill in America: A History of Their Cure and Treatment from Colonial Times.* New York: Columbia Univ. Press, 1949.

Drayton, Daniel. *Personal Memoirs of Daniel Drayton: Four Years and Four Months a Prisoner (For Charity's Sake) in Washington Jail.* Boston, MA: Bela Marsh, 1853.

The Early Love Letters and Later Literary Remains of Maria Bickford: Murdered in Boston, October 25th, 1845. Edited by a Friend of Her Youth. Boston, MA: Silas Estabrook, 1846). http://reader.library.cornell.edu/docview er/digital?id=sat:1907#page/1/mode/1up.

Eigen, Joel Peter. *Witnessing Insanity: Madness and Mad-Doctors in the English Court.* New Haven, CT: Yale Univ. Press, 1995.

Ela, David H. *A Vindication of the Result of the Trial of Rev. Ephraim K. Avery.* Boston, MA: Russell, Odiorne and Co., 1834.

Flanders, Judith. *The Invention of Murder.* New York: St. Martin's Press, 2013.

Freedheim, Donald K. *Handbook of Psychology.* Hoboken, NJ: John Wiley & Sons, Inc., 2003.

Griffin, Patrick. *The People with No Name: Ireland's Ulster Scots, America's Scots Irish, and the Creation of a British Atlantic World, 1689–1764.* Princeton, NJ: Princeton Univ. Press, 2001.

Grimsted, David. *American Mobbing 1828–1861.* New York: Oxford Univ. Press, 1998.

Grob, Gerald N. *The Mad Among Us: A History of the Care of America's Mentally Ill.* New York: The Free Press, 1994.

Haines, Michael R. "The Urban Mortality Transition in the United States, 1800–1940." *Annales de Demographie Historique* no. 1 (2001). https://www.cairn .info/revue-annales-de-demographie-historique-2001-1-page-33.htm#.

Haskins, George L. "The Beginnings of Partible Inheritance in the American Colonies." *Yale Law Journal* 51, no. 8 (1942): 1280–1315. *https://digitalcom mons.law.yale.edu/cgi/viewcontent.cgi?article=4259 . . . ylj.*

Head, Natt. *Report of the Adjutant General of the State of New Hampshire for the Year Ending June 1, 1868,* Manchester, NH: John B. Clarke, Printer, 1868.

Hershock, Martin J. *A New England Prison Diary.* Ann Arbor: Univ. of Michigan Press, 2012.

Horn, Mike. "A Rude Awakening: What to Do with the Sleepwalking Defense?" *Boston College Law Review* 46, issue 1, no. 1 (Dec. 1, 2004): 149–82.

Hurd, Henry Mills, William F. Dewry, Richard Dewey, Charles W. Pilgrim, G. Alder Blumer, and T. J. W. Burgess. *Institutional Care of the Insane in the United States and Canada.* Baltimore, MD: The Johns Hopkins Press, 1916.

Jimenez, Mary Ann. *Changing Faces of Madness: Early American Attitudes and Treatment of the Insane.* Hanover, NH: Univ. Press of New England, 1987.

Journal of the American Temperance Union 10, no. 9 (Sept. 1, 1846). http://books. google.com/books?id=JspOAAAAYAAJ&pg=RA1-PA133&dq=andrew +howard+murdered+phebe+hanson&hl=en&sa=X&ei=5DKeUr6bGq_ MsQTkqYGIDw&ved=0CC8Q6AEwAA#v=onepage&q=andrew%20how ard%20murdered%20phebe%20hanson&f=false.

Kasserman, David Richard. *Fall River Outrage, Life, Murder, and Justice in Early Industrial New England.* Philadelphia: Univ. of Pennsylvania Press, 1986.

Krueger, Glee. *A Gallery of American Samplers.* New York: E. P. Dutton, 1978.

Kuritz, Hyman. "The Popularization of Science in Nineteenth-Century America." *History of Education Quarterly* 21, no. 3 (Autumn 1981): 259–74.

Lawson, John D., ed. "The Trial of Abraham Prescott for the Murder of Mrs. Sally Cochran Concord, New Hampshire 1834." In *American State Trials; A Collection of the Important and Interesting Criminal Trials Which Have Taken Place in the United States, from the Beginning to the Present Day.* Vol. 5. St. Louis: F. H. Thomas Law Book, 1916.

Lebergott, Stanley. "Wage Trends, 1800–1900." In *Trends in the American Economy in the Nineteenth Century.* Princeton, NJ: Princeton Univ. Press, 1960. https://pdfs.semanticscholar.org.

Lifshutz, Jason I., and Walter M. Johnson. "History of Hydrocephalus and Its Treatments." *Neurosurgery Focus* 11, no. 2 (2001).

Lord, C. C. *Life and Times in Hopkinton, N.H.* Concord, NH: Republican Press Association, 1890.

Lyford, James O., ed. *History of Concord, New Hampshire from the Original Grant in Seventeen Hundred and Twenty-Five to the Opening of the Twentieth Century.* Concord, NH: Rumford Press, 1903.

MacNish, Robert. *The Philosophy of Sleep.* Glasgow: W. R. McPhun, 1834.

Masur, Louis P. *Rites of Execution Capital Punishment and the Transition of American Culture, 1776–1865.* Oxford: Oxford Univ. Press, 1989.

McFarland, Gerald. *The Counterfeit Man.* New York: Pantheon Books, 1990.

McKinnon, Susan. "Cousin Marriage, Hierarchy, and Heredity: Contestations over Domestic and National Body Politics in 19th-Century America." *Journal of the British Academy* 7, no. 20 (May 2019): 61–88. https://www.thebritishacademy.ac.uk › sites › files › JBA-7-p61-McKinnon.

Memorial Biographies of the New England Historical Genealogical Society. Vol. 6, 1864–1871. Boston: New England Historical Genealogical Society, 1905.

Moffitt, Terrie E. "Male Anti-social Behavior in Adolescence and Beyond." *Nature Human Behavior* 2 (Feb. 2018). https://www.ncbi.nlm.nih.gov/pmc/articles/PMC6157602/.

Moore, J. Bailey. *History of the Town of Candia, Rockingham County, New Hampshire from Its First Settlement to the Present Time.* Manchester, NH: G. W. Browne, 1893.

Nicholl, Sir John. *A Report on the Judgment in Dew v. Clark and Clark.* Edited by John Haggart. London: A. Strahan, 1826.

Noyes, Daniel J. *Memoir of Nathaniel Gookin Upham Read at the Annual Meeting of the New Hampshire Historical Society, June 14, 1871.* https://archive.org/stream/memoirofnathanieoonoye/memoirofnathanieoonoye_djvu.txt

Nylander, Jane C. *Our Own Snug Fireside,* New York: Alfred A. Knopf, 1993.

Olson, S., and D. R. Gerstein. *Alcohol in America: Taking Action to Prevent Abuse.* Washington, DC: National Academies Press, 1985.

Oppenheimer, Clive. "Climatic, Environmental and Human Consequences of the Largest Known Historic Eruption: Tambora Volcano (Indonesia) 1815." *Progress in Physical Geography* 27, no. 2 (2003): 230–59.

Parker, Rev. Edward L. *History of Londonderry Comprising the Towns of Derry and Londonderry, N. H.* Boston, MA: Perkins and Whipple, 1851.

Parker, Joel. *Report of the Trial of Daniel H. Corey on an Indictment for the Murder of Mrs. Matilda Nash at the Term of the Superior Court of Judicature Holden at Keene in the County of Chesire on the First Tuesday of October 1830.* Newport, NH: French & Brown, 1830.

Parker, Patsy. "The Historical Role of Women in Higher Education." *Administrative Issues Journal: Connecting Education, Practice, and Research* 5, no. 1 (Spring 2015): 3–14.

Perry, Claire. *Young America Childhood in the 19th-Century Art and Culture.* New Haven, CT: Yale Univ. Press, 2006.

Private Individual at the Bar. "Abr'm Prescott's Confession, of the Murder of Mrs. Sally Cochran, June 23, 1833." Copy of a broadside. New Hampshire Historical Society, catalog no. 1998–303. https://www.nhhistory.org/object /266238/copy-of-the-poem-abraham-prescott-s-confession-of-the-murder -of-mrs-sally-cochran-of-pembrok-nh.

Raiselis, Tara Vose. *From the Elegant to the Everyday: 200 Years of Fashion in Northern New England.* College Station, TX: Virtualbookworm Publishing, Inc., 2014.

Raiselis, Tara Vose, and Leslie Lambert Rounds. *Industry and Virtue Joined.* College Station, TX: Virtualbookworm Publishing, Inc., 2015.

Rapaport, Diane. *The Naked Quaker: True Crimes and Controversies from the Courts of Colonial New England.* Beverly, MA: Commonwealth Editions, 2007.

Reed, P. Holmes. "Insanity as a Defence in Criminal Law." Historical Theses and Dissertations Collection, Cornell Law Library, Scholarship@Cornell Law: A Digital Respository, 1895. https://scholarship.law.cornell.edu/his torical_theses/index.3.html.

Report Made to the Legislature of New Hampshire on the Subject of the Insane, June Session 1836. Concord, NH: Cyrus Barton, Printer, 1836.

Report of the Trial of Abraham Prescott for the murder of Mrs. Sally Cochran, of Pembroke June 23, 1833. Executed at Hopkinton, January 6, 1836. Manchester, NH: Daily Mirror Office, 1869.

Report of the Trial of Abraham Prescott, on an Indictment for the Murder of Mrs. Sally Cochran, before the Court of Common Pleas, Holden at Concord, in the County of Merrimack. On the first Tuesday of Sept., 1834. Concord: M. G. Atwood, and Currier & Hall. John W. Moore, Printer, 1834.

Ressler; R. K., and A. W. Burgess. "Crime Scene and Profile Characteristics of Organized and Disorganized Murders." *FBI Law Enforcement Bulletin* 54, no. 8 (Aug. 1985).

Ring, Betty. *Girlhood Embroidery.* New York: Alfred A. Knopf, Inc., 1993.

Rogers, Artemus, and Henry B. Chase. *The Trial of Daniel Davis Farmer for the Murder of the Widow Anna Ayer at Goffstown on the 4th of April A. D. 1821.* Concord, NH: Hill and Moore, 1821.

Rorabaugh, W. J. *The Alcoholic Republic: An American Tradition.* Oxford: Oxford Univ. Press, 1979.

Rounds, Leslie Lambert. *I My Needle Ply with Skill.* College Station, TX: Virtual Bookworm.com Publishing, 2013.

Rush, Dr. Benjamin. *Medical Inquiries and Observations upon the Diseases of the Mind.* Philadelphia: Grigg and Elliot, 1835.

Russell, Howard S. *A Long, Deep Furrow: Three Centuries of Farming in New England.* Hanover, NH: Univ. Press of New England, 1976.

Sammons, Mark J. "The District Schools of Early New England," Families and Children. In *Dublin Seminar for New England Folklife Annual Proceedings 1985.* Boston, MA: Boston Univ., 1985.

Sargeant, Honorable Leonard. *The Trial, Confessions and Conviction of Jesse and Stephen Boorn for the Murder of Russel Colvin and the Return of the Man Supposed to Have Been Murdered.* Manchester, VT: Journal Book and Job Office, 1873.

Steenburg, Nancy Hathaway. *Children and the Criminal Law in Connecticut: Changing Perceptions of Childhood.* New York and London: Routledge, 2005.

Sturmey, Peter. *Reducing Restraint and Restrictive Management Practices.* Basel, Switzerland: Springer International Publishing, 2015.

"Supreme Judicial Court of New Hampshire, State v. Pike." *American Law Register* 20, no. 4, New Series vol. 11, Apr. 1872, *University of Pennsylvania Law Review.* https://www.jstor.org/stable/3303702?seq=26#metadata_info_tab_contents.

Trial of Seth Elliot, Esq. for the Murder of His Son, John Wilson Elliot: Before the Supreme Judicial Court at Castine, October Term, 1824. Belfast, ME: Fellowes and Simpson, 1824.

Trial of Stephen and Jesse Boorn for the Murder of Russel Colvin. Rutland, VT: Fay & Burt, 1820.

True, D. Hack. *A Dictionary of Psychological Medicine.* London: J. & A. Churchill, 1892.

Ulrich, Laurel Thatcher. "Derangement in the Family: The Story of Mary Sewall, 1824–1825." In *Medicine and Healing.* Boston, MA: The Dublin Seminar for New England Folklife Annual Proceedings, 1990.

Waterman, Elijah. "A Sermon, Preached at Windham, November 29th, 1803, Being the Day of the Execution of Caleb Adams for the Murder of Oliver Woodworth." http://www.calebadams.org/sermon.htm.

Wells, Robert V. "Family Size and Fertility Control in Eighteenth Century America: A Study of Quaker Families." *Population Studies* 12, no. 1 (Mar. 1971): 73–82.

Wheeler, George A. *History of Castine, Penobscot and Brooksville, Maine.* Bangor, ME: Burr & Robinson, 1875.

NEWSPAPERS

Kennebunk Gazette and Maine Palladium
Maine Democrat (Saco)
New Hampshire Sentinel (Keene)
New York Times
Patriot (Concord, NH)
Portsmouth (NH) Journal of Literature and Politics

FURTHER READINGS

Abbott, Karen. "The Case of the Sleepwalking Killer." *Smithsonian Magazine,* Apr. 30, 2012.

Asher, Robert, Lawrence B. Goodheart, and Alan Rogers, eds. *Murder on Trial 1620–2002.* Albany: State Univ. of New York Press, 2005.

Baker, David. *Women and Capital Punishment in the United States: An Analytical History.* Jefferson, NC: McFarland and Company, Inc., 2016.

Bayles, Richard M., ed. *History of Windham County, Connecticut.* New York: W. W. Preston & Co., 1889.

Benedetto, Christopher. "A Warning to All Others: The Story of the First Executions in New Hampshire's History." *New England Ancestors,* Feb. 10, 2008.

Connor, Michael G. "The Risk of Violent and Homicidal Behavior in Children." http://www.oregoncounseling.org/ArticlesPapers/Documents/child violence.htm.

Cox, M., J. Chandler, A. Boyle, P. Kneller, and R. Haslam. "Eighteenth and Nineteenth Century Dental Restoration and Treatment and Consequences in a British Nobleman." *British Dental Journal* 189 (Dec. 9, 2000). https://www.nature.com/articles/4800839.

"Evidences of Insanity." *Boston Medical and Surgical Journal* 11, no. 23, Jan. 14, 1835.

Farmer, Daniel Davis. *The Life and Confessions of Daniel Davis Farmer Who Was Executed at Amherst, New Hampshire on the 3rd Day of January, 1822, for the Murder of the Widow Anna Ayer on April 4, 1821 to Which Is Added His Valedictory Address and Some of His Correspondence During His Imprisonment, 1822,* Amherst, NH: Printed by Elijah Mansur, 1822.

Halttunen, Karen. *Murder Most Foul: The Killer and the American Gothic Imagination*. Cambridge, MA: Harvard Univ. Press, 1998.

Hearn, Daniel Allen. *Legal Executions in New England 1623–1960*. Jefferson, NC: McFarland & Company, Inc., 1999.

Horwitz, Elinor Lander. *Madness, Magic, and Medicine: The Treatment and Mistreatment of the Mentally Ill.* Philadelphia: J. B. Lippincott Company, 1977.

Johnson, James, ed. *The Medico-Chiurical Review and Journal of Practical Medicine*, vol. 14. New York: Richard & George S. Wood, New York, 1831. http://books.google.com/books?id=rTrp4gRwGaUC&pg=PA254&lpg= PA254&dq=frederick+jensen+sudden+propensity+for+murder+or+suicide &source=bl&ots=XfJoEW2byj&sig=sKA5CeR41I_FuTqvCT8hbwOK 4pg&hl=en&sa=X&ei=Wy-iUr_sIdTekQfEpIHQCg&ved=0CCwQ6A EwAA#v=onepage&q=frederick%20jensen%20sudden%20propensity%20 for%20murder%20or%20suicide&f=false.

Ludlum, David M. *Early American Winters II 1821–1870*. Boston, MA: American Meteorological Society, 1968.

Lyon, G. Parker. *New Hampshire Annual Register and United States Calendar for the Year 1845*. Concord, NH: G. Parker Lyon, 1845.

Morris, Norvall, and David J. Rothman, eds. *The Oxford History of the Prison*. New York: Oxford Univ. Press, 1998.

Numbers, Ronald L., and Janet S. Numbers. "Millerism and Madness: A Study of 'Religious Insanity' in Nineteenth-Century America." In *The Disappointed*. Bloomington: Indiana Univ. Press, 1987.

Porter, Roy. *Madness A Brief History*. Oxford: Oxford Univ. Press, 2002.

Prince, Carl. "'The Great Riot Year': Jacksonian Democracy and Patterns of Violence in 1834." *Journal of the Early Republic* 5, no. 1 (Spring 1985): 1–19.

The Report of the Adjutant General for the State of New Hampshire for the Year Ending June 1, 1868. Manchester, NH: John B. Clarke, State Printer, 1869.

Report of the Trial of the Rev. Ephraim K. Avery, Methodist Minister, for the Murder of Sarah Maria Cornell, at Tiverton, in the County of Newport, Rhode Island, before the Supreme Judicial Court of That State, May 6, 1833: Containing the Evidence of the Numerous Witnesses Unabridged, and the Speeches of General Albert C. Green, Attorney General, the Hon. D. Pearce, and William R. Staples, Esq., Counsel for the Prosecution, and Those of the Hon. J. Mason, Richard R. Randolph, Esq., and Other Counsel for the Prisoner: Together with the Charge of His Honor Chief Justice Eddy, in Full, as Taken in Short Hand. New York: W. Stodart, 1833.

Rothman, David J. "Perfecting the Prison, United States 1789–1865." *The Oxford History of the Prison*, edited by Norval Morris and David J. Rothman, pp. 111–29. New York: Oxford Univ. Press, 1998.

Shirley, John M. *Reports of Cases Argued and Determined in the Supreme Judicial Court of New Hampshire*, vol. 50. Concord, NH: B. W. Sanborn & Co., 1872.

Starr, Douglas. *The Killer of Little Shepherds: A True Crime Story and the Birth of Forensic Science.* New York: Alfred A. Knopf, 2010.

Stearns, Ezra S., ed. *Genealogical and Family History of New Hampshire,* vol. 2. Chicago: Lewis Publishing Co., 1908.

Tucher, Andie. *Froth and Scum Truth, Beauty, Goodness, and the Ax Murder in America's First Mass Medium.* Chapel Hill, NC: Univ. of North Caroline Press, 1994.

Ulrich, Laurel Thatcher. *The Age of Homespun: Objects and Stories in the Creation of an American Myth.* New York: Alfred A. Knopf, 2001.

Wilson, Lisa. *A History of Stepfamilies in Early America.* Chapel Hill: Univ. of North Carolina Press, 2014.

INDEX

Abbot, Comfort, 70

Abbott, William, Jr., 8–9, 26, 43, 65, 70, 133–34

Abercrombie, John, 89–90

Adams, Caleb, 104–95

Adams Female Academy, 19

Adventures of Tom Sawyer, 115

Alabama, 73–74

Alabama, Supreme Court of, 74

alcohol: and crime, 67, 78, 201–2; consumption levels of, 118, 236n14; and sleepwalking, 206

Allenstown, New Hampshire, 39, 44, 130–31, 134

American Railroad Journal, 82

Anderson, Margaret, 18–19

Andover, Massachusetts, 55

Andover, New Hampshire, 58

Arnold, Edward, 198

Arthur, Chester, 215

attire: bloomers/drawers, 70; calash, 5–8, 65–68, 129–30, 133, 146–47, 157; comb, 5–8, 65–68, 129–30, 132–33, 146–47, 157, 165; day cap, 66; drawers, 70; dress, 4, 6, 8, 70, 100, 135, 147, 192; pantaloons, 48; shirt, 7, 9, 25–26, 48, 66, 92, 134; waistcoat, 48, 66

Austen, Jane, 100

Avery, Ephraim: newspaper coverage of, 3, 62, 156, 163, 207; trial of, 3–4, 30, 97–99

Ayer, Anna, 56

Badger, William, 168, 170, 174, 186

Bagley, Jonathan, 58

Barnum, John, 76

Bartlett, Ichabod: background, 49, 73–75; closing argument, 138–49, 151–53, 166; examining witnesses, 63, 66–67, 71, 116, 120, 123, 125; life after trial, 216; planning the defense, 77; reaction to verdict, 183

Batchelder, Jeremiah, 130, 144

bathing, 111

Beech Hill Golf Club, 214

Beede, Elizabeth, 234

Belden, L. W., 93–94, 232–33

Bellingham, John, 143, 199

Bickford, Francis, 35, 133

Bickford, James, 190, 245

Bickford, Mary Ann "Maria" Dunn, 189–93, 244n2

Blaisdell, Amos P., 34, 135

Blake, Hezekiah, 104, 106

Blake, Jeremiah, 107–8

Blake, John, 107

Blood, Priscilla, 190

Boorn, Amos, 149
Boorn, Jesse, 149–51
Boorn, Stephen, 149–50
Boston, Massachusetts, 10, 118, 122–23, 155, 190, 207
Boston Post, 175
Boyden, Wyatt, 58
Brown, Elizabeth, 201–2
Brown, Thomas, 201–2
Burgin, Hall, 130–31, 144–45
Burns, Samuel, 179–80
Burrows, George Man, 97, 102

Caldwell, David S., 59
Calef, Abigail, 31, 127
Carpenter, Abigail, 213
Carr, 45, 135
Carroll, 178–79
Carter, Elias, 188
Cartwright, Rosalind, 194
Chadbourne, Thomas, 124
Chandler, Moses, 124
Chapman, Elisha, 105
Chase, Rev., 178
Chase, Baruch, 56
Chase, Hannah Ralston, 56, 216
Chase, Horace G., 214
Chase, Robert Follansbee, 45, 172–73
Chase, Salmon P., 56
Choate, Rufus, 191–93, 207
Church, Methodist, 31, 214
Clark, Martha, 234
Clay, Henry, 216
Cochran, Betsy, 9, 19, 217
Cochran, Chauncey: and apprenticeship of Prescott, 39, 131–32; background of, 13–14, 20–21; church membership of, 41; and death of Sally, 6–8, 43, 147; and devil possessing Prescott, 76, 129; education of, 16–17; family history of, 10–14, 128; farm of, 21; inheritance of, 14; interest in Avery trial of, 3, 6, 163; January attack on, 25–28, 135; later life of, 212–14; marriages, 20, 212–13; neighbors of, 49, 133, 135; perception of attack on Sally of, 7, 72, 76, 162–64, 212; perception of Prescott, 28–31, 33, 39, 131; and prison interview of Prescott, 49, 129; and public sympathy for, 58–59, 78; recollection of Avery discussion, 162; refusal to pick strawberries by, 3–4; responsibilities of, 5, 22–23, 33, 42, 133; trial testimony of, 62–64, 101–2, 131–32, 162

Cochran, Giles Newton, 4, 62, 213
Cochran, James, Jr., 4–5, 8, 13–14, 215
Cochran, James, Sr., 13–14, 20
Cochran, Jane "Jenny," 11–13, 20, 215
Cochran, Jasper, 213–14
Cochran, John, 10–11
Cochran, Lettice Duncan, 4, 13, 20, 25–26, 31, 71, 215
Cochran, Mary Jane, 8, 12, 14, 71, 164–65, 215
Cochran, Moses, 11–13, 20, 215
Cochran, Norris, 49, 126, 128–29, 136, 155
Cochran, Sally: attack on, 5–6, 42–43, 50–51, 65–66, 135–36, 207–8; background of, 15–23; childbearing of, 23; clothing of, 4–5, 65–66, 100, 132; death of, 8–9, 158; defense of Prescott by, 31–32, 151; and discussion of Avery trial, 98–99, 163; education of, 16–19; examination of body of, 66, 68, 70, 147; family history of, 10–14; household responsibilities of, 22–24, 33, 40; injuries of, 66, 68, 147; management of household help and, 23; marriage of, 20, 96; possibility of a struggle of, 68–69, 135, 146–47, 163–65; public perception of, 127, 164, 189; relationship with Prescott, 28, 30–32, 40, 50–51, 64, 127; sampler of, 9, 17–20, 214, 217; sexual assault and, 50–51, 69–71, 157, 207–8; winter attack on, 25–27, 63, 135–36
Cochran, Samuel, 43
Cochran, Samuel, Jr., 132
Cochran, Sarah (daughter of Jasper), 214
Cochran, Sarah, 4, 213
Colburn, James, 59
Colvin, Russel, 149–50
Colvin, Sally Boorn, 149–50
Commentaries on Insanity, 97
Concord, New Hampshire, 3, 9, 60; as asylum site, 188; attorneys practicing in, 49, 75, 161, 216; newspaper of, 43, 63; physicians practicing in, 124; as trial site, 56–69, 117, 138
confession, false, 149–50
Corey, Daniel Haseltine, 86–88, 112, 231n4
Cornell, Sarah: examination of body of, 69–70, 98; murder of, 98; relationship with Rev. Avery and, 96, 99; reputation of, 98–99
Cornier, Harriet, 151–52
Court of Common Pleas, Merrimack County, 43, 49, 74, 86, 179, 200
criminal code, 46
Criminal Lunatics Act of 1800, 81

criminal offender, 44, 46, 67, 210
Critchett, Mary, 33, 36, 132, 145
Crockett, Simeon, 245n11
Crum, Hannah, 234n8
Culpepper, Colonel, 90–91
Currie, James, 112

Dartmouth College: lawyers educated at, 56, 74–75, 88, 161, 191, 193, 215; medical school of, 113, 123; weather records from, 47
death penalty: as a deterrent, 82, 153; mandatory for murder, 46, 71, 75; nature of, 140; New Hampshire abolishing use of, 205; New Hampshire use of, 57, 203; opposition to, 140–41, 148, 152, 170
Deerfield, New Hampshire, 34–35, 39, 113–14, 116, 130–35
dental care, 101–2
Dinsmore, Samuel, 186
dipsomania, 201–2
Dix, Dorothea, 185
Drayton, Daniel, 47–48
Drummond, Edward, 200
Durham, Monte, 204–5
Durham, New Hampshire, 55, 74
Dyce, William, 90

Eagle Hotel, 160
Eams, Fanny, 233n31
East Corinth, Maine, 41, 212–14
Eastman, Moses, 60, 74
Eastman, Timothy, 212
Edes, Thomas, 212
education, 16–20
Elliot, John Wilson, 77
Elliot, Seth, 77–78, 230n17
Epsom, New Hampshire, 35, 166, 173, 215
Evans, Andrew O., 130
execution: of Abraham Prescott, 161, 167, 176–80; crimes punishable by, 46; popularity of, 58, 78; preventive effect of, 83, 140, 170; public behavior during, 83, 140–41, 171; use of, 82, 104, 202, 210

Fain, 194, 197, 247n15
Falater, Scott, 196–97
Fall River, Massachusetts, 3, 69
Farmer, Daniel Davis, 56–57, 74, 76, 86
The Farmer's Cabinet, 16
Fellows, Jonathan, 134
Fifield, Joseph, 59
Fifield, Sally, 59

Foss, Andrew T., 178
Fowler, John L., 41, 49–51, 64–66, 128, 134, 136, 164
Fowler, William, 9
Fowler, Winthrop, 43
Franklin, Benjamin, 91
Franklin, New Hampshire, 58–59
Fraser, Simon, 194
French, Adeline, 202
French, Frank, 202
French, Hannah, 234n10
French, Mary, 70
French, Miriam, 36, 115
French, Widow. See French, Miriam

Garfield, James, 215
Gay, Maria, 212–13
Gay, William, 59, 213
George III, 81, 89, 160, 199, 205
Gericault, Theodore, 239
Giles Tavern, 49
Goodhue, Dr., 115
Goodhue, Mary, 165
Graves, William: background of, 36, 113–15; death of, 116; legal issues of, 114–15; medical care from, 36, 111, 155; students of, 114–16; testimony of, 115–16, 165; and theft of corpses, 114
Greeley, Horace, 169

Hadfield, James, 81–82, 89, 160, 199, 204–5
Hanson, Phebe, 57
Harris, John, 57
Harvard College, 55, 86, 113, 122, 217
Hill, Isaac, 174
Hodgdon, Caleb, 34, 110, 112
Hodgdon, Sally Prescott. See Prescott, Sally C.
Hopkinton, New Hampshire, 56; as site of execution, 177–78, 214; as site of jail, 43–45, 47–48, 52, 57, 134, 167; as site of riot, 166, 168, 171–74
Howard, Andrew, 57
humors, 38–39, 109
Huntoon, Hannah, 107, 234n10
Hutchins, Ida May, 213
hydrotherapy, 111

Industrial Revolution, 15, 28, 76
insanity: asylum treatment of, 183–86; case histories of, 99, 100, 106–8, 119, 194; changing perception of, 76, 81, 169–70, 174; duration of, 126–27; heritability of,

insanity (*cont.*)
96–97, 104, 120, 123–24, 154–55; home care and, 183–85; incarceration and, 185; legal test for, 77–78, 81, 142–44, 160, 199–205; monomania and, 119, 152, 165, 239n14; moral treatment of, 117, 185; as "multiform monster," 123; New Hampshire statistics of, 186–87; perceived causes of, 84, 101–3, 119, 123; physical restraint and, 183–83; poorhouse confinement and, 185; possession by the devil and, 7, 76, 105, 129, 169; potential for violence and, 142; and Prescott, 71; and somnambulism, 86, 93, 104, 119; and wandering, 117, 185
intercourse, 13, 137, 157, 241n32

jails and prisons: average intelligence of prisoners, 67, 210; Concord State Prison, 46, 49, 57, 128–29, 136, 202; as housing for the mentally ill, 185; Ipswich Prison, 47; jailors' stipends, 48; living conditions, 46–49; prisoner reform and, 46–47; Salem jail, 47
Jean-Georget, Etienne, 142
Jensen, Frederick, 143
Johnson, John, 131
Jones, Ann, 202–3
Jones, Hiram, 202–3
Jordan, William, 49
Journal of the American Temperance Union, 57
Joy, Timothy, 47
jurisprudence, 82, 85
jurors: behavior of, 78–79, 139, 160–61, 209; demographics of, 58–59, 162; duties of, 60; perceived ignorance of, 113, 168–70; rejected, 59–60; sequestration of, 60, 160–61

Kennebunk Gazette and Maine Palladium, 164
Kenyon, Lord, 199
Kiger, Joan, 194
Kimball, John (juror), 58
Kimball, John, 39, 130–32, 145
Kingsley, George O., 233n31
Knox, Maine, 77
Knox, William, 49, 129, 155

Lamson, Clarissa, 216
Lane, Isiah, 114
Lawrence, Joel, 190–91

Leach, Andrew, 43–45, 80, 134–35, 172–73
Leach, Clarissa Green, 173
Leach, Mary, 43–45, 134–35, 172–73
Lear, Eliza, 35
Lear, Lucy Salter, 35
Lear, Mary Lucy, 35, 223n3
Lear, Mary "Polly": age of, 36–37, 38; appearance of, 108; background of, 35, 223n3; death of, 215; testimony of, 37–39, 108–10, 131, 155
Lear, Samuel, 35, 223n3
legal proceedings against Abraham Prescott: appeal, 161–67; closing arguments in first trial, 138–57; coroner's inquest, 43; defense in the first trial, 60–72; defense's rebuttal witnesses in first trial, 128–37; governor's consideration of verdict, 170, 174–75; indictment, 49, 52; prosecution's opening statement in first trial, 79–103; prosecution's witnesses in first trial, 106–27; second trial, 161–67
Lincoln, Abraham, 56
Livingston, Edward, 140
Londonderry, New Hampshire, 11–12, 16, 18
Long, Howard, 205
Lovering, 175
Lowell, Massachusetts, 115–16, 235n3
Lynn, Massachusetts, 18

MacNish, Robert, 91
macrocephaly, 37–38, 224n13
Maine Democrat, 175, 179–80
Mansfield, James, 143, 160, 199
A Manual of Pathology . . . , 89
marriage, consanguinity in, 14, 96–97, 219n12, 220n19
Martin, Noah, 114
Martin, Samuel, 134
Martinet, Louis, 89
Mather, Cotton, 10–11
Maxwell, Theodore, 244n2
McDaniel, Samuel, 49–50, 136
McLean, John, 117–18
McLean Asylum, 117–18, 122–25, 185
McNaughton, Daniel, 200
Mendel, Gregor, 96
Merrill, Annis, 189, 191
Merrill, Dr., 115
Merrill, Silas, 150
Model Penal Code, 204
Moffit, Terrie, 227n25
mortality, childhood, 13, 224n8

mortality in childbirth, 13, 223n3
Mount Holyoke College, 17, 221n6

Nash, Daniel, 87
Nash, Elizabeth, 87
Nash, Matilda, 87
New England Historical and Genealogical Register, 216
New England Mutual Fire Insurance Company, 216
New Hampshire Asylum for the Insane, 183, 186–88
New Hampshire House of Representatives, 55, 74–75
New Hampshire legal code, 201–5
New Hampshire Patriot: and attorneys' letter, 168; and coverage of execution, 170, 180; and coverage of inquest, 43; and coverage of murder, 63 and coverage of trials, 79, 103, 139, 152, 161; and coverage of winter attack, 27; and response to riots, 174, 177
New Hampshire Senate, 55–56, 74
New Hampshire Superior Court of Judicature, 52, 57, 86, 161, 170–71
New York Evening Post, 150
Nichol, Sir John, 142, 199
Noyes, Parker, 74
Nutfield, New Hampshire, 11

Oberlin College, 17
Old North Meeting House, 57, 139, 141, 160–62
Onslow, Lord Thomas, 198–99
Otis, Betsy Thomas, 34

Paddock, Henry, 82
Parker, Joel, 86–88, 162, 166, 181
Parkman, George, 122–23, 125, 236n2
Parks, Kenneth, 195–97
Patterson, William, 190
Peaslee, Charles Hazen: and appointment of, 49, 73; background of, 75; death of, 215–16; and efforts to found insane asylum, 183, 187–88; and final statement, 138–39; opening argument of, 78–103, 162–63; and payment of, 74; and witnesses, 104–27
Pembroke, New Hampshire: and the Cochran murder, 3–4, 43; as home of the Cochrans, 11, 20–21, 212–13, 215; and jury selection, 59; and the Prescott family, 33, 130, 180

Perceval, Sir Spencer, 143
Perry, William, 126–27
Phillips Academy, 55
phrenology, 94, 143, 175
Pierce, Franklin, 215
Pike, Josiah Little, 201–3, 205
Pingry, Stephen, 59
Pinkerton Academy, 16–17, 19, 221n6
Poor, Mary, 106
Portsmouth, New Hampshire, 35, 49, 74–75, 86, 171, 188, 202, 216
Powell v. Alabama, 73–74, 229n3
Prescott, Abraham: appearance of, 60–61, 92, 125, 131–33; apprenticeship of, 40–41, 131–32; attack on Sally by, 6–7, 61–62, 68–69, 227n25, 228n31; background of, 33–36; behavior of, 3, 27–30, 32, 49, 64, 134; birth order of, 35; childhood illnesses of, 36–39, 109–11, 115–16, 165; claim of toothache, 7, 9, 101–3, 119; confessions of, 7, 9, 42, 49–51, 63, 136; defense's depiction of, 83, 145; education of, 17, 39, 84, 131; escape attempt of, 45, 135; execution of, 178–80; incarceration of, 43–44, 48–49; January attack by, 24–28, 63, 71; mental difficulties of, 67, 125–26, 134, 168–70, 209–10; mistreatment of animals by, 5, 28–29, 64, 133–35; motive of, 162–64, 175–78; reaction to sentence by, 161, 167; relationship with the Cochrans, 28–32; and sleepwalking, 131, 134, 207
Prescott, Abraham, Jr., 107
Prescott, Abraham, Sr., 34, 106–8, 134, 154–55, 185
Prescott, Alexander Otis, 35, 39
Prescott, Benjamin, 112
Prescott, Betsy, 34–35
Prescott, Chase: and Abraham's childhood, 37–39; and Abraham's sleepwalking, 28, 84, 131; background of, 34–37; and contract with Chauncey Cochran, 39–41, 131–32; finances of, 35–36; living arrangements of, 36, 39; testimony of, 111–12
Prescott, Chase, Jr., 34–35
Prescott, Josiah, 114
Prescott, Lucy, 106
Prescott, Marston, 106–8, 112, 116, 134
Prescott, Mary "Polly." *See* Lear, Mary "Polly"
Prescott, Moses, 106, 108, 116, 155
Prescott, Sally C., 34, 108, 110, 116, 155, 234n10

Pressey, John, 162
primogeniture, 11, 34

Richardson, William M., 86, 88, 158–60,
    162, 201, 216
Ricker, Mary W., 35
Rider, Jane C., 93–95, 184, 232n29
rioting, 172–74, 177, 243n10
Robinson, Belinda, 8, 26, 135
Robinson, Clarissa, 8, 26, 164
Robinson, Henry, 8, 129, 164
Robinson, Jonathan, 8, 26, 42, 64, 67, 133–
    35, 163–64
Robinson, Lucy, 8, 26, 135, 164
Robinson, Timothy, 8, 42, 129, 164
Robinson, William, 8, 164
Rowe, Joseph A., 58
Rowe, Mary Blake, 108, 110
Rowell, Benjamin, 44, 185
Rowell, John, 59
Rush, Benjamin, 90, 102, 184
Russel, Stephen, 245n11

Saco Museum, 214
sampler. See schoolgirl embroidery
Sanborn, Benning W., 130, 144
Sargent, Samuel, 8, 26–27, 43, 68–71, 129, 135
schoolgirl embroidery, 17–20, 217
Scotch-Irish settlers, 10–11, 14
"Scottsboro Boys." See Powell v. Alabama
Sebright, Sir John, 97
Sense and Sensibility, 100
Sewall, Henry, 184–85
Sewall, Mary, 184–85
Sewall, Susan, 184
Sewall, Tabitha, 184
Shakers. See United Society of Believers in
    Christ's Second Appearing
Shute, Samuel, 10–11
Simpson, O. J., 152
Simpson, Sarah, 75
Sleeper, Love, 107
sleepwalking: case histories of, 81–94, 119–
    20; defense in trials, 76–77, 189–97; fa-
    milial incidence of, 206; mental acuity
    during, 206; relationship to non-REM
    sleep, 194–95; statistics of, 194–95

Smith, Henry, 194
"Springfield Somnambulist." See Rider,
    Jane C.
Stebbins, Festus, 94, 232n29
Stinson, Abner P., 43, 49–51, 135–36
Straw, Ezra, 49
Sullivan, George, 55, 57, 63, 74, 154, 216
Sullivan, John, 55

Thompson, George C., 49, 136
Thompson, George Washington, 58
Thompson, John Adams, 58
Thompson, Joseph C., 58
Thompson, Walter Scott, 58
Thomsonian Botanic Watchman, 92
Tirrell, Albert Jackson, 189–94
Tirrell, Orient, 190, 193
Tuck, Samuel, 134

United Society of Believers in Christ's Sec-
    ond Appearing, 184
Upham, Nathaniel Gookin, 161, 191
US Constitution, 51, 73, 210
US House of Representatives, 86, 161, 215
US Supreme Court, 56, 73–74, 210, 229n3

Wadleigh, Benjamin, 86, 88
Webster, John White, 236n2
Webster, Nathaniel, 59
Welch, George, 194
Welch, Moses C., 104
Whig party, 74
Whipple, John, 55–56, 60–62, 161, 216
Whittemore, Aaron, 86, 88
Whitworth, Annie, 214
Wilmot, New Hampshire, 59
Wilson, Mary Anne, 115
Woodward, Oliver, 105
Woodward, Samuel B., 165, 192
Worcester State Hospital, 94, 118, 121,
    232n29
Worthen, Hannah, 234n10
Wyman, Rufus, 117–21, 123

York Institute. See Saco Museum